RED GOD OF WAR

Soviet Artillery and Rocket Forces

Other Titles from Brassey's

BAXTER
The Soviet Way of Warfare

CARTWRIGHT & CRITCHLEY
Cruise, Pershing and SS-20: The Search for Consensus:
Nuclear Weapons in Europe

COKER
A Nation in Retreat?: Britain's Defence Commitment

ERICKSON & SIMPKIN
Deep Battle: the Genius of Marshal Tukhachevskii

GOLDSTEIN
Fighting Allies: Tensions within the Atlantic Alliance

MAIN
Beam Weaponry

MYLES
Jump Jet, 2nd Edition

RUSI
RUSI/Brassey's Defence Yearbook, 1986

SIMPKIN
Race to the Swift: Thoughts on Twenty-First Century Warfare
Red Armour

WINDASS
Avoiding Nuclear War: Common Security as a
Strategy for the Defence of the West

RED GOD OF WAR

Soviet Artillery and Rocket Forces

by

CHRIS BELLAMY

BRASSEY'S DEFENCE PUBLISHERS
(a member of the Pergamon Group)

LONDON · OXFORD · WASHINGTON · NEW YORK
BEIJING · FRANKFURT · SÃO PAULO · SYDNEY · TOKYO · TORONTO

U.K. (Editorial)	Brassey's Defence Publishers, 24 Gray's Inn Road, London WC1X 8HR
(Orders)	Brassey's Defence Publishers, Headington Hill Hall, Oxford OX3 0BW, England
U.S.A. (Editorial)	Pergamon-Brassey's International Defense Publishers, 1340 Old Chain Bridge Road, McLean, Virginia 22101, U.S.A.
(Orders)	Pergamon Press, Maxwell House, Fairview Park, Elmsford, New York 10523, U.S.A.
PEOPLE'S REPUBLIC OF CHINA	Pergamon Press, Qianmen Hotel, Beijing, People's Republic of China
FEDERAL REPUBLIC OF GERMANY	Pergamon Press, Hammerweg 6, D-6242 Kronberg, Federal Republic of Germany
BRAZIL	Pergamon Editora, Rua Eça de Queiros, 346, CEP 04011, São Paulo, Brazil
AUSTRALIA	Pergamon-Brassey's Defence Publishers, P.O. Box 544, Potts Point, N.S.W. 2011, Australia
JAPAN	Pergamon Press, 8th Floor, Matsuoka Central Building, 1–7–1 Nishishinjuku, Shinjuku-ku, Tokyo 160, Japan
CANADA	Pergamon Press Canada, Suite 104, 150 Consumers Road, Willowdale, Ontario M2J 1P9, Canada

First edition 1986

Library of Congress Cataloging in Publication Data
Bellamy, C. W. (Christopher W.)
Red god of war.
Bibliography: p.
1. Artillery—Soviet Union.   2. Rockets (Ordnance) Soviet Union.
I. Title.
UF85.B45   1986   358'.1'0947   85-28002

British Library Cataloguing in Publication Data
Bellamy, Chris
Red god of war: Soviet artillery and rocket forces
1. Artillery—Soviet Union
I. Title
623.4'1'0947   UF8565.S/

ISBN 0-08-031200-4

The front cover shows a salvo from
Katyosha 132 mm multiple rocket
launchers, Great Patriotic War.

Printed in Great Britain by A. Wheaton & Co. Ltd Exeter.

FOR SALLY B
Sometime Comrade-in-Arms

Acknowledgements

I would like to thank: all my friends and teachers on the staff of the Polytechnic of Central London School of Languages for teaching me Russian and encouraging my interest in Russian history, literature and culture, especially literary sources of which I would otherwise have been unaware, and for advice on translation problems; my friends in Finland, especially the staff of the Military Museum (Sotamuseo) in Helsinki, for all their help and for making my trip there in 1980 so pleasant and productive; Ian V. Hogg and Dipl. Ing Franz Kosar for their invaluable technological and technical artillery expertise; Terry J. Gander for the same, and for pointing out that it really is not difficult to point a camera at a gun; to my friend Steve Kimminau for lending his professional photographic expertise; to the Public Relations staff of the Israel Defence Forces for their help and making my travels so fruitful; the staff of the British Library Reference and Photographic Services Divisions for all their help in finding sources and copying them; the Imperial War Museum, Departments of Photographs and Film for their help with visual evidence; the University of London Library, especially Brigitte Burrows on the International Loans desk, and the British Lending Library, Boston Spa, for getting all kinds of rare and exotic texts from abroad; the staff of the Ministry of Defence Whitehall Library, General, Military and Scientific and Technical Sections for their unfailing enthusiasm and help and especially Charles Potts, former head of the Military Section, for the most astonishing finds in the way of nineteenth- and early twentieth-century foreign publications and British Intelligence sources, the staff of the Soviet Studies Research Centre, RMA Sandhurst, for constant enthusiasm and extremely prompt assistance whenever I called for it; Christopher Duffy, Department of War Studies and International Affairs, Sandhurst who nurtured my interest in military history at Oxford 10 years ago and for advice and encouragement since, including putting me straight on the eighteenth century; the Librarian of the Royal Artillery Institution, Woolwich, for finding rare and unexpected documents; the stills library of the BBC, for topical photography; Associated Press, for the same; the National Film Archive and Contemporary Films for help with creative film; Collet's International Bookshop and the book Import

Department for help with more historical Russian books, to my friends Christopher F. Foss and Dick Woff, for their personal interest and help; Professor Bruce Menning of the Combat Studies Institute, Fort Leavenworth, for his enthusiasm and encouragement and for giving me the opportunity to try out my ideas on audiences in the USA, Major Roger Rains and the *US Field Artillery Journal* for putting their weight behind me, my professional advisers, friends and drinking companions Charles Dick and John Hyden for keeping me thinking; Dave Roberts, for lending a mathematician's expertise, the staff of Sky Photographic Services, Ramillies Street, for their extremely prompt and professional service at all times; the National Westminster Bank, Oxford 121 High Street Branch, for their constant forbearance and understanding that my schemes would come to fruition one day; my wonderful parents, without whom, needless to say, nothing would have been possible and again to my meticulous father for compiling the index, and last but perhaps most my gallant friend Miss Sally Barker, for typing large sections of the original manuscript which, although not used in that format, was crucial to the survival and evolution of the project. Thank you all: any mistakes or misunderstandings which may have crept in, as they may in a work of some scope, such as this, are mine.

King's Cross, London   CHRIS BELLAMY

Contents

List of Plates

List of Figures

Brief List of Soviet Terms

Some readers may be interested to know the Russian for certain important terms used in this book. To avoid interrupting the text with bursts of Russian, these terms are indicated by italics when they first appear in the text and in certain other places where precise terminology is important, which indicates that they can be found in the English–Russian glossary. Because Soviet military terminology is often much more precise than English and specific, some key phrases are defined here, to avoid misunderstanding. These can all be found in the glossary.

Arm	A sub-division of the Ground Forces, such as *Rocket Forces and Artillery*, Tank Troops, Signal Troops.
Formation	A division but, depending on their role, sometimes a corps or brigade.
Higher Formation	Usually an Army or Front but, depending on its role, sometimes a Corps
Operational Art	The manipulation of *higher formations* in the conduct of war and the training and theory pertaining to this.
Service	One of the five Armed Services of the Soviet Union, viz., *Strategic Rocket Forces, Ground Forces, Air Defence Forces, Air Forces, Navy*
Sub-unit	Usually an *all-arms* or *artillery battalion* and below.
Tactics	The employment of *formations* and smaller entities.
Theatre of Military Operations (TVD)	A large area of land or sea, embracing the operations of several Fronts. A TVD has a headquarters controlling its subordinate fronts, but is not believed to have its own assets.
Unit	Usually, a regiment, but sometimes a battalion acting independently can be a unit.

Introduction

Artillery kills. On major battlefields this century, more than any other weapon. Artillery shells inflicted over 58 per cent of casualties on British troops on the western front in World War I, and in the North African desert in World War II the percentage rose to 75 per cent. In Korea nearly 60 per cent of Americans killed in action fell to blast or fragments from artillery and mortar shells — mainly Soviet made. During the 4 years of combat on the eastern front in World War II, henceforward referred to by its Soviet name of the Great Patriotic War, 51 per cent of casualties sustained by the Red Army were caused by artillery fire, and in the last year of the war, 61 per cent. Whilst these statistics give the lie to the widespread view that artillery is only good for keeping people's heads down, they do nothing to convey the sheer horror of what artillery fire does and the psychological effect which multiplies that of its cold lethality many times. Those who have experienced large scale land warfare constantly recall the shattering noise of artillery fire and the sense of hopelessness that it creates among those on the receiving end. Whereas one can steel oneself to fight another man, artillery is a monstrous, apparently unstoppable machine, slicing mechanically through earth, rock, flesh, bone and spirit. Furthermore, it is not a clean way to die. Whereas men can sometimes come to terms with the thought of a swift bullet through the head, the sight of one's comrades blown apart, disembowelled, of bodies disinterred by shellfire and tossed around as gory playthings, is infinitely more crushing to morale. Those who have survived being under artillery fire describe a constant buffeting, or a hundred express trains screaming towards them. Artillery oppresses, jars, stuns and disorientates the enemy and lifts the morale of its own troops. Artillery and rockets provide the greatest firepower and sear a path for infantry, mechanised forces and armour both physically and spiritually. Throughout the centuries, no army has understood this better than the Russian.[1]

The Soviet Army, as it has been known since 1946, is the world's second largest, arguably the most powerful, and has more modern artillery than any other. It is evolving the ability to fight and win quickly an offensive war in Europe without resort to nuclear weapons and before the other side has a

PLATE 0.1.   Effect of fire. This photograph of the Winter War battlefield of
Kuhmo was taken in 1970, 30 years after Soviet artillery cut a swathe through
the forest. Only now is the vegetation beginning to grow back. The size of the
corridor can be gauged by the coaches in the distance. The way the treetops
have been torn off is particularly marked. (Sotamuseo)

chance to use theirs. It has therefore placed renewed emphasis on the
experience of the Great Patriotic War 1941–45, which was the most colossal
land conflict in human history in terms of people and resources employed.
The role of artillery in that war including multiple rocket launchers, is
exhaustively studied, drawn upon and developed. In the absence of nuclear
strikes, massive but precise concentrations of artillery and rocket fire must
facilitate and accelerate the advance of armour and motor rifle troops. In
the Great Patriotic War, it is estimated that Soviet artillery inflicted some
70 per cent of material and personnel losses on the Germans. This figure is
consistent with the others given at the beginning of this introduction, given

PLATE 0.2.   German soldier killed by Soviet artillery fire in the re-capture of
Velikiye Luki, January, 1943. This one has fallen in the entrance to a pill
box, smashed by Soviet shells. Marshal Voronov noted that most dead
Germans seemed to have artillery induced wounds, and the copious evidence
from Soviet newsreels bears this out. (Newsreel film, IWM)

that the Soviets placed relatively greater stress on artillery. *Rocket Forces
and Artillery*, as the arm is formally called, now comprise from 15 to 25 per
cent of the Soviet Army's manpower, but would provide 80 per cent of its
firepower in any conflict. This is a measure at once of the high priority
attached to artillery and also of how very economical it is in terms of
manpower. In front-line formations the predominance of rocket troops and
artillery is even more marked: in the offensively configured Third Shock
Army, the proportion of rocket troops and artillery rises to 28 per cent of
the total.

The latter figure is an indication of the inter-connected and mutually
supportive roles of artillery and armour. Artillery has been a cardinal
component of any Soviet armour heavy offensive since the 1930s, as
explained in Chapters One and Four, and for years now the Russians have
been stressing the need for a balanced, all arms team. In April 1984 the
armoured forces received a major blow to their status whilst the Rocket
Forces and Artillery received a unique honour in being allowed to retain the
prestigious special to arm rank, *Chief Marshal of Artillery* (see Chapter

Two). This is partly a reflection of the heightened role of this arm in the Theatre Strategic Operation, with its emphasis on deep battle where targets can only be engaged from the ground by indirect fire rockets and artillery.

Artillery is also closely connected with air power. The commander of the Group of Soviet Forces Germany (GSFG) until summer, 1985, Colonel-General M. Zaytsev (now replaced by Colonel-General P. G. Lushev) recently said that up to 50 per cent of firepower on the modern battlefield would be delivered by air. Given that the ground forces would provide the other 50 per cent, rocket troops and artillery would provide at least 40 per cent of the total firepower in a continental Theatre of Military Operations.[2] The newly enunciated Soviet concept of Integrated Fire Destruction of the Enemy envisages the careful co-ordination of Ground Forces' Rocket Forces and Artillery and air delivered firepower to achieve maximum value from each. Soviet officers are placing special stress on the integration of assault helicopters and ground artillery fire (see Chapter Four). Gunners have always played an important role in the development of the air arm over battle, both in the West and in the Soviet Union. Army aviation grew out of the need to spot for artillery and the modern assault helicopter can provide the same sort of fire support, further into the enemy depth and with greater flexibility, but without some of artillery's traditional qualities: mechanical certainty of delivery, relative immunity to weather and immediate counter-measures. The interworking of artillery and air is therefore a crucial issue.

The Soviet Rocket Forces and Artillery are certainly not resting on their laurels, however luxuriant those may be. The open military press runs numerous hard-hitting articles on a wide range of questions relating to artillery, and although this sort of self examination is healthy, one gets the impression that there are major weaknesses and problems in the organisation and training of this arm. At the time of writing the Rocket Forces and Artillery are undergoing profound changes, but because of the sheer size of the Soviet military establishment these will take many years to permeate the system. There was a 30 per cent increase in the numbers of artillery pieces (including multiple rocket launchers) deployed in Europe between 1978 and 1983 alone. In 1983, very senior officers in the three most important posts were replaced: The Chief and Deputy Chief of the Rocket Troops and Artillery and the Head of the Main Rocket and Artillery Directorate for Procurement (see Chapter Two). These were all in line for a move on grounds of age but the fact that they were moved at the same time suggests that the new Head of the Soviet Ground Forces, Marshal Vasily Ivanovich Petrov, was acting as a new broom. The new men will undoubtedly help bring in the new ideas which have been discussed in the military press in the last decade.[3]

Of course, an understanding of the Soviet Rocket Forces and Artillery is not only relevant to deterring or fighting a war between the superpowers and in Europe. Soviet artillery equipment, or designs based on it, is also used by the world's largest army, that of the People's Republic of China, and their employment of it owes much to Soviet precedent, for example, the emphasis on multiple rocket launchers. Even more closely modelled on the Soviet is the world's third largest army, that of Vietnam. It should not be forgotten that the regular North Vietnamese army which defeated the United States and South Vietnamese armies in that theatre was trained, equipped and led on Soviet lines. The North Vietnamese artillery was particularly effective, greatly feared and out-shot the latest and best that the West could provide (see Chapter Three). The sixth largest army, that of North Korea, is similarly equipped. The Arab states of the Middle East owe much to the Soviet Union in terms of military equipment and technique, and Soviet weaponry, including artillery has been used in anger there throughout the last three decades. The Israelis, pragmatic as ever, have not been slow to adopt captured equipment of Soviet origin, for which they have a high regard (see Chapter Three). The Iraqis have employed large amounts of Soviet-made artillery in Soviet style in the Gulf War; one correspondent witnessed a devastating bombardment by four regiments of heavy guns which was the nearest to a Soviet bombardment that he ever wished to experience.

PLATE 0.3.   Soviet made D-74 122 mm gun, maximum range 24 kilometres firing in support of Iraqi operations, Gulf War, April 1985. (With kind permission of BBC Television News)

The Iraqis, certainly, and probably the Iranians as well, have also made quite extensive use of Soviet made surface-to-surface missiles, apparently Scuds. This is the largest scale employment of such weapons since the Germans' use of V2s in World War II. Even with conventional warheads, these are capable of doing terrible damage, especially against large civilian targets. Nor are Soviet exports confined to obsolescent equipment. Syria has recently taken delivery of some of the latest SS-21 operational-tactical surface-to-surface missiles. The Soviet Union is the largest arms exporter to the Third World and Soviet advisers and practices go hand in hand with their equipment.[4]

It is therefore surprising that artillery in general and Soviet artillery in particular tend to receive relatively little attention in the Western military press. It is axiomatic that no arm of services can be considered in isolation, but where specialisation is necessary authors have tended to focus on, for example, armour or air forces. Artillery is less glamorous; its equipment is not normally at the very forefront of technological development and here perhaps is the crucial point — its action is difficult if not impossible to simulate in peace time, since it only manifests itself as fire. Apart from the occasional carefully staged firepower demonstration and rare opportunities for single batteries to work with supported arms in the expanses of the Canadian prairie, artillery is an unknown quantity for most Western soldiers and civilian analysts. Few people apart from those who are professionally involved have the opportunity to learn how artillery is employed on the battlefield. The artillery commander requires detailed technical knowledge as well as the tactical skills normally required of a soldier. Fire planning, the need to co-ordinate the requirements of the all-arms commander with the capabilities of the artillery, the need to distinguish between priorities when everyone is screaming for artillery support; none of this is as exhilarating or as comprehensible to the layman as 'two up and bags of smoke'. Besides giving the military professional the facts about the oldest and deadliest arm of the Soviet army, this book also explains the importance and key features of Soviet Rocket Forces and Artillery operations which will be of interest to the general reader and help the historian, the journalist and the student of Defence Studies. This will also shed light on the role of artillery in other armies, too: there are certain similarities between Western and Soviet ways of doing things, obviously. But there are also crucial differences. Too often, Soviet artillery developments, like all military developments, are seen through Western eyes, and through this mirror imaging the picture is in fact distorted.

One final point. During the 1950s and 60s the Rocket Forces and Artillery of the *Ground Forces* were somewhat neglected, but a new *armed service, the Strategic Rocket Forces*, grew out of them. It is as well to remember that the strategic nuclear missiles trained on western Europe and the USA are also manned by men wearing the traditional crossed gun badge of the Russian artillery (see Chapter Two). As the first chapter illustrates, the Russians learned a long time ago that they could not afford to be out-gunned by anybody. Exactly the same philosophy applies to nuclear missiles. The Ground Forces' Rocket Troops and Artillery whom this book is about, have responsibility for large operational-tactical missiles with a range of up to 1000 kilometres. Beyond that, the Strategic Rocket Forces take over. To someone on the receiving end, if these weapons were ever used, the point would seem rather academic.

The *Soviet Military Encyclopedia* defines 'Artillery' in three ways: an *arm of service*, a type of weaponry, and the science of making artillery weapons and their employment on the battlefield, embracing artillery *tactics* and *operational art*.[5] This seemed the best way of organising this book and modern Soviet Rocket Forces and Artillery, equipment and technique are considered in those three ways. The statistics at the beginning are justification enough for calling the chapter on equipment 'the deadliest weapon'. First, however, we need to take a look at the development of Soviet artillery and rocket troops up to their triumph in the Great Patriotic War, because this holds crucial lessons for today. Although the historical material has been packaged separately so that the historian and the modern professional will each have their prime area of interest readily to hand, it is vital to realise that Soviet officers do not see it that way. The Great Patriotic War in particular, is the source of much wisdom for present day operations and, conversely, discussion of present day issues takes place in terms of military-historical examples. The author has adopted the same approach: the historical chapter has been written with a constant eye on the present and all the points made are a clear mirror for our own time.

Notes

1.   58 per cent: *Medical Statistics: Casualties and Medical Statistics of the Great War (History of the Great War)* (HMSO, London, 1931), p. 40; North Africa and Korea: Colonel James Boyd Coates, Jr., *Wound Ballistics* (Office of the Surgeon General, US Government Printing Office, Washington DC, 1962), pp. 55, 755; Soviet experience, Colonel A. A. Sidorenko, *The Offensive* (Voyenizdat, Moscow, 1970), translated under the auspices of the United States Air Force, US Government Printing Office, Washington DC, 1976), p. 20; sense of hopelessness and fighting material, not men: Alistair Horne, *The Price of Glory: Verdun, 1916* (Penguin, London, 1978), p. 190: shells playing with bodies, p. 188; constant buffeting, Nicolas Downie's description of Soviet heavy mortar fire in Afghanistan, *Sunday Times Magazine*, 7 December, 1980; hundred express trains, interview with former *Wehrmacht* officer.

2.   70 per cent of losses: Lieutenant-General of Artillery A. Sapozhnikov, '*Divizion, osnovnaya ogneveya yedinitsa artillerii*' (Battalion: Main Artillery Fire Unit') *Voyenny Vestnik (Military Herald,* henceforward *VV*), 2/1982, p. 59; 15 per cent, David C. Isby, *Weapons and Tactics of the Soviet Army* (Jane's London, 1981), p. 161; 25 per cent Colonel Kurt Hoffmann 'An analysis of Soviet Artillery Development', *International Defense*

Review, 6 (December)/1977, reprinted in *Special Series 7: Artillery Systems*, p. 9 of the latter; 80 per cent of firepower Lieutenant-General I. Anashkin, Deputy Commander of Artillery and Rocket Troops (see Chapter Two) *'Za kompleksnoye resheniye problemy'* ('For an all-embracing Solution to the Problem'), *VV* 10/1976, p. 72; 28 per cent: Major-General M. J. Tomlinson, 'Handling Artillery within the Corps', *British Army Review*, December, 1983, p. 7; 50 per cent of firepower provided by air, General of Tank Troops M. Zaytsev *'Organizatsiya PVO — vazhnaya zadacha obshchevoyskogo komandira'* ('The organization of Air Defence — a crucial Task of the All-arms Commander'), *VV* 2/1979, p. 23.

3.   30 per cent Increase, *Soviet Military Power, 1983* (Secretary of Defense, Washington DC, 1983), p. 40. On command changes see Chapter Two.

4.   Equipment, see Chapter Three; bombardment by four regiments, interview with Major-General Edward Fursdon, *Daily Telegraph* correspondent; surface-to-surface missiles, see Chapter Three; SS-21s to Syria: 'Moscow to deploy Modern Missiles', *Guardian*, 12 October, 1983, p. 8; on strength of Asian armies, *The Military Balance* (International Institute for Strategic Studies (IISS), London), various years; Soviet Union greatest arms exporter to Third World, Thomas Ohlson and Evamaria Loose-Weintraub, 'The Trade in Major Conventional Weapons', *SIPRI Yearbook*, 1983 (Stockholm Peace Research Institute, 1983), pp. 269–73.

5.   *Sovetskaya voyennaya entsiklopediya* (*Soviet Military Encyclopedia*; henceforward *SVE*), Vol. 1, (1976), p. 272.

1.

A Tradition of Excellence

'The Russian artillery is of the most powerful description. No other army moves with so many guns and with no other army is it in a better state of equipment, or is more gallantly served'.

GENERAL SIR ROBERT WILSON, 1810.

PLATE 1.1. A Tradition of Excellence. This photograph of manoeuvres in 1903 illustrates several key factors in the evolution of Russian and Soviet artillery. The terrain is flat, there is no natural cover, and the officers are anxiously scanning the horizon for enemies coming from any direction. The long range, flat trajectory fire of the guns is the only defence. (British Library)

Distant Thunder

The Russians first used guns to defend Moscow against the forces of the Tartar Khan Tokhtamysh in late summer, 1382. That at least is the conclusion to be drawn from medieval chronicles which were, admittedly, compiled some time after the events which they claim to describe. It was a punitive raid; two years before Prince Dmitry of Moscow had rebelled against his suzerain lords of the Golden Horde and defeated Khan Mamay in the titanic battle of Kulíkovo field on the banks of the river Don. Now,

9

Moscow held out for four days but was eventually captured by a ruse. Dmitry hastened there to find it a smouldering ruin with 24,000 corpses still to be buried. Dmitry would probably have drawn small comfort from the fact that on this occasion the steppe nomads had encountered something which was soon to swing the military balance against them and play a major role in the evolution and survival of the Russian state: artillery. There is no record of firearms having been used at Kulíkovo in 1380 and the Soviet army accordingly celebrated the 600th anniversary of Russian artillery in 1982. A special series of articles commemorating the jubilee appeared in the influential professional journal *Military Herald*, beginning in August, 1980. While these aimed to inspire pride in the glorious history of the Russian Senior Service, officers were also encouraged to enter a jubilee competition which entailed a searching examination of their present day competence. Russian scholars used to think that guns were first brought to Russia by merchants from the West in 1389, and for this reason the 500th anniversary was celebrated with equal enthusiasm in 1889. The question of the dates seems somewhat esoteric, but the amount of attention which it has generated is an indication of the affection with which the Russians have always regarded their artillery arm and the high priority they attach to it.[1] This has been at least partly conditioned by the circumstances of artillery's appearance and early use.

Although there is a cryptic reference to a thundering sound emanating from the city of Bolgary on the river Volga in 1376, which alarmed the Russian besiegers, it is almost certain that guns were first used by the Russians against their enemies to the east and not the other way round. Artillery was the weapon of the settled community, because whereas torsion and counter-poise engines of war were constructed from readily available materials, guns required huge quantities of metal and advanced production techniques. The metal had to be mined, refined and concentrated in one place. The development of Russian and Soviet artillery is of course intimately connected with that of the industrial base. Because urban communities had the technological knowledge and resources to invest in artillery whereas the nomad had not, the traditional military advantages of physical prowess and instinct which the latter imbibed with his mother's milk were outweighed. The Tartar-Mongols did not make much use of artillery, even after they had plenty of time to get acquainted with it, and the great military commander Timur (lived 1336 to 1405) did not employ guns to any extent, even for besieging cities. This is because the highly mobile, predominantly cavalry tactics of the Mongols and the successor tribes were unsuited to the use of the artillery of the time, and because the break up of the once cohesive Mongol Empire inhibited the creation of an industrial base comparable to that of late medieval Europe.[2]

The Russians, on the other hand, were quick to exploit the new weapon.

A powder and gun manufacturing industry was set up during the reign of Vassily I, who ruled from 1389 to 1425, and we know that there was a gunpowder factory in Moscow by 1400 because in that year it blew up killing some 200 people. Guns were particularly effective against the Tartar-Mongol tribes. Moscow's artillery armament is reported to have been the main factor which deterred Khan Yedigey from attacking the city in 1408, and in 1451 the capital defended itself against Khan Mazovshey with firearms, this time successfully. This was, incidentally, the first time the Russians used hand guns as well as the larger artillery pieces. Many of the Tartar-Mongol tribes, particularly the Nogays, were more afraid of gunfire than were Europeans or Turks. The reason why the Russians put so much stress on *artillery*, as opposed to small arms, apparently, was that until the eighteenth century, at least, the powerful composite bows used by the Tartars actually out-ranged infantry muskets. Artillery was therefore the only weapon which gave the Russians the crucial advantage of range, something which was even more important in the flat, open expanses of the steppe than in the closer country of western Europe. Artillery was a secret weapon, the one thing that really frightened the Mongols, and as such acquired a special place in Russian folk memory. The 'Tartar Yoke' thus cradled Russian and Soviet artillery, as it shaped many aspects of modern Russia.[3]

The development of Russian artillery received extra impetus from Ivan IV the Terrible (ruled 1533 to 1586), who took a personal interest in it as did a later dictator, Josef Stalin. Ivan enjoyed watching firepower demonstrations in order to see 'what his gunners can do', which involved firing at huge earth bunkers until they were flattened. Ivan's artillery was equally effective when used in anger. It played a major role in Ivan's victories including the capture of the Tartar city of Kazan' in 1552, and the film maker Eisenstein clearly drew the parallel with the decisive role of artillery in his own time in the film *Ivan the Terrible* made during the Great Patriotic War (see Plate 1.2). In 1558, during the Livonian War, the commander of Narva, which was being besieged by the Russians, signalled the Grand Master of his order saying that the garrison would not be able to endure the unusually intense Russian bombardment for much longer. Then, as now, the size of the Russian artillery force impressed foreigners: in 1576, Kobenzel, the Habsburg Emperor's ambassador to Moscow reported that the Tsar of Muscovy had 'artillery and firearms of all sorts in abundance', such as he had never seen.[4]

In the early sixteenth century the Russian artillery was organised on a guild or corporate basis, as in other countries (for example, the Honourable Artillery Company in England). Unlike the musketeers or strel'tsy, known to posterity mainly for their revolt against Peter the Great, who were formally established in 1551, it is not known when the organisation

PLATE 1.2.   The Firepower of Holy Russia. Sergey Eisenstein stressed the
role of artillery in Ivan the Terrible's victories in his film *Ivan the Terrible*
(Part One, 1944), a clear parallel with the part it played in those of his own
time. It was particularly important for capturing fortified cities like the Tartar
stronghold of Kazan', which affirmed Ivan as lord of all European Russia.
(With kind permission of Contemporary Films Ltd.)

responsible for artillery was founded. 500 light gunners were formed into an
organised body in Pskov as early as 1510, and 'gunners' and 'light gunners'
are referred to in a corporate sense in 1545. The separate estate or guild of
artillerymen or pushkary was therefore senior to the strel'tsy, reinforcing
the Soviet artillery's claim to be the senior arm. The gunners enjoyed
considerable privileges in exchange for their services and the corporate
spirit was still strong in the 1690s. The guild's headquarters was the
Artillery Chancellery in Moscow, which was extant by 1581 although, once
again, we do not know when it was founded. When Peter I the Great
(reigned 1682–1725) began his military reforms he seems to have left the
gunners alone. In 1702, the office of Master General of the Ordnance was
superimposed on the Artillery Chancellery but otherwise the organisation
remained unchanged. When this is compared with the creation of Western
style infantry regiments under Peter and his father Aleksey Mikhaylovich,

who reigned from 1645 to 1676, and the abolition of the Strel'tsy after their abortive revolt, it is clear that the artillery does indeed enjoy the longest continuous tradition of any service or arm of service in the Russian and Soviet armed forces.[5]

The survival of the artillery guild was partly a result of their greater professionalism. In the campaigns against the Crimean Tartars in 1687 and 1689, the Russians disposed of a very large force of cavalry and infantry, but they were poorly disciplined and it was the artillery alone which repelled the Tartars' attacks. In the second campaign the Russians fielded 700 guns, an astonishing number for the time. There are many subsequent examples of the Russian artillery making up for inadequacies in the other arms, echoing Napoleon's view that 'the more inferior a body of troops the more artillery it requires'.[6]

Peter the Great was another key figure in the evolution of Russian artillery, although he was evidently happy to build on earlier experience. For example, the Russian envoy in Paris, Kurakin, wrote to the Tsar about new guns he had seen which could be loaded at the breech. Peter replied that rapid firing guns with a drop breech had been known in Russia for a long time, but had not been adopted because they became clogged with saltpetre after a few rounds. These were the guns now in the Artillery Museum in Lenigrad. One of these, dated 1615, is rifled and all three are breech loaders one of which is illustrated here (Fig. 1.1 and Plate 1.3). The

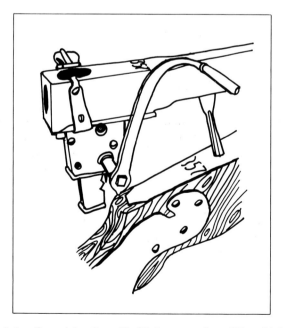

FIG. 1.1.   Breech loading rifled light gun, reign of Tsar Aleksey
Mikhaylovich, *c.* 1660.

PLATE 1.3.   Breech loading rifled light gun, *c.* 1660.

other two were made during the 1660s or 1670s. Primitive breech loaders, with removable chambers had been known in Europe since the fifteenth century, but the sophisticated lever mechanism on the later guns does seem remarkably advanced, as does the idea of a rifled cannon (rifled small arms had been made in the early sixteenth century). The Russians claim that these show how advanced their artillery technology was in the seventeenth century, but one of the guns bears an inscription in German, indicating that it was either made in Germany or by a German in Russian employ. Russian claims to have been 'ahead of the times' in any field should be treated with caution. The same goes for Onisim Mikhaylov's *Rules for Military Ordnance and Other Matters, touching on Military Science*, published in Russian in 1621. This is vaunted as one of Europe's first treatises on artillery, but the text itself makes it clear that it was compiled from foreign studies.[7] Nevertheless, the Russians did undoubtedly produce some new and original ideas, and their extraordinary ability to assimilate foreign talent was in itself a great asset, a trait which remains today. Peter the Great, for example, formed companies of light guns to support cavalry. The Russians claim that these were the first true 'horse artillery', but this may be stretching the point, and Russian horse artillery really began with Count P. A. Zubov's company in 1794.[8]

When it was first invented, artillery had been primarily for the attack and defence of fortified positions. Field artillery, able to manoeuvre and influence a mobile battle, first appeared in the Thirty Years' War (1618–48), and its development owed much to Gustavus Adolphus of

Sweden. Yet it was against the Swedes that Russian field artillery was to have its first major success, at Poltava, on 27 June (8 July) 1709, during the Great Northern War of 1700–1729. The attack of the Swedes, whose military reputation was still exorbitant, was broken up by a sieve of redoubts but they reformed for a final assault on the main Russian force. At a range of 600 metres The Russian artillery opened a withering fire with 72 guns and 120 rounds of ammunition for each. The Swedes came on suffering terrible casualties as the cannon shot swathed through them, and as they drew close the Russian artillery switched fire on to the Swedish second line, preventing it reinforcing the first which clashed hand-to-hand with the Russians. This must be one of the first examples of a form of 'Follow On Forces Attack' (see Chapter Four)! The Swedish King Charles XII had horses shot from under him by Russian artillery, and Peter the Great himself acknowledged that artillery had been 'the arbiter of victory'. New regular regiments of artillery were not formed until 1712, so Russian expertise with this arm at Poltava owed much to the old pushkary.[9]

The Later Eighteenth Century

Artillery was the arm which underwent the most significant development in this period, in all European armies. Technological improvements facilitated the tactical handling of the arm. In Russia, the former are associated with the name of the seventh Master General of the Ordnance from 1756, Field-Marshal Count Peter Shuvalov (lived 1710–1762). Many of the ideas may in fact have come from his subordinates Major M. V. Danilov and Colonel S. A. Martynov. Round shot was the most effective weapon at extreme range, its kinetic energy would carry it through several lines of men, slicing a body that got in its way in half. At shorter range, grape shot and canister were relatively more effective, but with a line of men as a target up to a quarter of the grape or canister projectiles in a salvo fell short and another quarter whistled over their heads. In order to maximise the effect of canister and grape, Shuvalov (or Danilov) devised a weapon called the Secret Howitzer, with a flattened bore, designed to discharge a lethal spray of bullets at about waist height. The first model was made as early as 1753, and the first production batch of 70 was rolled out just before the Seven Years' War began, in 1756. A few were used at Gross-Jägersdorf in 1757, and they were employed on a larger scale at Zorndorf in 1758. The Secret Howitzer did not always come up to expectations, but one of Frederick's officers described it as a devastating weapon, capable of sweeping away a whole platoon with a single round. Even more significant was the unicorn howitzer, so called because of the ornamental handles. In order to achieve greater range, the unicorn had a conical chamber for powder rather than the cylindrical one. Unicorns were made in various sizes

FIG. 1.2.   Secret howitzer.

and the heavier ones proved excessively cumbersome. This led to allegations that unicorns in general were inferior to conventional artillery. Shuvalov was enraged at this and arranged for tests to be carried out under the supervision of four senior officers. The reports varied from adequate to fairly enthusiastic and all agreed that unicorns were better than the weapons they were designed to replace. The lighter unicorns did meet the need for lighter and more versatile artillery, and their plunging trajectory was particularly useful for firing over the heads of one's own troops. The Russians used them in this way at the battle of Paltsig or Kay (modern Pałcł, in Poland) in July, 1759. The position of the Russian guns on the right did not give a commanding view over the battlefield and contemporary maps show them firing over trees, so the Russians must have been using a primitive form of *indirect fire* targeting. Indirect fire means firing at targets which the gun layer and commander cannot see themselves, and is the normal mode of operation for field artillery in Western armies today (see below and Chapter Four). An instruction issued by Major-General Aleksandr Glebov, commander of the Russian artillery in the field from January 1760, indicates that this was a regular practice. Glebov's ideas on the employment of artillery were very advanced for the time: he created an artillery reserve, capable of intervening in emergency or exploiting success, and deployed artillery in depth to deal with flanking attacks. Glebov also issued orders setting out the relationship of artillery with other arms. At the highest level, the chief of the field artillery reported directly to the Commander-in-Chief, and by the same token other artillery officers accepted the orders of the local senior commander, whilst continuing to report to the Chief of Field Artillery. This is essentially the same as the control of artillery sub-units today (see Chapter Four).[10]

The high quality of the Russian artillery of this period comes out most clearly from the events of 1(12) August, 1759 in the confused battle of Kunersdorf. Frederick the Great carried out one of his famous oblique attacks against a strong Russian and Austrian position, but for some reason the allied command had assumed he would attack from that direction all the time. In a report to the Empress Elizabeth, as crisp and as fresh as if it was written yesterday and illustrated with detailed maps, the Russian commander, General Saltykov, describes how the enemy cavalry and artillery suffered especially from the 'large battery of newly invented guns and Shuvalov howitzers disposed in the centre of the army'. It must be rare to find such a clear admission by an eighteenth-century soldier of the ability of new technology to influence the outcome of a battle decisively.

Two important influences in the later eighteenth century were Field-Marshal Count Pyotr Rumyantsev-Zadunayskiy (lived 1725–1796) and the military genius Aleksandr Suvorov (lived 1729 or 1730–1800). Rumyantsev issued *Instructions to Battery Commanders* in 1788, which paid particular

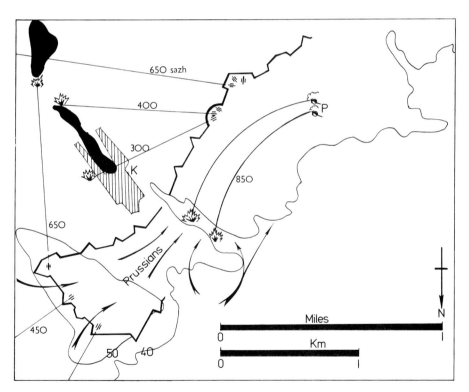

FIG. 1.3.   Battle of Kunersdorf (Kunowice), 1(12) August, 1759. K = Kunersdorf; P = letter used by Saltykov to indicate battery of 'newly invented guns and Shuvalov howitzers' posted on a hill. Ranges are given in *sazhen*, as on the original map. One *sazhen* equals 2.13 metres. Source: Korobkov, diagram 5.

attention to using artillery at optimum ranges, and not opening fire too soon. Suvorov was quite clear about the need to concentrate fire at the decisive point, in spite of his famous statement that the bullet was a fool and the bayonet thoroughly reliable. At the storming of the Turkish fortress of Ismail on the Danube in December 1790, the majority of the land guns (67 out of a total of 110) and the entire firepower of the fleet (500 guns) was concentrated in support of an amphibious assault on one side, the land guns firing over the ships from across the river. It was a classic example of the concentration of artillery on a narrow breakthrough sector, so typical of Soviet artillery employment today (see below and Chapter Four).[11]

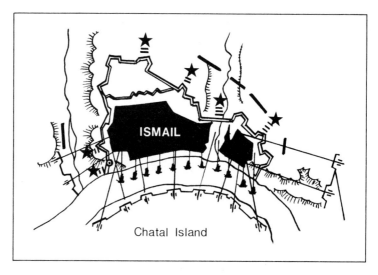

FIG. 1.4.   The capture of Ismail, 10–11 December, 1790: Concentration of overwhelming firepower at the enemy's weakest point. Stars = Redoubts with artillery built close to the Turkish fortifications to act as springboards for the assault. Gun symbols indicate batteries.

The Revolutionary and Napoleonic Wars

The French Revolutionary and Napoleonic Wars were enormously important for the way in which artillery came to be used on the battlefield, although these changes were facilitated by technological developments in the eighteenth century. In 1776 the French introduced the Gribeauval system with improved and more manoeuvrable guns. These inspired one of the greatest influences on Russian artillery, Count Aleksey Andreyevich Arakcheyev (1769–1834). In 1792 Arakcheyev was posted to the infamous Gatchina corps, the private army of the heir apparent to the throne, later Paul I. Arakcheyev used the opportunity to experiment with guns of especially light construction and their use as horse artillery. Arakcheyev was an objectionable and repulsive person, but as a professional artillery officer he certainly knew his business. He became master General of the Ordnance in 1799, and after a brief period in retirement because of a scandal, returned to the colours in 1802, as head of a commission charged with working out new designs for artillery. These became known as the Model 1805 or 'Arakcheyev pattern' guns. These were based on the Gatchina experimental designs and were more mobile than their predecessors without any loss in performance. This was achieved by having a hollow (split) trail, and by reduction of superfluous ornament. The Russians lost an enormous quantity of artillery at the Battle of Austerlitz in 1805, which proved to be a blessing in disguise as the new Arakcheyev systems were ordered *en bloc* to replace them. The Arakcheyev gun carriages remained standard until 1845, a measure of their quality and also of the fact that there was little technological change from then until the introduction of rifled ordnance. Napoleon, himself an artillery officer, was impressed by the Arakcheyev guns and ordered them to be copied.

Besides his technological innovations, Arakcheyev introduced important tactical and organisational reforms. In 1806, he ordered that instead of splitting up artillery regiments into penny packets, each infantry division should have an artillery brigade and that each corps should have an artillery general to take command of all its artillery. The Russian artillery thus acquired a centralised system of control, which facilitated the massing of large numbers of guns at decisive points, something which Russian and Soviet artillerymen have stressed ever since. He also introduced theoretical examinations for artillery officers, a scientific system of artillery intelligence, and in 1808 founded the *Artillery Journal* and a Committee for artillery studies. He was thus the founder of the modern Soviet artillery's formidably scientific, if sometimes excessively theoretical approach to training. The Prussian general Gneisenau believed that Arakcheyev had laid the foundations for the development of the Russian armed forces, and had created 'the superb Russian artillery' which was instrumental in driving Napoleon out of Russia in 1812 and the subsequent operations which led to his defeat.[12]

Another key figure is Aleksandr Ivanovich Kutaysov (lived 1784–1812), who was appointed Arakcheyev's 'Quartermaster Lieutenant' in 1798. Cultured and intelligent, a linguist and poet, he complemented the gauche Arakcheyev ideally. Kutaysov took part in the Polish campaign of 1806–7 as a Major-General, where he used artillery to great effect. The Russians had 500 guns with them in this campaign, and used that many at the battle of Eylau (6–7 February, 1807). Here, the Russian artillery gave 'a lesson in technique to the French', hitherto regarded as the foremost exponents of the art. Sir Robert Wilson, an independent if admittedly Russophil observer, was greatly impressed, as the opening quotation shows.

After hostilities ceased, Kutaysov travelled to France, where he could discuss military matters with Napoleon's generals. French and Russian ideas for using artillery developed together, a reciprocal exchange of ideas. Kutaysov returned to Russia in 1811, and was appointed to command the artillery of Bagration's First Western Army in 1812. On the eve of the Patriotic War, he issued his *General Rules for Artillery in Field Combat*, which are some of the earliest surviving regulations for the tactical employment of large numbers of guns anywhere. Kutaysov paid particular attention to the massing of artillery against a breakthrough sector and to the creation of an artillery reserve which, he said, could comprise horse artillery whose speed and lightness enabled it to move swiftly to various points. This shows how the Russian concept of 'mass' need not involve the ponderous assembly of ground forces but in fact depends on mobility and agility for the rapid concentration of combat power. This thought influences Soviet artillery and rocket design and employment today (see Chapters Three and Four). Kutaysov also stressed the need to choose the right sort of shot for a given target at a given range. In the offensive, the artillery's main task would be to destroy the enemy's artillery, which is particularly interesting as the British Royal Artillery did not begin to consider counter-battery fire a worthwhile operation until the 1840s. Howitzer batteries should be sited 'behind small mounds, just big enough to cover them, because all their fire, apart from case-shot, would be *plunging fire*'. This is a clear provision for some form of indirect fire.

Kutaysov would doubtless have made the Russian artillery even more progressive and competent had he not been killed at Borodino on 26 August (7 September), 1812, in the attempt to re-take the Rayevsky redoubt. His death is, however, very much in the tradition of the Russian artillery. No matter how technically brilliant or senior, an artillery officer is a soldier first and foremost and leads from the front. This theme is constantly repeated; it recurs in General Skobelev's orders in Central Asia in 1880; 'artillery must have a soul; the gunner is not simply a mechanic', and in the aggressive handling of modern Soviet artillery, with its willingness to take up direct fire positions.[13]

During the Napoleonic Wars, artillery became the decisive arm. At Borodino, the Russians deployed 640 guns, the French, with Napoleon himself an artillery officer, 587. Furthermore, the Russian artillery had longer range. Artillery caused the majority of fatal casualties in the battle. The following year, in the assault on Warsaw, the Russians employed 120 guns massed in one 'Grand battery'. The experience of the Napoleonic wars was analysed by another important figure in the evolution of Russian artillery thinking, Lieutenant-General Nikolay Aleksandrovich Okunev (1788–1850). In 1831, Okunev published a book in French, *Memoranda on the Change which Artillery Used Correctly Will Produce on Modern Grand*

Tactics. Artillery was not merely a 'supporting arm', but could achieve decisive results by itself, which he supported with examples from Russian campaigns in Poland. The phrase 'Grand Tactics', of course, implied the conduct of an entire battle. The secret of success, Okunev believed, was an enormous massed battery of 80–100 guns. In order to survive the artillery had to be fearless; it was necessary to swamp the enemy with fire before he had the chance to retaliate. In this, Okunev anticipated the later Soviet

Генералъ-лейтенантъ
Н. А. Окуневъ
(т. XVII, стр. 117)

PLATE 1.4.   Nikolay Aleksandrovich Okunev, Prophet of Firepower Superiority and the First Strike. (British Library)

concept of *fire superiority* and Soviet thinking on nuclear strategy. Okunev's work was influential being translated into English in the 1840s.[14]

The Mid Nineteenth-Century Technological Revolution

The general adoption of rifled, breech loading ordnance, explosive shells, the ability to mass produce them, and large conscript armies to use them could only be revolutionary. The Russians had begun experimenting with rifled artillery for general use in 1856, and a small number of Rifled Muzzle Loaders were produced in 1860. The Russians were not convinced of the superiority of rifled ordnance in all cases until after 1866, when the Battle of Königgratz demonstrated once and for all the superiority of Prussian rifled guns over Austrian smoothbores. The first rifled breech loaders adopted for general service in Russia were the 1867 pattern, of various calibres. Russian artillery development and procurement received added impetus in 1862, when the *Main Artillery Directorate (GAU)* was set up, as one of the first products of War Minister Dmitry Milyutin's famous reforms. The organisation has a continuous history from then until the present day (see Chapter Two). The *GAU* was responsible not only for artillery guns and ammunition but for small arms as well, a reminder of the influential position of the Russian and Soviet artillery within the military system as a whole.[15]

The revolution led to a flowering of Russian inventiveness. This consisted, then as now, not so much in being at the very forefront of technology but in making clever use of existing technologies or components, making things simpler than corresponding foreign equipments and in modifying foreign ideas. For example, although the Russians did not invent the multi-barrelled machine gun, they were the first army to employ it in significant numbers, in their Central Asian campaigns where these weapons proved most effective in breaking up massed attacks by Turcoman cavalry. These weapons were of course regarded as artillery pieces, mounted on high wheeled carriages and deployed in batteries. The Russians referred to them as *rapid firing guns* at the time, although the same term was later applied to the Quick Firing Field Guns introduced at the end of the century. Dr. Gatling first patented his invention in 1862, and in 1864 the Russian General Gorlov was sent to the USA to work on the development of a repeating rifle with the US government. It appears that the Russians took more notice of the American Civil War than other European armies. Gorlov became interested in Gatling's invention and began work on a version modified to take the 0.42 inch cartridge of the Russian Berdan infantry rifle. He also added a number of improvements, which gave the Gorlov modified Gatlings superior performance.[16]

One extremely talented Russian engineer of this period was Vladimir Stepanovich Baranovsky (1846–1879). In 1872, Baranovsky built the first of his remarkable 2.5 inch (63.5 mm) rapid firing guns, which embodied virtually all the features of a modern field gun. The barrel was a steel tube, loaded through a screw breech which operated as shown in the photograph (Plate 1.5). The firing mechanism cocked itself when the breech was opened. The gun had a safety mechanism to prevent firing should the breech not be fully closed and an automatic ejecting mechanism. It fired *fixed ammunition* — a shell and tin cartridge case combined. Most notable was the recoil mechanism, shown below (Plate 1.6). This was the first truly modern recoil mechanism in the world. The barrel recoiled independently of the carriage, its movement being checked and then being returned using hydraulics and a steel spring. The gun was also fitted with an optical sight, as it had a range of 8 kilometres, well beyond that of normal human eyesight. A small number of these revolutionary weapons were despatched to the front in the Russo-Turkish War (1877–78), where they were tested before Rushchuk. Some of the shells, which were rather fragile, were damaged and were returned to Russia for testing. Baranovskiy himself was examining one in 1879, when it exploded and the inventor was killed. Because of the complexity of the system and the accident, only one battery of mountain artillery was equipped with the system, known as the M-1883, both in Russia and abroad. There is no doubt that Baranovskiy's gun, which embodied features which were not to be fully incorporated in other guns until the late 1890s, was 20 years ahead of its time. The French M-1897

PLATE 1.5.   Baranovskiy Field Gun showing the operation of the breech mechanism. This elegant gun was 20 years ahead of its time. (Author's photograph, with kind permission Sotamuseo)

PLATE 1.6.   Baranovskiy recoil mechanism. (Author's photograph, with
kind permission Sotamuseo)

'Canon de 75' was the first widely produced gun to incorporate them all.
These features were not again incorporated in Russian field artillery until
the appearance of the 76.2 mm M-1902.[17]

As a result of the lessons of the Russo-Turkish War, the Russians also
introduced a Field Mortar, the 6-inch M-1885. This was fitted to a wheeled
carriage known as the 'M-1889'. This was the first heavy mortar ever to be
designed for mobile field operations. The M-1889 carriage also incorporated an early recoil control device, an ingenious 'spade brake'. This was
an early compromise between having the whole gun and carriage recoil
uncontrolled and later developments where only the barrel recoiled, and
was designed by the then Colonel Robert Durlyakher (born 1856). This was
an interesting example of a weapon designed specifically in response to new
requirements, in this case those imposed by strong field fortifications. The
M-1885 was, however, an evolutionary dead end, as Quick Firing field
howitzers would soon appear to fulfil the same function. Durlyakher
designed many ingenious gun carriages, and in 1900 the French awarded
him a gold medal for his work. His articles were translated into German and
French, indicating that his inventions were as advanced as any being
produced by those countries.

This tradition was continued by General Engelhardt, who began working
on a Quick Firing gun for general service in 1896 (nearly 20 years after
Baranovskiy's brilliant but ill-fated design had been accepted into service).
Engelhardt originally planned an 87 mm gun, but the model finally adopted
was of 76.2 mm calibre. This was the M-1900 pattern Field Gun, which

came to be the mainstay of the Russian Field Artillery during the Russo-Japanese War. Foreign observers described it as a 'really excellent gun' which should have given the Russians a great advantage over the Japanese — if it was used properly.

At the same time, Engelhardt was already working on an improved gun, the M-1902, which is possibly the most famous Russian gun of World War I, Russian Revolution and Civil War. It appears in many Revolutionary paintings as a symbol of the fighting determination of workers and soldiers. Impartial and informed observers described it as 'the most powerful field gun in existence'. The Russian artillery, and the army as a whole, were not short of good equipment.[18]

Rocketry

The Imperial Russian artillery in the nineteenth century also enjoyed the benefit of the world's most advanced rocketry. From the beginning the Russians regarded rockets as logically belonging to the artillery. Although Peter the Great had shown some interest in rockets, the Russians' particular aptitude for rocketry can be traced back to Aleksandr Dmitrievich Zasyadko (1779–1837). Zasyadko's rockets built after the Patriotic War of 1812 were superior in range to any others in the world. Zasyadko rockets were used in the Caucasus in the Russo-Turkish War of 1828–9. Zasyadko had a particularly brilliant pupil, in Konstantin Ivanovich Konstantinov

PLATE 1.7.   M-1900 pattern field gun: a 'really excellent gun'. (Author's photograph, with kind permission Sotamuseo)

PLATE 1.8.   M-1902/3 pattern field gun (usually referred to as the M-1902 although the first versions had axletree seats and no shield). 'The most powerful field gun in existence', in 1906. (Author's photograph, with kind permission Sotamuseo)

(1817–71). Konstantinov became head of the St. Petersburg Rocket factory in the 1840s and 1850s, and his rockets were used in the Eastern War of 1853–6, mainly against the Turks but also at Sevastopol. They were particularly useful in mountainous areas, especially the Caucasus, as they could easily be carried where artillery could not penetrate, and the Russians therefore paid great attention to them. A two inch diameter rocket with a 12 pounder shell attached had a range of about 600 metres. Konstantinov published a series of lectures on rockets and rocketry, which he considered would play a very important part in future wars. The problem of throwing a very large body with a very high velocity would, he believed, be solved using the projectile power of rockets, and not guns. He would thus have predicted that a rocket would be used to put the first man on the moon, rather than a giant shell fired from a gun. The Russians clearly recognised the enormous military potential of rockets in the 1860s, and the Soviet Union has striven to develop that potential to its utmost.[19]

The Scientific and Industrial Base

Given the backwardness of the Russian economy in the nineteenth century, it may seem surprising that they were able to manufacture weapons so numerous, so advanced, and of such quality. The reason is, of course, that the Tsarist economy, like the Soviet, concentrated resources in the defence sector. The best scientific brains were also employed on defence work, and this accounts for the high level of competence in the defence related industries, particularly metallurgy. The mass production of cast steel, so vital for the further development of artillery, was started in Russia by P. M. Obukhov. Obukhov's first factory for the manufacture of steel guns opened in 1860, and his big St. Petersburg gun factory (now the Bol'shevik factory) in 1863. In 1862, at the World Exhibition in London the Obukhov firm was awarded a gold medal for a heavy gun which had fired over 4000 shots without bursting. Obukhov's works and the Putilov factory (established in 1801, but bought by the engineer N. I. Putilov in 1868) became the principal armaments producing firms. The Putilov factory was renamed 'Red Putilov' from 1922–34 and then became the Kirov factory, the name it bears today.

Visitors to Russian arsenals in the 1860s remarked on the notable 'tenacity and toughness' of the steel, and in 1868 the Russian military scientist General Chernov discovered that the crystalline structure of steel changed at a certain temperature, but that this temperature varied with carbon content. This was the phenomenon known as the eutectoid temperature, the discovery of which is normally attributed to the Englishman Sir William Roberts Austen, in 1888. In 1871, an 11-inch gun made by the German firm of Krupp burst during firing at Kronstadt. A board of enquiry found that this had been caused by an internal flaw in the ingot from which the defective part had been cast. According to a British report, the Russian authorities 'seemed convinced that when guns on the same system are made entirely in the Russian foundries the recurrence of such an accident would be precluded'. The Russian armed forces also benefited from the services of no less a physicist than Dmitry Mendeleyev, who devised the periodic table of the elements. Smokeless powder as a propellant was introduced in various European countries in the 1880s. In fact, it was not 'powder' at all but a completely new type of explosive. In 1890, Mendeleyev developed a new type of smokeless power, pyrocollodion, and in 1892 organised its production. From 1890–95, he was consultant at the Naval Ministry's scientific-technical laboratory.

This concentration on the defence industries produced an imbalance in the economy, which meant that whilst the Russian army might be well equipped to fight a short war, the country did not have the industrial depth and flexibility to fight a long one. This proved disastrous in World War I; whereas other European countries and the USA could mobilise their industries to meet the unexpected demands of total war, the Russians had little industrial capacity immediately available in reserve.[20]

The Modern System of Indirect Fire

Although primitive and improvised systems of *indirect fire* had been in use for many years, these had all relied on a line of markers from the gun position to a point from which the target was clearly visible. They were therefore unsuitable for use in a mobile battle or for rapid lateral shifts of fire. The improvements in field artillery could not be used to full effect without indirect fire; there was little point in having a gun like the Russian M-1877 87 mm field gun with a range of four miles, if its effective range was limited to that of human eyesight and the visible horizon. The introduction of the modern system of indirect fire, enabling guns to fire on a target from all corners of the battlefield, using data computed from a map if necessary, was arguably the single most critical development in the history of land warfare in this period. Without it, World War I could not have been fought as it was.

The Germans were the first to advocate indirect fire for field artillery in a big way, because of their experience in the Franco-Prussian War of 1870–71. In addition to the problem of finding positions for a large number of guns, all of which could see the enemy, the Prussian artillery had suffered grievously from the fire of the new rifled small arms and machine guns. The Russians had a tradition of using indirect fire in the field, and the fortress artillery of Sevastopol had also used indirect fire against the besiegers in the Crimean War.

The essence of the modern system is to point the guns in a convenient direction towards the enemy ('*centre of arc*'), using a compass or some other method. An *aiming point* is selected, and an indicator on the sight turned to point at it. To turn the gun through a given angle, the pointer is moved through that angle but in the opposite direction, and then brought back on to the aiming point by turning the gun. The gun is now pointing in the desired direction. Readers who are unfamiliar with gunnery may find the explanation in the box useful. With the first indirect fire sights the pointer could only be moved through a few degrees. Later, the pointer could be turned through a full circle, which meant that the gun could too. The approximate direction and range to the target are worked out from the map and observers' corrections passed to the gun by flags or, later, telephone and ultimately radio.

The Russians were quick to appreciate the need for such a system. In 1882, Karl Georgiyevich Guk (1846–1910), a Lieutenant-Colonel at the Mikhail Artillery Academy, wrote a book called *Indirect Fire for Field Artillery*, which described all the essentials of the modern system. He considered laying guns in a given direction by compass, which he did not recommend because of the error caused by the presence of steel guns. He illustrated the use of aiming points and dealt with problems of crest clearance, and devised an elaborate system of signals for passing corrections

Basic Gunnery — Indirect laying

The technique, which is still used today is to select an aiming point, measure the angle between the target and aiming point, pass it to the guns, displace the gun's sight by the required angle and then bring it back onto the aiming point by moving the gun. It is particularly interesting that Guk showed the method that is still used by the Russians today, that is, all the guns used the same aiming point and were deployed in a straight line. The western practice, since at least 1910, has been to pass the line individually to each gun and then for each gun in turn to call out the reading on the head. When the guns were laid on the director at these angles, they would all be parallel.

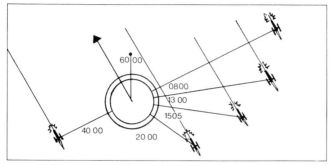

FIG. 1.5.

One of the notable idiosyncracies of Soviet artillery is its predilection for deploying in line. One of the reasons for this is that it is much simpler to orientate the guns quickly if they are deployed in a straight line, with the same aiming point. If the aiming point is in line with the row, parallelism will be automatic:

FIG. 1.6.

Where the guns are in line, but the aiming point is in another position, the procedure is still relatively simple. The commander of the first gun (the right hand gun in Russian batteries) would read the directions to the other guns in the line on his dial sight: 'Second gun, 45–05, third –45–00.' The gun line commander would then order 'Second gun, *uglomer* 15–05, third gun, 15–00, lay on the first'. After this all three guns would be parallel. An aiming point would then be selected: the cottage chimney. Each gun would lay the sight on it. The gun commanders would then read out their respective angles to it: No. 1 gun, 30–05, for example.

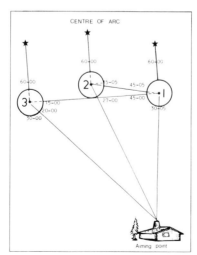

FIG. 1.7.

from the Observation Post to the guns. He also predicted, correctly that when the guns retired behind the masking hills, the forward observers who manipulated their fire would become prime targets. Guk's work was on a par with the most advanced foreign thinking, and an original contribution to artillery technique. Many, of course, were suspicious of indirect fire, believing that gunners would sacrifice effect for safety, a belief which Guk strongly contested.

Indirect fire suddenly became a major issue in the mid-1890s. In 1896, the Russian Artillery Committee decided to introduce a special indirect fire sight, modelled on the German *Richtfläche*. This was not a full circle, but a circular sight was introduced in 1902 and an improved one in 1905 (see Figs. 1.8 to 1.10 and Plate 1.10). These early non-optical sights were known as goniometers in English and *uglomery* in Russian. The *uglomer* was a standard fitting on the M-1900 pattern Field Gun (Plate 1.9). When war broke out in 1904, the Russians therefore had artillery officers who were practised in indirect fire, but they were reluctant to employ it in practice at first (Plate 1.11). However, at the battle of Tashichao, on 11 July Old Style (24 July New Style), 1904, Lieutenant-Colonel Pashchenko of 9 East Siberian battalion hit the Japanese with deadly indirect fire from behind a crest and high vegetation, drawing their return fire on to dummy positions

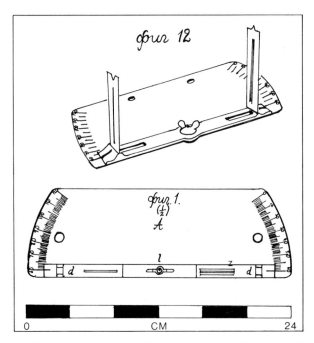

Fɪɢ. 1.8.   Sight for horizontal indirect laying, modelled on the German, introduced in 1896 and approved in 1898.

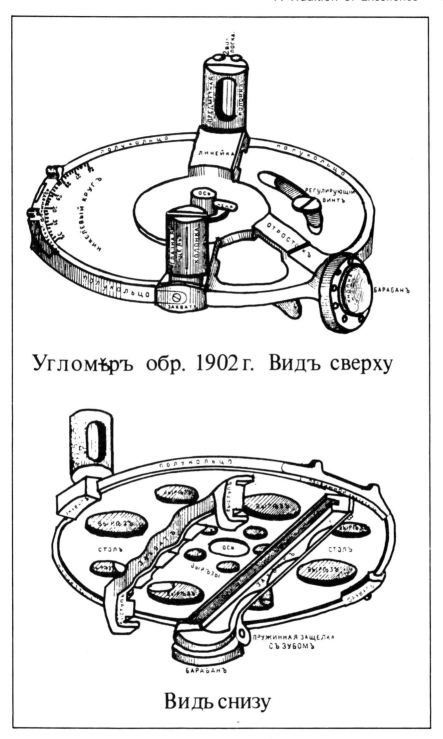

Fɪɢ. 1.9.   1902 pattern non-optical dial sight (*uglomer*).

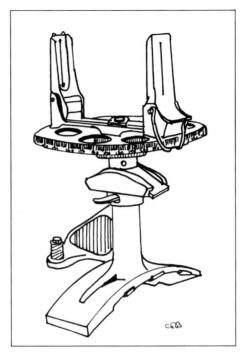

FIG. 1.10.   Model 1905 non-optical dial sight (*uglomer*). This was quickly
replaced by the Goertz panorama sight. Model 1906.

PLATE 1.9.   The mounting for the non-optical dial sight on the M-1900
pattern gun. (Author's photograph, with kind permission Sotamuseo)

on the forward slope of the crest. The Russians used indirect fire on a large scale at Liao-Yang at the end of August, and in October Pashchenko's commanding officer, Colonel Slyusarenko tracked the Japanese across the terrain in another striking demonstration where the gun crews saw nothing of the enemy, but their fire 'swept around like brooms'. From Liao-Yang on, indirect fire became the normal mode of operation. The Russians did not invent it but they made a major contribution to its development and were the first to use it *as the rule* in war.[21]

PLATE 1.10.   M-1877 pattern field gun with 1905 pattern *uglomer* or non-optical dial sight. (Sotamuseo)

Relations with other Arms

The tradition of intellectual and professional excellence founded by Arakcheyev and others was maintained, and the legacy of Arakcheyev was evident in the high social position enjoyed by the Imperial artillery. In the 1880s, those who graduated from the Officers' Artillery School with first class certificates were promoted Second Lieutenants and were given seniority above those who had graduated from the War Schools for infantry

PLATE 1.11.   Russian artillery making a lighthearted attempt at digging on manoeuvres in August, 1903. The smiles, the white tunics and suicidal open position would all soon be swept away by the harsh realities of modern war. (British Library)

and the Corps of Pages with 'excellent' grades the year before. Given that the Corps of Pages was the 'most aristocratic Cadet school in Russia', the very high status of the Artillery School's best graduates can be appreciated. A British observer in China during the Boxer rebellion of 1900 remarked that the Russian artillery officers considered themselves more professional and better educated than those of the other arms, although he himself did not notice much difference. Among the Russian artillery's most distinguished officers was Count Leo Tolstoy, the writer. Tolstoy did not regard his artillery service in the Caucasus and at Sevastopol merely as a patriotic chore; he was a professional officer who wrote technical papers on artillery problems. His experience shows through in *War and Peace* and other novels and stories.

Although this tradition made for very good guns and very good technical gunnery, it proved counter-productive to some extent as it hindered co-operation with the other arms. This became a particular problem when indirect fire enabled the artillery to move back from the front line, whereas previously it had been in the front line, or even deployed in front of the infantry. The gunners' ethos and method of operation were suddenly transformed, as the cartoon from the artillery school magazine of 1905 shows. Soldiers of other arms began to resent the gunners, while the gunners became preoccupied with technicalities and forgot about tactics. This happened in the French army as well, where the artillery also enjoyed elite status. The Russian artillery resented attempts to subordinate batteries to infantry commanders, and at the highest level the Inspector-General of Artillery, Grand Duke Sergey Mikhaylovich, refused to obey the orders of Sukhomlinov, War Minister from 1909–1915. Visitors remarked that officers of the different arms hardly seemed to be members of the same army. Sergey Mikhaylovich's aide was an officer called Smyslovskiy, and

Техника прогрессирует

ТЕПЕРЬ
NOW

ПРЕЖДЕ
THEN

Fig. 1.11.   The March of Technology — the effect of the introduction of
indirect fire on the artillery's ethos, temporarily, at least.

the British Military attaché in Petrograd at the beginning of World War I, Colonel Knox, commented that 'both of them represent the views of the hide bound gunner who is so obsessed with science that he never thinks of the necessity for practical co-operation with the infantry'.

The lack of co-operation worked both ways. Foreign observers at manoeuvres in 1866 noticed 'the little use made of the large force of artillery', and there were numerous examples of General officers failing to use their artillery in the Russo-Japanese War. One General, on seeing a battery taking up an indirect fire position, ordered it forward on to a ridge. When he was told that it was not necessary for the guns to see the target, he refused to believe it. There was a tendency to keep large numbers of guns in reserve, in order to exploit success which rarely materialised. General Kuropatkin could have used many more guns at Liao-Yang, and at Mukden many guns were kept back with the result that there was not the proper proportion of guns to infantry. In one Corps at the battle of the Sha-Ho, an entire brigade of thirty-two of the new M-1900 Quick-Firing Field Guns was kept well away from the field.

After the war, attempts were made to improve infantry–artillery co-operation, and an order to this effect was issued in 1907. This proved to be ambiguous, however, and in some formations the artillery remained aloof whilst in others infantry captains were allowed to give instructions to artillery batteries. By the time of the Great War, an improvement was nonetheless apparent.[22]

The Beginning of World War I

The Russians went to war in 1914 prepared for a short and mobile clash on the flat plains of Poland. They had planned for the wrong war. The Russian artillery had 7900 pieces of ordnance to the Germans' 6700, and given the Germans' commitments in the West this should have given the Russians a convincing superiority. However, most of the Russian pieces were field guns, designed to fire fast and flat, whereas the Germans had more heavy field howitzers, which would prove invaluable in trench fighting. The Russians had laid in a shell reserve of 1500 shells per gun, the Germans 3000. However, many of the Russian shells did not reach the artillery because of the chaotic distribution system, and within three weeks of the start of the war alarmed telegrams were flying to Petrograd warning of the huge expenditure of ammunition. This was the beginning of the notorious 'shell shortage'. Soon there were tales of Russian gunners fighting hand-to-hand having run out of ammunition. Shell shortage was not peculiar to Russia; Britain and France also both experienced munitions crises in 1915, and in all three countries the problem was not really solved until 1916. The British were still short of ammunition at the battle of the Somme, although admittedly the 'norms' of shell required by the British and French were higher than the Russian. The density of artillery, as of all arms, remained substantially less in East than in the West throughout the war. In the opening phases, German artillery was responsible for 45 per cent of casualties inflicted on the Russians, which British observers considered to be a function of shell shortage and the consequent inability of the Russians to beat down the German guns. In fact, this percentage was less than that (nearly 60 per cent) later found to apply in the West, and this was probably due to the more mobile and extended nature of the fighting. Even so, it is considerable given that, as Major-General Headlam noted in 1917, the density of artillery fire was nowhere near that experienced in France.

In spite of the shell shortage and the appalling strategy and generalship, the tactical and technical performance of the Russian artillery are rarely criticised. Of course, standards varied with individual units and the availability of ammunition was very much dependent on the luck of the draw. The south-west front seems to have been well favoured throughout. Professor Bernard Pares noted in early 1915 that the accuracy of the Russian artillery was one of the striking features of the campaign. Russian batteries were very seldom dismantled by the enemy. The Austrians often placed batteries on the crests of hills and suffered severely from the accurate fire of the Russian artillery. In March and April, 1915 the Russians made a number of attacks on this front, each preceded by a 'very strong' artillery preparation. The effect of this on the Germans was very marked. German officers taken prisoner testified to extremely large losses and described the intensity of artillery fire as equal to that which they had encountered in France. Sometimes they even said that they believed French guns and gunners to be serving opposite them on the Eastern Front, which was, of course, not the case.[23]

Brusilov's Offensive, Summer 1916

The superb handling of the relatively limited force of artillery which was available to support Brusilov's offensive on the South-West Front in 1916 is one of the Imperial Artillery's finest achievements. It is also the prologue to Soviet employment of artillery on the battlefield. Brusilov himself later joined the Red Army, after much soul searching, as did the senior engineer, Velichko. The fate of Lieutenant-Colonel V. F. Kirey, the Chief of artillery of Ninth Army is unknown, although the two very important pamphlets which he wrote in 1916 and 1917 were published by the Red Army in book form in 1926 and again in 1936, with an introduction by the chief of the Red Army's artillery, Yuri Sheydeman, also an ex-Tsarist officer (see below).

The fire support plan for Brusilov's offensive has a striking antecedent in the German Gorlitse-Tarnuv offensive of the previous year. The skilful co-ordination of artillery fire with the movement of the other arms was developed by the German Bruchmüller, and his methods have much in common with those used by the Russians in 1916; the concentration of fire on carefully selected and reconnoitred targets and the careful briefing of artillery and infantry officers together. Ex-Imperial officers working for the Soviets certainly studied Bruchmüller's methods after 1918, but it is not at all certain whether and, if so, how the Russian offensive of 1916 was modelled on the German of 1915. Brusilov, it is true, was very nearly cut off by the German enveloping movement, and might have had good reason to study the reasons for its success, but the Russians could well have evolved their ideas independently.

One of the main reasons for the success of the Brusilov breakthrough was the good co-operation between artillery and infantry, a far cry from the distrust that existed before the war. The same thing is constantly stressed by the modern Soviet artillery (see Chapter Four). Kirey constantly hammered home the need for co-operation and interworking, and in the second of his pamphlets, on artillery in the defence, he put the point in the bluntest terms. Artillery officers should personally reconnoitre every height and

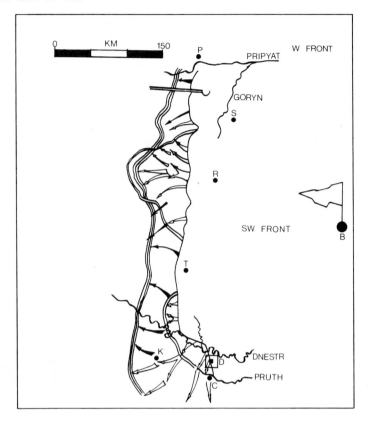

FIG. 1.12.   Brusilov's Offensive, South West Front, from 22 May (4 June),
to 31 July (13 August) 1916. B, Berdichev (HQ of SW Front);
C, Chernovtsy; D, Dobronouts; K, Kolomyya; P, Pinsk; R, Rovno; S, Sarny;
T, Ternopol. Front line as at 21 May, O.S. ——— Extent of Russian
advance to 2–3 June. ═══ Extent of Russian advance to 31 July. ═══

depression, and visit every trench. They should on no account become
alienated from the infantry officers, and should give orders on the ground,
not over the telephone or off a map. Otherwise, said Kirey, for every drop
of artilleryman's sweat saved, the infantry would weep tears of blood.

In this offensive, the Russians achieved a very effective concentration of
fire by working out the artillery fireplan with great care. Just how detailed it
was can be seen from a section reproduced in Kirey's book. The principle
employed was ruthless realism; some Russian planners had been using
French norms and criteria, which were clearly inapplicable and unneccessary
on the Russian front, where formations, guns and ammunition were all
fewer and further between. Kirey stressed the need to start with the number
of guns and shells available, and work back from there. This accords with
the modern Soviet principle of Operational Art and Tactics of 'adjusting
ends to means', expressed by Colonel Savkin in 1972. Another modern

Soviet officer, Colonel Sidorenko drew attention to the fact that the breakthrough was calculated 'by shells and metres of operation', and that special attention was paid to a narrow *breakthrough sector*, both characteristics of the modern Soviet offensive. Also notable is the great depth of the attacking force. In all breakthrough operations, the main problem is not so much to achieve the initial penetration of the forward edge of the defence, as to keep up the momentum of the attack right into the enemy depth, and to provide fire support for it. In Brusilov's Offensive, the former was achieved by holding reserves in bunkers constructed very close to the front line and the latter by having light mountain guns to accompany the infantry right through the defence. This coincides exactly with the later Soviet idea of the *Deep Operation*, and with the modern emphasis on maintaining fire support all the way through the enemy deployment (Integrated Fire Destruction of the Enemy — see Chapter Four).

The Ninth Army's attack, on the extreme left flank, took place on a sector 14 kilometres wide from the River Dnestr to point 458 (see Fig. 1.13), with a main 'breakthrough sector' of three and a half kilometres, from point 216 to point 218. On this frontage Kirey had 211 guns — a low density by western front standards. Kirey was anxious to keep the bombardment short for four reasons. First, the more prolonged the bombardment, the more time the enemy will have to bring up reserves and concentrate the artillery. Secondly, the Russians were short of ammunition. Thirdly, there was a very real danger of wearing out the guns, and fourthly surprise would be lost.

The ability of artillery to fire indirect was utilised to the full. Targets were carefully located and surveyed and batteries situated as far forward as possible 3 to 4 kilometres from the forward enemy positions — for greater accuracy. The batteries were not 'massed' in one place but deployed according to their individual tasks so that it was possible to mass the fire of the majority of them on the most important points of the enemy position.

Each artillery group (battalion battery or section) had a precisely defined task; the suppression of enemy strong points, breaching obstacles, and so on. Close links with the infantry were established in particular having forward observation officers in the front line, to correct the fire.

Before the operation many doubted whether it could succeed. How could the Russians achieve a breakthrough with a comparatively light density of ordnance when the French and British in the West had failed with so much more? The Russian Eighth Army had 704 guns, not significantly superior to the Austro-Hungarian forces' 600. The Ninth Army had 59 heavy guns to the opposition's 150. But 55 of those were to be on the narrow breakthrough sector, with 104 light and mountain guns. As a result the Russians' bombardment was shatteringly effective. On Eighth Army's sector forward trenches were levelled and dugouts caved in under the impact of heavy

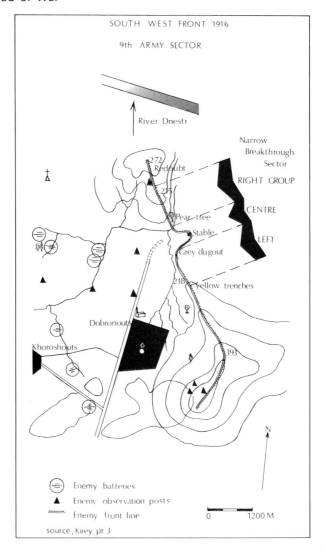

FIG. 1.13.   Brusilov's Offensive, 1916, breakthrough on 9th Army Sector.

shells. On the Ninth Army's front, the Austrian commander, Pflanzer-Baltin, was not to know that the guns firing at him were virtually all the Russians had. He remarked on 'the enemy's great superiority in long range heavy artillery . . . of unprecedented effectiveness'. In fact, the Russians were inferior in this respect. It was a perfect example of concentration of force, and of how 'mass' could be achieved by 'unprecedentedly good timing and thoughtful preparation'. The care with which the fireplan was worked out, combined with measures to ensure that the infantry received fire support right through the assault, meant that the Russians achieved a breakthrough and subsequent advance that were spectacular by World War I standards.

In his book, Kirey also dealt with the role of artillery in repulsing tank attacks. Although he had never seen a tank, he was quick to appreciate their potential and the way in which they might be employed for deep penetration tasks. He suggested that tanks which broke through the forward lines should be engaged by the anti-aircraft guns assigned to protect bridges, key junctions and so on, and that anti-tank combat would mainly be by direct fire. He therefore anticipated later theories of tank employment and World War II practice, German and Soviet, in using anti-aircraft guns against them. In this, and in the employment of artillery on the battlefield generally, Kirey and his colleagues were the originators of modern Soviet ideas and methods.[24]

The Last Days of the Imperial Artillery

A number of technical improvements took place later in the war. Russian artillery conducted their first *registration point* shoot in 1916. Although the best way to bring artillery fire on to a target is for an observer to adjust on to it, it is not always possible for the observer to see the objective, especially in long range counter-battery fire. Also, surprise is lost. The method used is therefore to adjust on to a neighbouring registration point, the distance and direction of which from the target is known, in order to iron out all the errors, and then to switch on to the desired target. Nevertheless, the Russians remained rather weak in this very important area. Their gun positions were generally well selected and arranged, and as long as observation was possible all ranks were thoroughly proficient. When required to fall back on air observation, air photographs or shooting entirely from the map 'they had neither the equipment or the knowledge'. In the West there had been rapid development in his area. However, conditions were quite different in the east. On the south-west front, the terrain was very mountainous and, of course, troops were far thinner on the ground. In some other ways the Russians were remarkably professional: their maps were 'excellent', their instruments simpler and more workable and the panorama sketches drawn by observation post officers 'of higher average merit' than British.

Gun positions were frequently well-camouflaged, although the Russians would promptly proceed to compromise them by driving sledges right up to them, leaving prominent tracks which enemy aeroplanes could see. In spite of Lenin's famous statement that the Army 'voted for peace with its feet', there were no signs of collapse on the south-west front in March, 1917, and the Russian artillery continued to conduct itself coolly and competently into

September. It was only after the Bolshevik seizure of power that officers there were ordered to dismiss their batmen and go home.[25]

The Imperial Russian artillery had much in common with the Soviet artillery, whose direct ancestor it was. Its equipment was abundant, technologically advanced and of good quality. This was achieved by concentrating resources and talent at the expense of the rest of the economy. Its officers were an intellectual, technical and social elite. The Russians made original contributions to artillery technology, technical gunnery (indirect fire) and the operational employment of artillery. In the stress they placed on mass artillery fire, the concentration of fire on a narrow breakthrough sector and their emphasis on the combination of mass *and* mobility, the Imperial Artillery clearly anticipated the Soviet artillery's operational ideas. The main problem was in ensuring co-operation with the other arms. The best Imperial officers insisted that artillerymen should work closely with the other arms, just as modern Soviet officers constantly reiterate the need for artillerymen to be completely *au fait* with combined arms tactics and for officers of other arms to understand what artillery can do.

Soviet Artillery

To some extent the Soviet artillery has inherited the Imperial artillery's professionalism, whilst shedding its isolation. The Imperial artillery influenced the artillery of the Red or (as it was known from 1946), Soviet army directly for two main reasons. Firstly, the experience of World War I was studied exhaustively by the Red Army and, secondly, because a great many Imperial officers joined the Reds, often rising to very high ranks.

The Russian Civil War began on 9 December, 1917, with Kaledin's operations against Rostov. Whether former officers and NCOs joined the Red Army or the White (counter-revolutionaries) depended largely on geography and who happened to be in power where: a pistol pointed at the head was frequently most persuasive. The Reds had very few guns available at first, since most of the artillery was in frontier areas which the Reds did not control. In December, 1917, the College of People's Commissars for Military and Naval Affairs was set up, and on 1 January, 1918, a number of authorities, corresponding to those of the old War Ministry were created, among them that of the Inspector General of artillery. On 15 January this was renamed the 'All-Russian College for the Organisation and Direction of the Red Army', and the Workers' and Peasants' Red Army ($RKKA$) was officially founded. The College comprised eight sections, including the armament section, dealing with artillery. The old Main Artillery Director-ate (GAU) was subordinated to this. The staff of GAU, including many very senior officers and Civil Servants, were summoned and told that they would now use all their energies working for the Bolshevik government, and that no resignations would be accepted. Two commissars were appointed to supervise the head of *GAU*, but otherwise the organisation continued to operate as it had done under the Tsar. While the Bolsheviks paid great attention to the organisation of the centre, that at the front remained most irregular. It was not until March, 1918, that the Higher War Council set out the prescribed organisation for a Soviet infantry division, including its artillery complement of 68 guns (including eight Anti-Aircraft).[26]

Meanwhile, at the end of 1917, the Volunteer Army, the most important element of the White forces, began to form on the river Don. If anything the Whites were even worse off for equipment than the Reds at this stage, although they possessed much greater military skill. Later, the Whites received much material aid from the Germans and the Entente, and a number of foreign weapon types entered Red Army service by this route when they were subsequently captured. Both Red and White artillery usually operated in the *direct fire* mode. It was extremely difficult to find concealed positions in the totally flat steppe where most of the fighting took place, and experience showed that in manoeuvrist war the main thing was to open fire first and fastest. The side which did so could paralyse the enemy as Okunev had envisaged a century before, and guns with shields were designed for this purpose. Direct fire is obviously more efficient and effective than indirect, especially for units lacking technical training, which was a problem for both sides. In these circumstances, the Whites' superior basic military training and discipline gave them the advantage, battery for battery, but organisation and political will told in the end.[27]

Imperial influence on the Red Army was probably greater in the artillery field than anywhere else. This was partly because of the specialised nature of the gunner's black art, which made the Reds more dependent on specialised knowledge there than elsewhere, but it must be said that the Soviets acquired some artillery experts who were exceptionally able and energetic officers by any standards. Two of them, Imperial Lieutenant-General Yuri Mikhaylovich Sheydeman and Imperial Colonel Vladimir Davydovich Grendal', have their contribution to modern Soviet artillery described in Chapter Two. Sheydeman and Grendal' were among the highest ranking Imperial officers to exercise direct control over Soviet forces; former Tsarist full generals like Brusilov and Mikhnevich were employed on military academic work while many of the more prominent commanders in other arms had been Tsarist NCOs or at most very junior officers, like Tukhachevskiy. Sheydeman and Grendal' authored many of the most influential artillery manuals in the 1920s, and Sheydeman presided over analysis of particular problems which had been revealed by the Great War: the use of air photographs, correcting fire from aircraft, compensating for meteorological conditions and sound ranging. At the end of 1922, Sheydeman also had armoured forces placed under his direction, another indicator of the pervasive influence of the Soviet artillery within the military system as a whole.

Other Imperial officers made a striking contribution as well. The Soviets were fascinated by the possibilities revealed by the German Paris Gun which bombarded the French capital from March to July 1918 at a range of 120 kilometres. As a direct result a special subcommittee of the Main Artillery Directorate's Artillery Committee was set up to study ways of increasing the range of artillery to 100 kilometres and beyond. On 17 December, 1918, at Lenin's personal command, this became the Commission for Special Artillery Experiments (KOSARTOP). KOSARTOP played a major role in the development of new artillery systems, including the first all Soviet artillery piece, the model 1927 infantry gun. The potential of super long range artillery continued to fascinate the Soviets and in 1927 a former Imperial colonel, V. Vnukov, published a book on the feasibility of firing at ranges of over 100 kilometres. He examined electric guns, using linear induction motors to propel projectiles as well as conventional ordnance. He concluded that such weapons were most likely to be of value against strategic targets, and that air attack was generally a more economical method of attacking such objectives. However, such artillery might be significant if the enemy had a clear superiority in the air. This clearly illustrates the contribution of Imperial officers to the Soviet army, not just in conventional areas but also as highly futuristic thinkers. This interest in super long range artillery must have created a favourable climate for the development of long range missile systems, which were envisaged by Tukhachevskiy from at least the mid 1930s. In the 1920s, the new Soviet regime was genuinely receptive to creative and futuristic ideas of all kinds, and these were particularly welcome in the military sphere for two reasons: first, to overcome the apparent dichotomy between mass and mobility and, second, to circumvent the massive conventional superiority enjoyed by the main adversaries of the regime, the victors of World War I. There is direct continuity between the systems foreseen or devised in this period and modern Soviet ordnance, and their further evolution is described in Chapter Three.

Another influential former Imperial officer, General Golovin, published a milestone article in 1925. He also analysed World War I experience and, in opposition to those who believed that this was irrelevant to the war of manoeuvre which the Soviets expected and wished to fight, stressed that artillery was even more important now, to preserve one's freedom of manoeuvre and deny it to the enemy. Manoeuvre meant above all manoeuvre of fire, and the most important guarantee of this was long range, something which the Soviets clearly still believe in today. The initial collision between opposed forces in any future war should be pursued with the utmost savagery, and therefore everything had to be thrown into a massive *fire blow* right at the start. For this reason, the World War I norm of at least 18 batteries to an infantry division should be adhered to. Artillery's principal tasks were support of the infantry and counter-battery fire. Golovin also stressed the role of chemical weapons and co-operation with aircraft. Only one ingredient of modern Soviet artillery thinking was missing: the need to clear the way for armour.[28]

Artillery in Soviet Operational Art

In 1924 the Red Army held the All-Union Artillery Conference, attended by many who were to steer the subsequent development of Soviet operational art, including the fiery genius Mikhail Tukhachevskiy. A paper of Tukhachevskiy's on Manoeuvre and Artillery was read and the conference also considered one on combat with enemy aviation, tanks and armoured vehicles. The conference contributed directly to the Frunze Army reforms of 1924–25 and the subsequent 1927 Field Regulations. The Frunze reforms established an infantry-artillery concept which developed naturally into the later all-arms offensive. The principles for employing artillery stated in the Regulations were, first, its employment in strict conformity with all-arms formations (primarily infantry at this stage), permitting full co-operation with them throughout the entire battle and unbroken support, second, massing of fire, third, suddenness of action and flexibility of fire. These principles still apply today. The reforms also made important organisational changes such as the establishment of a single divisional artillery regiment and the creation of target acquisition battalions, which facilitated the evolution of this essential and demanding service during the Great Patriotic War.[29]

Most details of modern Soviet artillery philosophy and employment become recognisable in the late 1920s and 30s. It was then that two major factors in modern war, tanks and aircraft, began to be considered seriously. Then, also, modern offshoots of field artillery began to appear: anti-tank artillery, recoilless guns and multiple rocket launchers and self-propelled (SP) guns. Mortars and anti-aircraft artillery (AAA) had been playing a significant role for longer, but also became more important during these years. The Soviets began to think about using artillery in the way they do today: adapting it to a war of manoeuvre, using it to 'clear the way', not just for infantry as in World War I, but also for tanks, conducting .long range counter-battery (CB) fire, interdicting (isolating) a particular part of the battlefield with a fire screen, and in all this possibly using chemical munitions and stressing the complementary and interacting roles of ground artillery, AAA and aircraft.

Many of the characteristics of modern Soviet artillery can be seen in the recommendations made by Vladimir Triandafillov, a founding father of Soviet military thought and art. Triandafillov, who lived from 1894 until his death in an air crash in 1931, published his seminal *Character of the Operations of Modern Armies* in 1929. Triandafillov saw clearly from World War I experience the need for artillery to accompany advancing troops through the enemy defence, 'not just with fire but also with wheels'. Huge quantities of artillery were essential for the successful breakthrough of positions held by infantry armed with the heavy weapons of modern war. Triandafillov calculated that the infantry in a modern division, attacking an enemy division deployed across a front of 8 to 12 kilometres could launch their offensive on a sector of 1500 to 2000 metres. The artillery in such an attacking division was sufficient to engage targets on a front of 500 to 800 metres (East European armies) or 800 to 1000 metres (Western armies). With eminent logic Triandafillov concluded that in order to obtain the optimum balance between artillery and infantry the quantity of artillery needed to be doubled relative to the infantry. This may be the reason for the colossal Soviet artillery build-up in the 1930s and the high proportion of artillery to other arms in the Soviet army today when compared with western armies. Triandafillov also noted the Polish regulations which recommended placing a whole artillery battalion in support of each battalion in the first wave of an attack, something which the Soviets continue to do today. He also laid down norms for the amount of artillery required to support an offensive: normally 50 to 60 guns per kilometre of front rising to 75 if counter-battery fire had to be carried out simultaneously. A corps attacking on a 5 kilometre sector would thus require some 300 guns, which meant reinforcing it with four to seven artillery regiments. This density of artillery was generally attained by Soviet forces during 1942 and greatly exceeded by the end of the war (see below).

Trandafillov noted how some people advocated using tanks to provide some of the fire support, but, like all Soviet military thinkers and in contrast to some of the tank prophets in the west, he was cautious about the ability of the tank to substitute for artillery. He assessed that two tank battalions might substitute for one artillery regiment, but in common with Soviet views to this day, massed artillery was still required to suppress anti-tank defences.

Triandafillov noted the absence of a 'strategic' artillery reserve in East European armies and the important role that such a force of heavy artillery had played on the western front in World War I. This was the origin of the artillery reserve of the supreme high command (ARVGK) of the Great Patriotic War. Finally, Triandafillov envisaged large scale use of chemical weapons and set out the amounts of artillery required to obtain the requisite concentrations of different types of chemical agents.[30]

These views and those of later Soviet theorists and practitioners contrasted with those who pinned all their hopes on the interaction of armour and aircraft and on what later came to be called Blitzkrieg in the West. These tended to relegate artillery to a lower position and even to regard it as somewhat out of date. During this period, artillery in the German army was decentralised. This was considered possible because, they thought, air forces could take over many of the tasks which had previously been the preserve of massed artillery, leaving artillery to deal only with opportunity targets; those which were identified by the advancing ground forces when the attack had started. In order to be able to keep up with motorised infantry and tanks, and to be able to operate off the roads, thereby reducing its vulnerability to air attack artillery would become self-propelled, although no army had much SP artillery at the beginning of World War II. It was even predicted that great artillery barrages like those of World War I would become 'merely interesting phenomena of the past'.

Some in the Red Army also adopted this view but neither top artillery man Voronov nor Stalin was persuaded. During the 1920s and 1930s the Soviets carried out large-scale and imaginative experiments in the combined arms offensive. However, the Soviet form of Blitzkrieg, unlike the German, always retained artillery as a cardinal component, along with motorised infantry, tanks, engineers and aircraft as Triandafillov had envisaged. The Soviet Field Service Regulations of 1936 stressed that artillery still provided the greatest firepower and opened the way for the tanks. The artillery would destroy machine and anti-tank guns; the tank attack *had to be secured by organised artillery fire and could not proceed without it*. Artillery was formally recognised as the *main source of firepower*, although because of fashionable views its role tended to be underestimated in practical exercises. In 1938, Stalin reaffirmed that artillery remained an important, indeed decisive, factor in war, and that the Red Army should give it special attention. However, even Stalin's blessing did not make the artillery immune from its opponents. The organisational changes in the period immediately before the war are connected with political and personal rivalries rather than with the requirements of Operational Art. Most anomalous was the decision in 1940 to abolish the post of Head of Red Army Artillery, and to split its functions between the General Staff and the Main Artillery Directorate. The post was re-established in July 1941, and given to Voronov.[31]

The Artillery Field Service Regulations of 1937 and the Gunnery Regulations of 1939 reflected the all-arms philosophy of the 1936 Field Service Regulations. The latter stressed the need for the impetus of the offensive to be maintained right through a deep defence and into the enemy's operational depth; the '*deep operation*'. This required several sorts of artillery; artillery for close support of infantry (*PP*); long range artillery for CB fire (*DD*), and heavy artillery for destroying the enemy (*AR*). The 1941 regulations further recommended anti-tank and AA artillery groups. Artillery helped the offensive along in the traditional three phases: *preparation*, *support* and *accompaniment*. Support was carried out using either a rolling barrage or successive concentrations of aimed fire (Chapter Four). Then, as now, the main form of operation envisaged was the offensive, and the Red Army was much less suited to operating on the strategic and operational defensive. This is why, having lost the initiative, the Red Army did not acquit itself as well as it might have against the Germans in the early part of the war. However, there is always a symbiotic relationship between attack and defence, not at least since every thrust is open to counter-attack, and the regulations also gave instructions for the defensive use of artillery. At extreme range the enemy would be met by long range fire blows, then by concentrated fire, and finally static and mobile barrages.[32]

Voronov had been a Soviet military 'adviser' on the Republican side in the Spanish Civil War (1936–9), and this influenced the employment of Soviet artillery. His experience in Spain had shown him that special anti-tank guns were not essential to defeat tanks, and that ordinary field guns could do the job perfectly well. This was particularly true of Russian guns which traditionally had low silhouettes and high muzzle velocities. Also, because of the sheer size of the Soviet artillery arsenal, the Red Army could use its artillery both after the fashion of the Great War, for massed indirect fire, and in the decentralised direct fire mode. In 1937, Soviet Russia was reported to have 9200 Field and heavy guns, roughly twice as many as Nazi Germany and over three times as many as France. By June 1941 the Soviets had 67,000 guns, howitzers and heavy mortars (excluding 50 mm mortars and AAA). Using some of this force in the direct fire role was partly a function of the manoeuvrist nature of the early stages of the Great Patriotic War as in the Civil War, and of the particular threat from armour. It was also simpler and quicker to teach, saved time and ammunition on the battlefield and helped circumvent shortages in communications and optical equipment vital to indirect fire.

Soviet artillery had proved particularly useful in the Winter War against Finland, for the breakthrough of the heavily fortified Mannerheim line. One of the reasons why Soviet artillery acquitted itself relatively better than armour or infantry in the Winter War and the early days of the Great Patriotic War was that its effectiveness depends largely on the technical competence of NCOs and relatively junior officers. It does not depend to such an extent on higher tactical or operational flair on the part of generals. Therefore, the purge of 1937–38, which struck the most senior ranks most cruelly, had relatively less impact on the artillery. Nevertheless, as noted above, all-arms commanders must make the most effective use of artillery, and at the beginning of 1941 there was a lamentable lack of artillery awareness at the MV Frunze all-arms Military Academy. This prompted Voronov to write a paper on the role of artillery in Blitzkrieg style war. He was half way through it when the Germans attacked. The survival of Voronov, whom Stalin liked, was also fortuitous for the Soviet artillery, as was that of Nikolay Dimitriyevich Yakovlev (1898–1972), the very able head of *GAU* during the war. Yakovlev had been Head of Artillery of the Kiev Special Military District, a particularly important MD where senior posts were reserved for those who were going places. Yakovlev was appointed on 16 June, less than a week before Hitler unleashed Barbarossa.[33]

The Great Patriotic War: First Period
(22 June, 1941–19 November, 1942)

In the early stages of the war, Soviet guns in direct fire positions were responsible for the majority of German tank losses. Tanks which broke through the first echelon of Soviet defences were engaged by the anti-aircraft guns of the second, an example of the interaction of ground artillery, AAA and air which was to characterise Soviet operations throughout. Another example of this was the use of ground artillery to impede German operations from advanced airfields. In the attack on Smolensk, in August, 1941, the German fighter-bombers operated from air-strips only about six miles behind their forward troops, so as to achieve the closest possible co-operation. Then, Soviet long range artillery forced them to abandon this tactic, the Soviets claiming to have destroyed 150 aircraft by this method in one day. The Soviet artillery like all arms, suffered catastrophic losses, as the German forces penetrated into Soviet territory, sometimes as fast as a 100 kilometres in one day. In order to preserve the valuable *heavy* and *super heavy artillery*, and to increase the manoeuvrability of Soviet formations, the amount of artillery in an infantry division was reduced from 280 pieces (including mortars) to 132, and the equipment thus released was formed into units of the *Artillery Reserve of the High Command*. The number of such artillery units rose from 110 in June 1941 to 255 on 1 December. The road-bound heavy artillery was just too vulnerable, but Yakovlev, who was in charge of the operation, knew that it would be needed when the time came to counter-attack. The new rocket launchers were deployed in 'Guards Mortar Regiments', the majority being sent to the Moscow defensive zone.

On 10 January, 1942, Stalin issued his directive 'On the *artillery offensive*'. This stressed the need to concentrate artillery on the main breakthrough sector, and for artillery to keep up unbroken support throughout the entire period of the offensive. Artillery and mortar fire should move with the infantry and tanks into the attack, and from one objective to the next. New gunnery regulations (PS-42) were also issued. These included provisions for directing artillery fire from tanks equipped with radios, to facilitate the co-ordination of *moving barrages* and *successive concentrations of aimed fire* with the movements of advancing troops, simplified rules for conducting fire by heavy artillery and army assets, an expanded section on counter-battery fire, including 'norms' of shell expenditure (see Chapter Four), and regulations for direct fire against moving targets.[34]

Centralisation and Concentration

As the front stabilised, the Soviets, with their centralised artillery command structure intact, enjoyed an advantage over the Germans in the conduct of massed and counter-battery fire. In the German army, the complex duties of artillery co-ordination were assigned to individual and separate officers; artillery chiefs of staff under the commanders of all-arms units. The Soviets' experience of the fighting led to more and more centralisation. Whereas in 1941 only 8 per cent of Red Army Artillery was High Command Reserve, by August, 1945, it was 35 per cent. In Autumn 1942, the Soviets re-established the artillery division (not to be confused with the *divizion*, or battalion), an artillery formation which had first appeared in 1819. This was designed to provide a massive force of artillery to reinforce formations on main axes. In 1942, an artillery division comprised eight regiments, in 1943–45, six or seven artillery brigades, or up to 364 guns, mortars and rocket launchers. There were also Guards Mortar divisions, comprising three regiments of Rocket launchers (288 equipments in 1943) each. Artillery and Guards Mortar divisions were first used for CB fire and destruction of the most important enemy targets. From 1943 artillery divisions were usually united into *Breakthrough Artillery Corps* (*AKP*), although some remained independent. AKPs were first introduced in Spring, 1943, to deal devastating blows on main axes of advance. At first a Corps comprised two artillery breakthrough divisions and one rocket launcher division, 1000 equipments in all. In 1944, there were two divisions in a corps. Numbers two and seven Artillery Corps took part in the great defensive battle of Kursk (July and August, 1943). During the defence of Leningrad in 1943, a Front CB artillery group was formed, comprising three artillery regiments, a naval rail gun brigade, and the guns of the Baltic Fleet. In 1944, this was reformed into an AKP. In the Berlin offensive operation in 1945, six AKPs participated, three from the Belorussian Front and three from the First Ukrainian. In all, ten such Corps were formed during the war, but afterwards they were disbanded.

There were also Artillery Groups, which were *ad hoc* formations comprising a variable number of units. At Stalingrad, in September 1942 a *Front Artillery Group* was formed, comprising 250–300 guns. From mid 1944, artillery groups were established in most combined arms formations and units of the first echelon. There were regimental, divisional, Corps and Army groups and also divisional, Corps, Army and Front *anti-aircraft groups*.

PLATE 1.12.   Rare photograph of Soviet counter-battery fire striking a German gun position, Eastern Front, 1941–45.

In addition to the artillery reserve of the High Command, which was the Front's reserve, the Soviets also formed a strategic *artillery reserve of the Supreme High Command*. At first, there were only independent regiments of the Supreme High Command reserve, but from 1942 brigades and divisions were formed and from 1943, AKPs.

The prime purpose of these concentrations of artillery was to break through the German lines. However, artillery *counter preparation* was also very important. This is defined as dealing a heavy blow to the enemy while he is deploying for an offensive. The German offensive at Kursk on 5 July, 1943 was subject to a counter preparation by artillery and aircraft unequalled in the history of war. 3000 pieces of ordnance were employed over the entire front, which weakened the Germans' offensive significantly.

The Soviets place great emphasis on the quantity of artillery brought to bear in various offensive operations in the war, and especially on the density of artillery per kilometre of Front. Details of the major Soviet operations are given in the table. After the battle of Stalingrad, the

Type and Density of Artillery on Breakthrough Sectors in Selected Operations of the Great Patriotic War

Offensive operation	Unit or Formation	Breadth of sector, km	Total guns, mortars, rocket launchers	Breakthrough sector, km	Total guns, mortars, rocket launchers on breakthrough sector	Density of artillery of 1 km of breakthrough sector			
						Operational		Tactical	
						General	Over 76 mm / Over 76 mm without rocket launchers	General	Over 76 mm / Over 76 mm without rocket launchers
Stalingrad counter-offensive 19–20.11. 42	5TA	35	2166	10	1067	107	$\frac{103}{64}$	—	—
	119RD	5	570	5	554	—	—	111	$\frac{102}{64}$
	421 RR	2	183	2	183	—	—	91	$\frac{87}{60}$
	65A	12	2405	9	1980	220	$\frac{203}{122}$	—	—
Kursk counter-offensive 7–8.43	11GA	36	3703	14	2516	180	$\frac{170}{142}$	—	—
	8GRC	3	930	3	734	—	—	245	$\frac{235}{227}$
	11GRD	1.5	—	1.5	381	—	—	254	$\frac{233}{225}$
	5GA	16	2325	6	1610	268	$\frac{260}{190}$	—	—
	33GRC	6	1680	6	1610	—	—	268	$\frac{260}{190}$
Belorussian operation 6.44	65A	24	2146	8	1572	197	$\frac{185}{140}$	—	—
	18RC	8	1572	8	1572	—	—	197	$\frac{185}{140}$
	37GRD	2	500	2	470	—	—	235	$\frac{214}{169}$

L'vov-Sandomir 7.44	60A	30	2641	8.3	2183	264	$\frac{250}{209}$	—	—
	28RC	4	—	4	1090	—	—	272	$\frac{256}{215}$
	302RD	1.5	—	1.5	489	—	—	326	$\frac{320}{280}$
Yassy-Kishinëv 8.44	37A	9	2272	6	1877	313	$\frac{266}{235}$	—	—
	6GRC	5.5	956	2.5	900	—	—	360	$\frac{336}{305}$
Petsamo-Kirkeness 10.44	14A	up to 60 (Arctic conditions)	2454	9	1540	171	$\frac{153}{114}$	—	—
	131RC	7	710	4	684	—	—	171	$\frac{150}{123}$
	10GRD	2	460	2	440	—	—	220	$\frac{210}{156}$
Vistula-Oder 1.45	8GA	30	2846	7	2438	348	$\frac{327}{291}$	—	—
	29GRC	2.5	1090	2.5	1051	—	—	420	$\frac{396}{369}$
	27 GRC	1.8	540	1.8	517	—	—	287	$\frac{277}{250}$
	76GRR	0.8	—	0.8	250	—	—	312	$\frac{300}{270}$
Berlin 4.45	5SA	9	2825	7	2430	347	$\frac{308}{265}$	—	—
	13A	9	2403	9	2356	252	$\frac{242}{230}$	—	—
	102RC	5	1373	5	1350	—	—	270	$\frac{252}{240}$
	147RD	1.5	458	1.5	450	—	—	300	$\frac{280}{260}$
	64ORR	0.8	—	0.8	—	—	—	300	—

(Source: Peredel'skiy et al., pp. 130–35)

Germans adopted a defensive system with continuous trenches, echeloned in great depth, and concrete strong points. This necessitated more numerous and powerful artillery. Heavy rocket launchers, like the BM-31 introduced in 1942, proved excellent weapons for dealing with such fortifications, without sacrificing too much mobility, as did the M-1943 160 mm mortar. Rocket launchers and mortars were favourite weapons, delivering a powerful projectile from a light launcher, and the plunging trajectory of the 160 mm mortar was especially useful. The Germans had nothing to compare with it, and when they first came under fire from it thought they were under air attack.[35]

The Russians' use of massed artillery reached its peak in 1945, when they enjoyed numerical superiority and command of the air. However, the difficulties of planning artillery operations on this scale should not be underestimated. It involved the most complex fire planning, transport to move artillery over long distances and close co-operation with supported arms. To take the example of the Vistula-Oder operation in January 1945, this involved the movement of one Breakthrough Artillery Corps, one anti-tank brigade, five rocket launcher brigades, two gun artillery regiments and three rocket launcher brigades from the reserve of the High Command to 1 Belorussian Front, and similar forces to 1 Ukrainian Front. The fire preparation was planned to last for two hours and thirty-five minutes with 7600 guns and mortars on a 33 kilometre breakthrough sector (33,500 pieces were involved in all). The density of artillery was 223 guns and 30 rocket launchers per kilometre. Such elaborate preparations were difficult to conceal from the enemy. The ordnance needed for the assault on Berlin was often hidden under loads of agricultural produce, and on one sector of the Belorussian Front over 700 guns, 500 rocket launchers and about 4000 tractors and soft skinned vehicles were moved under loads of hay and building materials.

Of course, no matter how much artillery is deployed, it can be ineffective if poorly directed. Centralised control of artillery enabled it to benefit from the work of specialised reconnaissance and target acquisition battalions. By the end of the war the Soviets were able to plot the positions of at least 70 per cent and sometimes 80–90 per cent of targets before an offensive began. The Soviets used sound ranging a great deal to locate enemy artillery and mortars. The timing and distribution of fire was also important. Soviet bombardments comprised periods of intense bombardment (*fire blows*) interspersed with less intense shelling. The variations in intensity and type of fire in some major operations are shown in the table. Variations in the pattern could be very effective; in one offensive by 5 Guards' Army a fire blow was delivered after the supported arms had already entered the German defence, and Germans who had come out of their protective dugouts were taken by surprise. Another tactic was to cease firing on a very narrow sector, and begin the assault, along this corridor while it appeared to the enemy that the bombardment was still in full swing.

German officers who experienced the Soviet bombardments agree that they were devastating. Anti-tank weapons were soon shot to pieces, however well sited or dug in, and reserves were 'battered to pulp'. The best antidote was counter battery fire at an early stage and with plenty of ammunition, and air strikes by the Luftwaffe.

The Soviet view is that *fire superiority* in the GPW was achieved primarily by massed artillery fire, in concert with air strikes. When artillery and air strikes were employed simultaneously, aircraft generally attacked enemy positions in the second and third lines of the defence, while artillery hit those in the first line. When employed consecutively, artillery and aircraft sometimes both attacked the same targets, although about 70 per cent of Soviet artillery in the war was of less than 100 mm calibre, able to hit targets up to a depth of about 5 kilometres. Experience showed that after the initial artillery and aviation *preparation* and initial *support* of the attack, fire support petered out when the advance reached a depth of 3 to 5 kilometres. For this reason it was necessary to have self-propelled assault guns to continue to help the tanks and infantry. In the most successful operations the Russians had one self-propelled gun to every two tanks. The first widely deployed self-propelled gun was the SAU-76, introduced in 1942. In 1943, 85 mm, 100 mm and 152 mm systems were introduced. The heavy assault guns ISU 122 and ISU 152 were designed specifically for the support and accompaniment tasks.

As the war progressed, the Soviets tended to make their bombardments shorter but more intense. This can be seen from the chart for counter-battery fire, and the same was true for other targets. The total time for artillery preparation, support and accompaniment did not decrease significantly, but proportionally more time was devoted to fire blows. In the Berlin Operation in 1945, 80 per cent of the time was given to them and only 20 per cent to *deliberate fire*.[36]

It would be impossible to do justice to the Soviet experience of employing artillery during the Great Patriotic War in a book this size. However, a number of key operations have been selected as examples. These are all offensive operations from the last period of the war: offensive, because that is the type of operation which causes us greatest concern, and from the last period of the war because that is when the density of artillery available and the morale and expertise of the Soviets approximate most closely to those which would obtain in a future European conflict. These campaigns are studied by Soviet senior officers in minute detail and they continually stress the relevance to future operations.

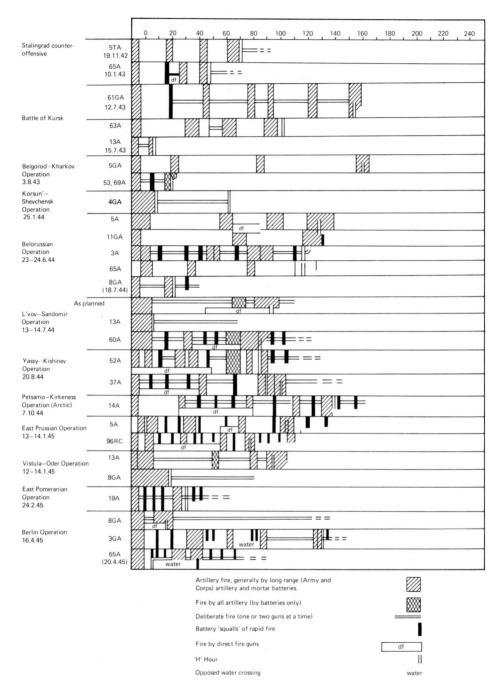

FIG. 1.14.   Suppression of enemy batteries during selected operations of the Great Patriotic War: type and duration of counter battery fire (Simplified). Time shown in minutes along the top.

The Belorussian Strategic Offensive Operation
23 June to 29 August, 1944

This one is particularly interesting because of the land area it covered, approximating to that of a future Soviet Theatre Strategic Operation (see Chapter Four), because of the operational manoeuvre of artillery over long distances, and the employment of mobile groups, the prototype of the modern Operational Manoeuvre Groups (OMGs). Much of the terrain is a combination of forest and swamp, notably the gigantic Pripyat marshes. It is therefore revealing with regard to Soviet expertise in inhospitable areas. These can all be seen from the maps (Figs. 1.15 and 1.17).

The four Fronts disposed of 13 artillery and rocket launcher divisions and 20 anti-aircraft artillery divisions. As with all successful Soviet operations

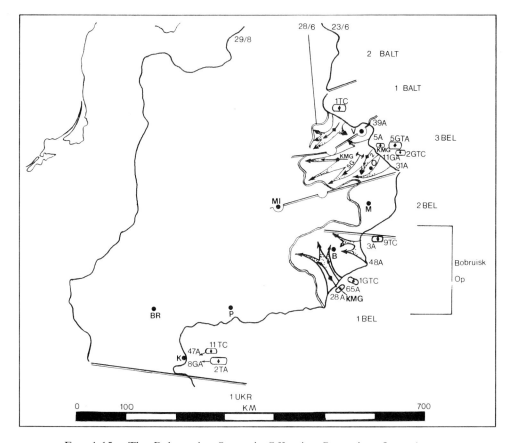

FIG. 1.15.   The Belorussian Strategic Offensive Operation, June–August, 1944. Balt, Baltic Fronts; Bel, Belorussian Fronts; Ukr, Ukrainian Front; B, Bobruisk; BR, Brest; K, Kovel; M, Mogilev; Mi, Minsk; O, Orsha; P, Pinsk; V, Vitebsk; A, Army; C, Corps; G, Guards; T, Tank; KMG, Cavalry-mechanised group (Konno-mekhanizirovannaya gruppa).

the majority of this force was boldly and ruthlessly concentrated on very narrow sectors: 80–90 per cent of the artillery on breakthrough sectors covering 11–20 per cent of the general area of the offensive. The grouping of artillery was not uniform: it varied with the opposition expected, the terrain ahead and the ability of the Soviets to deploy artillery into the area and supply it. Thus, 6 Guards Army of 1 Belorussian Front had four gun artillery brigades providing long range fire, while 5 Army of 3 Belorussian Front had two gun artillery divisions and two brigades. Of eleven breakthrough Armies, eight had rocket artillery divisions, the exceptions being 6 Guards, 31 and 28. Five armies had special 'Destruction Groups' and two, breakthrough groups. The variety of equipment and organisation within an army can be seen from the detailed chart. (Fig. 1.16) We can therefore not expect any fixed organisation or command and control relationships in future Soviet war formations. Likewise, the duration and type of fire during the artillery preparation phase varied. 1 and 2 Belorussian Fronts had a two hours five minutes preparation, 1 Baltic two hours fifteen minutes and 3 Belorussian two hours twenty minutes. The fire preparation phase began with a five to fifteen minute fire blow on targets at a depth of 2 to 6 kilometres, followed by regular fire. The much trickier support phase, as the troops went into the attack and passed through the deep defence was generally planned using successive concentrations of fire (see Chapter Four), over a one hour period at a depth of one and a half to two kilometres. The exception was 2 Belorussian Front where a new type of fire was tried out for the first time: the double barrage. This became more and more common later in the war as the Germans went over to a linear defence. In the accompaniment phase, as the troops pushed on into the enemy depth, barrage fire was also used, to protect the penetration corridors against counter-attacks.

In order to guarantee co-operation between artillery and the other arms as they pushed through the deep defence, commanders at all levels were briefed together using detailed sand models on which they worked out precise courses of action. There was also close co-operation with the air forces, who were (and are) regarded simply as long range artillery, especially in having ground artillery suppress anti-aircraft defences, a characteristic of today's integrated Fire Destruction concept.

The artillery fire was directed with flexibility and skill. Thus, in 3 Belorussian Front's area, artillery preparation for 72 and 65 Corps drew German return fire for some five minutes which enabled the Russian artillery reconnaissance to pinpoint new targets, and the fireplan was altered accordingly. One sharp infantry battalion commander noticed that the Germans were quitting their trenches long before the end of the artillery preparation phase. It was halted, not an easy task given the level at which it was controlled, and the infantry went into the attack at once.

	Close support (PP) Groups — Rifle Bn	Close support (PP) Groups — Rifle Regt	Breakthrough Group — Rifle Div breakthrough sub group	Breakthrough Group — At disposal of arty cdr rifle corps	Guards Mortar (MRL) Group	Long Range (DD) Arty Gp
In divisions			**In Corps**		**In Army**	
97 GRR (3 km) — PP Gp 97	545 mor regt: 36 x 120 mm mor	204 how arty regt: 28 x 122 mm gun	1 gds rifle div			
95 GRR — PP Gp 95	1 bn, 64 gds arty regt: 8 x 76 mm gun, 4 x 122 mm how	168 light arty regt: 24 x 76 mm gun	101 how arty regt: 28 x 203 mm how, 6 x 280 mm mor	117 hy how art bde, 316 special hy arty bn: 22 x 203 mm how, 6 x 280 mm mor		Subgroup 16 gds rifle corps: 114 gun arty bde, 523 gun arty regt. 16 k 122 mm gun, 34 x 152 mm gun-how
99 GRR — PP Gp 99	2 and 3 bns 186 gds arty regt: 16 x 76 mm gun, 8 x 122 mm how	35 gds arty regt (allocated to 2nd echelon): 24 x 76 mm gun, 12 x 122 mm how	16 GUARDS RIFLE CORPS			
79 GRR (1 km) — PP Gp 79	219 Light arty regt: 24 x 76 mm gun				18 gds rifle div	
75 GRR (0.5 km) — PP Gp 75	2nd bn of 1 gds arty regt: 8 x 76 mm gun, 4 x 122 mm how	187 gds arty regt (allocated to 2nd echelon) 24 x 76 mm gun, 12 x 122 mm how	33 gds mor bde, 207 gds arty regt: 28 x 122 mm how 80 x 120 mm mor	20 hy how arty bde, 245 independent super hy arty bn: 24 x 203 mm how, 6 x 280 mm mor	Subgroup 8 gds rifle corps; 317 gds mor regt: 20 x BM–13 4 x BM–8	Subgroup 8 gds rifle corps; 6 gds gun arty bde, 1093 corps arty bde, 149 army gun arty bde, 402 independent super hy arty bn: 12 x 122 mm gun 76 x 152 mm gun-how 6 x 152 mm gun (BR–2)
11 GRR (1 km) — PP Gp 11	1 and 3 bns, 76 gds arty regt: 16 x 76 mm gun, 8 x 122 mm gun how	24 gds arty regt (allocated to 2nd echelon): 24 x 76 mm gun, 12 x 122 mm how	8 GUARDS RIFLE CORPS / 5 gds rifle div			
243 GRR (2.5 km) — PP Gp 243	1 Bn 186 gds arty regt: 8 x 76 mm gun, 4 x 122 mm how	52 gds arty regt (allocated to 2nd echelon: 24 x 76 mm gun, 12 x 122 mm how				
245 GRR — PP Gp 245	2 and 3 bns, 64 gds arty regt: 16 x 76 mm gun, 8 x 122 how	1618 light arty regt: 24 x 76 mm gun	1158 how arty regt 1185 how arty regt 1209 how arty regt (60 how arty regt): 84 x 122 mm how	hy 102/how arty bde 93 hy how arty bde, independent rly bty, 226 special super hy arty bn: 28 x 152 mm	Subgroup 36 gds rifle corps 67 and 42 gds oor regt, 11 gds mor bde, 24 gds BM–13, 280 x M–31 fixed rkt launchers	Subgroup 36 gds rifle corps: 53 gun arty bde, 2 x bt btys 46 special super hy arty bn, 1165 corps arty regt: 16 x 122 mm gun, 35 x 152 mm gun-how, 4 x 152 mm gun BR–2
247 GRR — PP Gp 247	1619 light arty regt: 4 x 76 mm gun reserve: 24 x 76 mm gun	1 guards anti-tank arty regt: 20 x 76 mm gun		gun-how, 24 x 203 mm how, 2 x 305 mm how 6 x 280 mm mor	83 gds rifle div	
49 GRR (2.5 km) — PP Gp 49	1 and 2 bns, 44 gds arty reft: 16 x 76 mm gun, 4 x 122 mm how	3 bn 44 gds arty regt, 1 bn 1620 light arty regt:	36 GUARDS RIFLE CORPS / 244, 247 250 mor regts (20 mor bde): 90 x 120 mm mors			
46 GRR (2.5 km) — PP Gp 46	3 bn 44 gds arty regt, 1 bn 1620 light arty regt: 20 x 76 mm gun, 4 x 122 mm how	3 gds anti-tank arty regt: 20 x 76 mm gun				
43 GRR — PP Gp 43	2 bn 1620 light arty regt: 12 x 76 mm gun	6 gds anti-tank arty regt: 20 x 76 mm gun				

FIG. 1.16. The Belorussian Strategic Offensive Operation, Artillery Grouping of 11 Guards Army, 23 June 1944.

The performance of the rocket artillery was particularly noticeable. The recently introduced self-propelled BM-31-12, firing twelve rockets with a 300 mm warhead, proved very effective. On 3 Army's sector of 1 Belorussian, a battalion of these fired on a German centre of resistance near Berdichev. Seventy per cent of the deep timber and earth dugouts were destroyed completely. 1 Belorussian also used rocket launchers in an innovative way for so-called dispersed battery salvos. The rocket launchers would fire together with the gun artillery at the same objectives every five to seven minutes. This was exceptionally effective, presumably because it combined the constant regular pounding of tube artillery with the devastating shock of a rocket salvo.

Maintaining support for infantry and tanks as they pressed on into the enemy depth was particularly difficult because of the marshy terrain, intersected by numerous rivers and crossed by few tracks. The guns were frequently manhandled forward through the swamps and gunners constructed their own rafts.

PLATE 1.13.   Red Army officers examine the crater made by a Soviet 300 mm (diameter of warhead only) M-31 rocket. A slit trench would be little protection against a near-miss by one of these.

As the Soviet forces, all-arms and artillery, passed German units and encircled them, the Germans fought ferociously to escape. This frequently brought them into contact with Soviet artillery units who fought back with their guns and rocket launchers in the direct fire mode, small arms and the bayonet. One encirclement of particular interest is the Bobruisk operation of 23 to 28 June, which is often considered as a separate operation within the Belorussian strategic one. Between 14 and 19 June, the Russians planned to bring in 67 train loads of artillery to stations between Shatsilki and Kalinkovich. The loading was too much for the Belorussian railway, however, and the more mobile assets (120 mm mortars, 76 mm guns and 122 mm howitzers) were dropped off up to 200 kilometres away and told to get there under their own steam. On a sector about 100 kilometres wide the Soviets amassed four million shells, not counting Front reserves.

On day two of the Bobruisk operation, the cavalry-mechanised group which had been waiting between 65 and 28 Armies and which might therefore be equated with a Front OMG, was pushed into the gap created

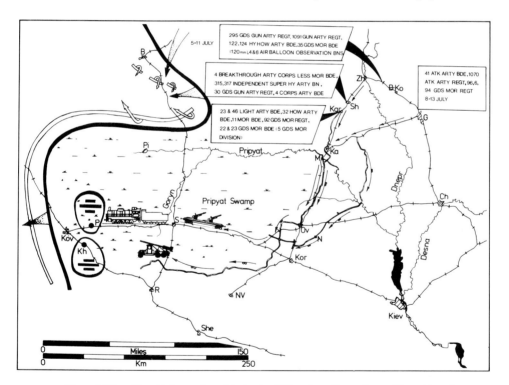

FIG. 1.17. The Belorussian Strategic Offensive Operation: Operational Manoeuvre of Artillery, July 1944. B-Ko, Buda-Koshelevo; Ch, Chernigov; G, Gomel; Ka, Kalinkovichi; Kar, Karpovichi; Kh, Khalevi (Goloby); Kor, Korosten; Kov, Kovel; M, Mozyr; N, Narodichi; NV, Novograd-Volynski; Ov, Ovruch; P, Povorsk; Pi, Pinsk; R, Rovno; S, Sarny; Sh, Shatsilki; She, Shepetovka; Zh, Zhlobin.

by the two Armies' success, with orders to head in the general direction of
Bobruisk. The mobile group's artillery comprised one anti-tank artillery
brigade, three rocket launcher regiments and a battalion of 3 rocket
launcher brigade. These were the most mobile systems available and, in the
case of the rocket launchers, those with the highest firepower to weight
ratio. It is believed that the mobile group's artillery had remained silent and
not been used in support of the initial breakthrough, to avoid compromising
surprise and to preserve ammunition. The mobile group was thus launched
into the enemy depth undetected and fully bombed up. The lessons for the
artillery component of a modern OMG are obvious.

Perhaps the most spectacular aspect of the Strategic operation was the
operational manoeuvre of elements of 1 Belorussian's artillery, including 4
AKP, in the area south of Bobruisk. The manoeuvre was carried out by rail
and road over a distance of some 600 to 660 kilometres between 5 and 13
July. Only the strictest control and most careful planning could prevent a
traffic jam involving 35,000 motor vehicles and 3500 artillery pieces. This, it
must be remembered, was carried out in an area much wilder than western
Europe: the roads marked on the map are little better than farm tracks. As
a result, artillery strength on 1 Belorussian's left wing was increased from
5500 to 9000 units, and a density of 180 to 240 guns, mortars and rocket
launchers per kilometre of Front achieved. The manoeuvre was also carried

PLATE 1.14. An armoured train, bristling with anti-aircraft guns, stands
guard as ML-20 152 mm gun howitzers move up. Judging by the pneumatic
tyres, this was taken very late in the war (IWM).

out, apparently, without the Germans' knowledge. The subsequent attack was successful.

Marshal of Artillery Kazakov, commenting on the Bobruisk operation, and Colonel-General of Artillery Mikhalkin summarising the Belorussian operation as a whole, have both explicitly underlined their relevance for the employment of artillery today.[37]

The Yassy Kishinëv Strategic Offensive Operation, 20 to 29 August 1944

This is of great interest as an operation with Grand Strategic as well as purely military objectives. The aims were: to destroy the German-Rumanian Army Group Southern Ukraine, to liberate the Moldavian SSR, and thus to split the German-Rumanian alliance. It succeeded. Its main interest for the employment of artillery arises from the rigorous denuding of sectors other than that where the breakthrough was to take place, the elaborate and efficient deception plan, and the battle in the enemy operational depth.

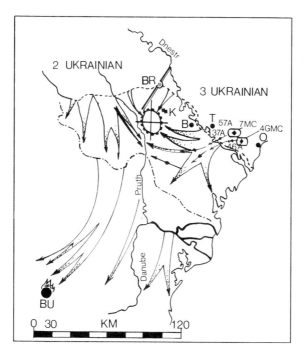

FIG. 1.18. The Yassy-Kishinëv Strategic Offensive Operation, 20 to 29 August, 1944, showing formations mentioned in the example. B, Bendery; BR, Bravicheny (inclusive to 2 Ukrainian Front); BU, Bucharest (rising on 23 August); K, Kishinëv; O, Odessa; T, Tirasopol. Soviet forward line, 19 August ----- . Soviet forward line, 24 August —·—·— .

The operation was carried out by 2 and 3 Ukrainian Fronts. 3 Ukrainian's artillery commander was Colonel-General of Artillery Mitrofan Nedelin, later to be the first commander of the Strategic Rocket Forces (see Chapter Two). As was usual in the war, the Stavka of the Supreme High Command in Moscow sent a representative to advise the Front commander. The Stavka representative on this occasion, Marshal Timoshenko, was taken aback by Nedelin's radical proposal to strip non-breakthrough sectors of virtually all their artillery, leaving only about seven guns per kilometre over a 126 kilometre sector. 73 per cent of the entire Front artillery assets were allocated to the breakthrough sectors of 57, 37 and 46 Armies, 18 kilometres wide in all, giving a density of about 250 guns, mortars and rocket launchers over 76 mm calibre for each kilometre there. At first Timoshenko argued that this was too great a risk, in case the Germans identified the direction of the thrust. Nedelin explained that he was currently fooling the Germans that 7 Artillery division, recently arrived from the Karelian Front, was concentrating on the Kishinëv sector. A battery of heavy artillery was firing desultorily, to lead the Germans to believe that they were adjusting targets prior to an attack south of Bendery. Timoshenko was convinced and the War Soviet unanimously accepted the plan. Fortunately, the Germans were convinced as well.

The artillery preparation phase was to last one hour forty-five minutes. It began with a short fire blow by all the artillery and BM-13 rocket launchers, followed by forty-five minutes of deliberate fire. There was also a fifteen minute switch by 40 per cent of the entire artillery force on to objectives in the dummy sector. As in the Belorussian operation, the support phase comprised a mixture of barrages and successive concentrations of aimed fire to a depth of one and a half to two kilometres. The OMG style penetration by 4 Guards and 7 mechanised corps was to be supported by all the High Command Artillery Reserve, plus two units from 37 and 46 Armies: one anti-tank brigade, two light and one howitzer regiments, one mortar and rocket launcher regiment and one anti-aircraft division. The high level of air defence underlines the modern view that OMGs are particularly vulnerable in the insertion phase (see Chapter Four).

Nedelin's earlier deception measures were reinforced by a complete dummy concentration in the Kishinëv area. There were numerous fake rail movements and large numbers of vehicles headed into the area by day, returning at night, and mock tanks and guns were constructed while the heavy artillery battery fired on enemy permanent fortifications. Of the 170 artillery and mortar regiments, 113 were regrouped for the offensive during the first days of August. Artillery regiments and battalions moved by night over farm and forest tracks with lights extinguished, and were carefully camouflaged at dawn until nightfall. The artillery of 37, 57 and 46 Armies adjusted targets from 14 to 19 August, using only calibres which had been there previously and the same pattern of activity as they had while holding in defence. At 0800 hours on 20 August bombers and fighter-bombers began their attack and over 6200 guns and heavy mortars and 460 rocket launchers opened fire. The sky over the entire area was completely filled with smoke and dust and the grass blackened with soot. By the end of the day 37 and 46 Armies had penetrated 11 to 12 kilometres and, in a Russian general's words, favourable conditions had been created for the insertion of the Front's mobile formations. At the head of 4 Guards mechanised corps column were three anti-tank artillery regiments and one rocket launcher regiment, the same sort of systems which had supported the mobile groups in the Belorussian operation. Once again, the insertion was supported by the Front's heavy artillery, but the mobile group's own had kept silent.

The defence crumbled rapidly and on 21 August it became obvious that an encirclement of the enemy in the Kishinëv area was in the offing. In contrast to the careful pre-planning of the breakthrough, which required highly centralised control, circumstances now demanded decentralisation. Nedelin ordered his three Army artillery commanders to reinforce all-arms regiments with divisional artillery, to give every infantry battalion an artillery battalion and every infantry company a battery. The division's artillery commander retained only one dedicated artillery regiment. Gun artillery brigades and rocket launcher battalions remained under corps artillery commanders. In other words, the whole pattern of command and control shifted in accordance with the changed circumstances and the need for rapid exploitation and pursuit. On 23 August, forces from 2 and 3 Fronts met on the river Pruth, and the first phase of the operation was over. As Soviet forces closed in on the encircled German 6 Army, fighting took on a highly unpredictable character and artillery units often engaged the Germans with direct fire and, once again, in hand-to-hand fighting. The operation indicates that the Soviet artillery had a genius for deception and surprise, and the flexibility to adjust command and control procedures rapidly in response to changed circumstances during the fighting.[38]

The Vistula-Oder Offensive Operation,
12 January to 3 February, 1945

The aim of this was to defeat German forces in Poland. It was executed by 1 Belorussian and 1 Ukrainian Fronts, with the left wing of 2 Belorussian and the right of 4 Ukrainian.

The density of artillery on key sectors exceeded that in any other operation, except the Kiev in 1943. On 8 Guards Army's sector of 1 Belorussian there were 350 pieces per kilometre of Front (that is one every 3 metres: literally wheel to wheel), of which 95 per cent was over 76 mm calibre. Once again, shock groups were protected by dense anti-aircraft

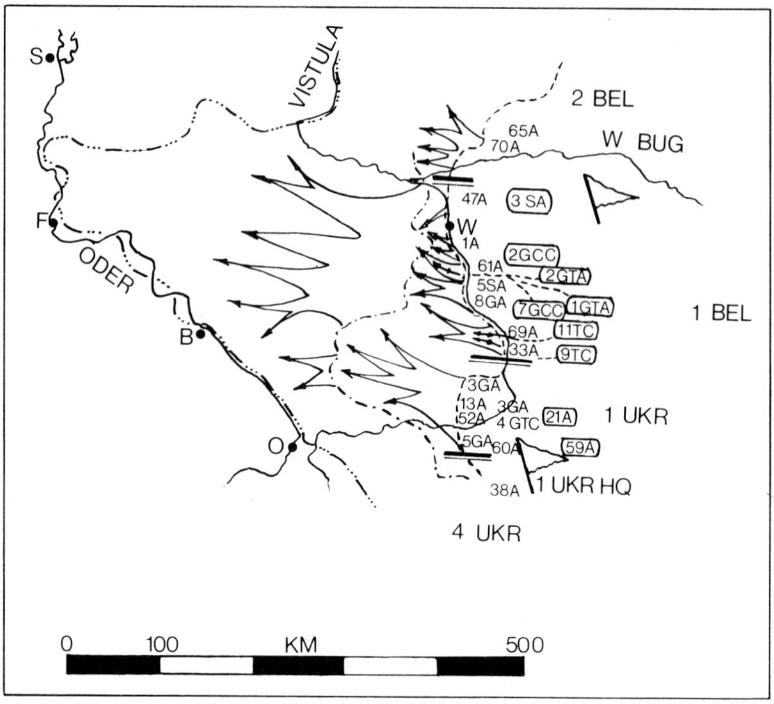

FIG. 1.19. The Vistula-Oder Offensive Operation, 12 January to 3 February, 1945. Bel, Belorussian Fronts; Ukr, Ukrainian Fronts; B, Breslau (Wroclaw); F, Frankfurt an der Oder; O, Ostrava; S, Szcecin; W, Warsaw; SA, Shock Army; G, Guards; T, Tank; M, Mechanised; C, Cavalry or corps; CC, Cavalry Corps. Soviet forward line, 12 January ------ . Soviet forward line, 18 January —·—·—·. Soviet forward line, 3 February —···—···—···.

cover, up to 40 anti-aircraft guns per kilometre. The system of establishing task-oriented groups of artillery at each level from regiment upwards was further developed. In 5 Shock Army three army level groups were created: a breakthrough group, a long range (primarily counter-battery) group and a rocket launcher group.

1 Belorussian Front's artillery preparation and support was planned with two variants, depending on whether or not the attack of the first battalions was successful. The first envisaged a twenty-five minute preparation followed by a one hour support plan with a single barrage moving ahead of the troops. If the attack after the first twenty-five minute preparation failed, a further seventy minute preparation would be fired followed by a double barrage. 1 Ukrainian Front had a one hour forty-seven minute preparation including one seven minute fire blow by the entire Front artillery on German batteries, anti-tank guns and observation posts only. This has been described in a modern article as a *fire strike*, not blow, a new concept (see Chapter Four), indicating a massive and decisive stroke to excise one

particular element of the enemy force. If the enemy air threat permitted, the Russians also planned to use some of the anti-aircraft artillery for counter-battery fire.

One gun per battalion was designated as the adjusting gun. These registered targets before the operation commenced in such a way as to appear as an individual roving gun. Then, in the freezing pitch dark of early morning on 12 January forward battalions of 1 Ukrainian began reconnaissance by battle, supported by successive concentrations of aimed fire. By 1000 hours they had penetrated to a depth of 3 kilometres, forcing the Germans to reveal many of their dispositions. Then the hundred and seven minute preparation of the main forces' attack began: a fifteen minute fire blow on targets throughout the tactical depth, then forty minutes of deliberate fire. Then came the seven minute strike on the enemy artillery network, which neutralised it as intended. Then came another thirty minutes of deliberate fire and a fifteen minute fire blow. At this stage, according to prisoner reports, large numbers of the Germans became disorientated and began streaming, panic stricken, to the rear. As the Russians came forward they were preceded by a double barrage. As the battle unfolded in the enemy depth there were numerous meeting engagements with enemy reserves, where artillery fought decentralised and using direct fire.

1 Belorussian's offensive began after a twenty-five minute fire preparation. During this period alone the Front's artillery fired 315,000 projectiles weighing nearly 5500 tons, of which 15 per cent were rockets. The main forces' attack was supported by successive concentrations of fire. On this front, the targets were almost completely obscured by smoke and dust as soon as the Russian artillery opened up, and could not be adjusted subsequently. The great accuracy of the target data and firing large concentrations of artillery at each target ensured that the fire was effective, however. Artillery was also ruthlessly concentrated against particularly tough objectives. To deal with one stubborn centre of resistance in the Grabuv region, 5 Shock Army's artillery commander gave permission for three artillery brigades comprising 180 guns to concentrate on one objective. After the Russian artillery fired 1150 shells in five minutes, resistance ceased. Artillery also played a major role in the capture of the fortress city of Poznan. 29 Guards and 91 rifle corps who were ordered to take the city disposed of 1400 guns, mortars and rocket launchers of which 1200 were 76 mm calibre and over. No fire preparation at all was carried out against the forts: a three to five minute fire blow was delivered as the troops rushed the forts, until they blocked the line of fire. Within the streets of the town the heavy 203 mm guns were frequently used for direct fire, as were individual *katyusha* rockets which were fired from their packing cases. The main fortress of Poznan, the Citadel, was stormed on 18 February, 1945

after a four hour bombardment by artillery including heavy and super heavy pieces.

At the end of January, 1945 forward Soviet units reached the river Oder and the German border. The scale of the operation can be judged from the fact that the Soviet anti-aircraft artillery shot down some 500 enemy aircraft, or one third of the total lost by the Luftwaffe to air and ground fire during the full course of the Battle of Britain. On both Fronts, surface to surface and anti-aircraft artillery combined fired some six million shells, bombs and rockets. Of the three and a quarter million fired by 1 Belorussian, the majority were fired in the first three days of the operation, that is, during the breakthrough of the tactical zone and the insertion of mobile groups into the fissures. This is drawn to the attention of modern Soviet officers, because it indicates that vast expenditures of ammunition occur during the initial attack from a static position, but that as the battle becomes more fluid far less ammunition is required.[39]

The Battle for Berlin, 6 April to 8 May, 1945

This is particularly relevant because it was the final operation of the European war, because of the density of artillery employed and the lessons for fighting in large urban areas. On 16 April 214 German divisions still faced Soviet forces to the east of the capital of the Third Reich. Around Berlin there were a million German troops and within the city there were a further 200,000 *Volksturm*, including fanatical units of the Hitler Youth. The battle for Berlin was by no means the last gasp of a German army stuffed with old men and children, and the capture of the city no walk-over. The operation was entrusted to 1 and 2 Belorussian and 1 Ukrainian Fronts, supported by 18 Long Range Air Army.

The first phase of the operation was the breakthrough of the Oder-Neisse line, from 16 to 19 April. On 1 Belorussian Front the attack began before dawn on 16th, the enemy defences being illuminated and blinded with powerful anti-aircraft searchlights. On the Front's main axis was 8 Guards Army, who were ordered to break through on a 7 kilometre wide sector. When they had carried the first and second lines of the deeply echeloned defence, 1 Guards Tank Army would be brought in. The well built German stone houses had been turned into strong centres of resistance and the Germans knew the Russians had to come from the Küstrin area, so surprise could not be achieved.

The Soviets concentrated 310 guns, mortars and rocket launchers on each kilometre of the breakthrough sector, rising to 325 on individual corps' sectors. Most of the artillery was deployed between 1 and 7 kilometres from the forward edge of the enemy defences, so the whole forward area was crammed with artillery, whole battalions and sometimes even regiments

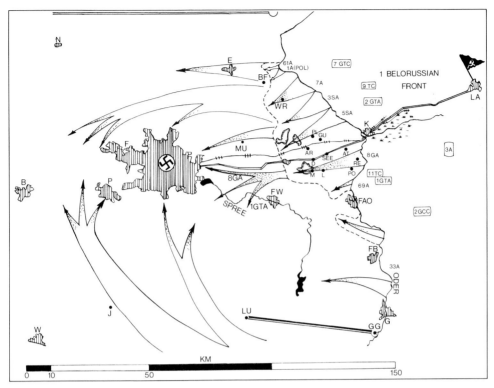

Fɪɢ. 1.20.   The Berlin Operation, 16 April to 8 May, 1945: Operations of 1 Belorussian Front to 19 April and subsequent general action (simplified). Places in path of 8 Guards Army are shown in some detail so as to place the detailed artillery plan (Fig. 1.21) in context. AR, Altrosenthal; AT, Alt Tucheband; B, Brandenburg; BF, Bad Freienwald; D, Diedersdorf; E, Eberswalde; F, Falkensee; FB, Furstenberg (Eisenhuttenstadt); FW, Furstenwald; G, Gubin; GU, Gusow; GG, Gross Gastrose (southern boundary of 1 Belorussian); J, Juterbog (on west of 1 Ukrainian's encirclement of Berlin from the south); K, Küstrin (Kostrzyn); L, Lietzen; Landstadt (now Gorzów Wielkopolski), 1 Belorussian Front HQ; Lu, Lübben (on southern boundary of 1 Belorussian); M, Marxdorf; Mu, Müncheberg; N, Neuruppin; P, Potsdam; PL, Platkow; PO, Podelzin; RE, Reitwein; SEE, Seelow; W, Wittenberg (Lutherstadt); WR, Wrietzen. Line reached by Soviets, 19 April - - - - -. High ground in path of 8 Guards Army ⌇⌇⌇ .

begin located on one gun position. This was possible because the German Air Force had been virtually destroyed by this time, but would be suicidal in a war against a sophisticated enemy today. Artillery groups were set up from regimental to Army levels, each one capable of firing at the request of the senior all-arms commander in support of all-arms units at the level below. Thus, the regimental artillery group could be ordered to fire in support of a rifle battalion by the rifle regiment commander, a system which

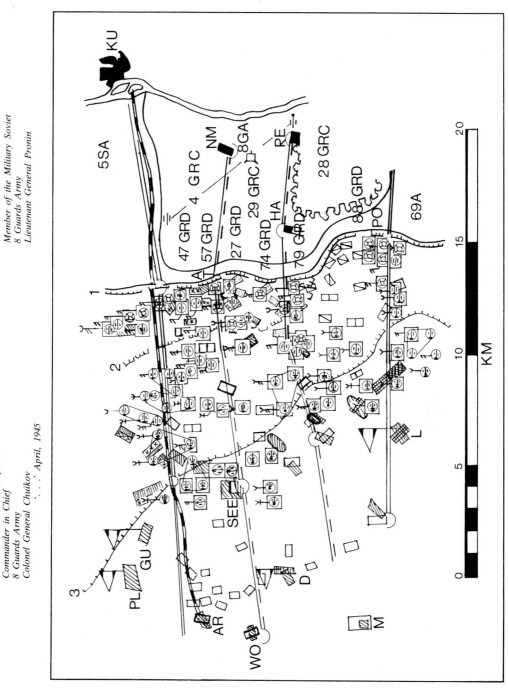

'I confirm'

Commander in Chief
8 Guards Army
Colonel General Chuikov

Member of the Military Soviet
8 Guards Army
Lieutenant General Pronin

'. . .' April, 1945

Artillery Commander 8 Guards Army
Major General of Artillery Pozharskiy

Chief of Staff
Colonel Khizhnyakov

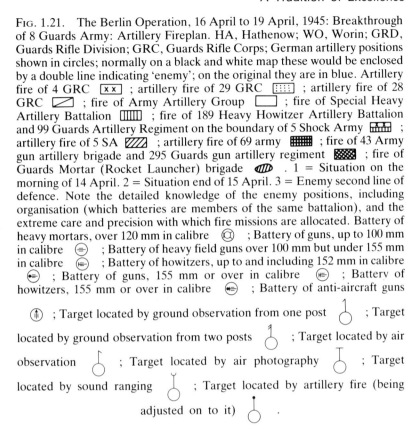

FIG. 1.21.   The Berlin Operation, 16 April to 19 April, 1945: Breakthrough of 8 Guards Army: Artillery Fireplan. HA, Hathenow; WO, Worin; GRD, Guards Rifle Division; GRC, Guards Rifle Corps; German artillery positions shown in circles; normally on a black and white map these would be enclosed by a double line indicating 'enemy'; on the original they are in blue. Artillery fire of 4 GRC [x x] ; artillery fire of 29 GRC [:::] ; artillery fire of 28 GRC ⬜ ; fire of Army Artillery Group ⬜ ; fire of Special Heavy Artillery Battalion ⬛ ; fire of 189 Heavy Howitzer Artillery Battalion and 99 Guards Artillery Regiment on the boundary of 5 Shock Army ▦ ; artillery fire of 5 SA ▨ ; artillery fire of 69 army ▦ ; fire of 43 Army gun artillery brigade and 295 Guards gun artillery regiment ▩ ; fire of Guards Mortar (Rocket Launcher) brigade ⬯ . 1 = Situation on the morning of 14 April. 2 = Situation end of 15 April. 3 = Enemy second line of defence. Note the detailed knowledge of the enemy positions, including organisation (which batteries are members of the same battalion), and the extreme care and precision with which fire missions are allocated. Battery of heavy mortars, over 120 mm in calibre ⊚ ; Battery of guns, up to 100 mm in calibre ⊜ ; Battery of heavy field guns over 100 mm but under 155 mm in calibre ⊜ ; Battery of howitzers, up to and including 152 mm in calibre ⊜ ; Battery of guns, 155 mm or over in calibre ⊜ ; Battery of howitzers, 155 mm or over in calibre ⊜ ; Battery of anti-aircraft guns ⊛ ; Target located by ground observation from one post ⓞ ; Target located by ground observation from two posts ⓞ ; Target located by air observation ⓞ ; Target located by air photography ⓞ ; Target located by sound ranging ⓞ ; Target located by artillery fire (being adjusted on to it) ⓞ .

Combinations of symbols indicate that a target has been located by more than one method.

guaranteed close co-operation with the infantry and tanks. It was envisaged that in the exploitation phase, as battle developed in the enemy depth, artillery battalions from the regimental artillery group would be given to all-arms battalions of the first echelon. Once again, command and control relationships were not fixed, but were altered according to circumstances. The preparation phase would last half an hour, with Army artillery firing at targets to a depth of 15 to 16 kilometres.

On 14 and 15 April, some of the Soviet divisions launched forward battalions to conduct reconnaissance by battle, preceded by a ten minute fire blow by one third of the Army artillery. As a result of this, the Germans withdrew their main forces by 2 to 3 kilometres to what had been the middle line of defence. It was clear to 8 Guards Army's commander that there was no time to lose, and he determined to attack before dawn on the 16 April.

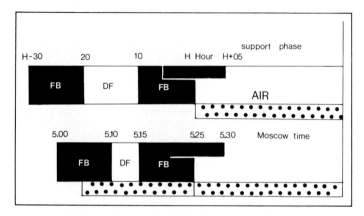

FIG. 1.22. Berlin Operation: Artillery Support Graphic. FB, Fire Blow; DF, Deliberate Fire. 1. Plan 2. As executed. Source for Figs. 1.21 and 1.22: Peredel'skiy *et al.* plan 4.

This gave the artillery commander, Pozharskiy, only a few hours in which to make the necessary topographical reconnaissance, draw up the fire plan and move the artillery of the forward divisions into position. Anxious as ever to post their artillery as far forward as possible for flexibility and accuracy, the Russians moved the divisional artillery up by the same distance that the Germans had withdrawn.

Because the artillery would be firing only 150 metres in front of the advancing troops, accuracy was very important. One innovation was that the guns were specially zeroed on the range to iron out errors and thus guarantee to hit target co-ordinates accurately at night. At 0300 hours local time on 16 April the artillery of 3 Guards Army brought down the first ten minute fire blow on all parts of the enemy defence to a depth of 10 to 12 kilometres. The main targets for army artillery were enemy artillery batteries and anti-tank weapons, plus regimental and divisional command posts. Meanwhile the Corps and Division artillery groups fired on enemy mortar batteries and defensive positions, and the regimental artillery the forward enemy trenches. At 0510 the army artillery went over to *deliberate fire*, which was a quarter to half as intense, in order to give the gun detachments a breather before the second fire blow at 0515. This time the rocket artillery joined in, rockets and guns firing on the most important objectives *all as one*. By 0525 the Germans had suffered between 30 and 75 per cent losses in personnel and equipment in the first line of defence, and the infantry and tanks attacked. The Regimental, Divisional and Corps artillery groups shifted to the support phase, while the Army Artillery Group continued to pound enemy batteries until 0530, thus masking the end of the preparation phase and covering the capture of the first line of enemy trenches. This mingled with the beginning of the forward marching support phase which had started at 0525. The Russian artillery brought down a double rolling barrage to a depth of 2 kilometres. Having overcome the first line of defences, the attackers moved forward hugging the barrage, and meeting little resistance. The longer range army artillery then carried out successive concentrations of aimed fire over the next 4 kilometres. 79 Guards Rifle Division was halted when it came under especially heavy mortar fire. The rolling barrage advanced a kilometre, and then the divisional commander ordered it to be brought back. Then it was moved forward again, this time with the infantry following. At this point some of the advancing Soviet forces lost their way and co-ordination between artillery fire and the advancing troops was temporarily lost. New targets in the enemy depth had to be reconnoitred, and this took place during the night of 17 April.

Meanwhile at 1015 on 17 April, Soviet artillery and air had pounded the German Müncheberg division which had taken a stand on high ground. Once again, successive concentrations of aimed fire were used to support the attack, to a depth of 5 kilometres. The Soviet artillery fire was corrected by observers in tanks and by tank brigade commanders personally, who were trained in controlling artillery fire. This was obviously a major improvement on the situation at the beginning of the war. Support was of the mixed type, combining double and single rolling barrages and successive concentrations of aimed fire to a depth of 4 to 6 kilometres. The support and accompaniment phases merged into one: a single rolling wave which swamped the defenders and in whose wake the mobile formation, 1 Guards Tank Army, was committed to the breach, a day after the offensive had begun. The breakthrough of the second line of the German defences became a logical continuation of the accompaniment of forces which had broken through the first: the artillery offensive had acquired its own momentum.

Between 19 and 25 April Soviet forces encircled Berlin, while 8 Guards pushed forward some 50 kilometres to the edge of the city. The Russian plan for the capture of the city itself envisaged breaking it up into small blocks and then destroying them in detail, 300 per day. In these circumstances, artillery was frequently used in the direct fire role. One technique was to employ artillery in teams of two light and one heavy pieces. The two light weapons would fire smoke rounds rapidly at a German-held building, to blind the defenders. Under cover of the smokescreen, a 203 mm howitzer was then rolled out to face the building and, as soon as the smoke began to clear, levelled it with a few rounds.

German resistance was fanatical, but the Russians, scenting imminent victory, piled on resources lavishly though not recklessly. Along the Avenue *Unter den Linden*, 500 pieces of artillery were drawn up along a stretch of less than a kilometre. Sometimes, a hail of a thousand shells crashed down on a single group of houses. So terrifying was the effect of this that, out of a group of 130 survivors taken prisoner in the cellars of the Air Ministry, *seventeen had gone mad*. As the good soldier Tërkin would have said, '*nashi byut, teper'-kayuk*': 'Those are ours: for Fritz it's — curtains'.[40]

During the Great Patriotic War, Soviet artillery strength increased to five times its 1941 level, or about 335,000 guns, howitzers and heavy mortars. Soviet industry provided the Red Army with about 360,000 of these weapons, of which 188,000 were guns and howitzers (there was considerable attrition), over 10,000 self-propelled rocket launchers and between twelve and fourteen million rockets. In the Belorussian, Vistula-Oder and Berlin operations the Russian artillery deployed 31,000, 33,500 and between 42,000 and 45,000 guns, howitzers, mortars and rocket launchers respectively. 1800 Soviet artillerymen, including Marshal Voronov received the coveted award Hero of the Soviet Union, 1,600,000 received decorations of various kinds and 500 units received the proud title Guards. On 19 November, 1944, the anniversary of the beginning of the Stalingrad counter-offensive, Stalin issued his order number 225 establishing that date as artillery day, praising artillery as the arm which had achieved dominance on the field of battle, halted the enemy at a critical hour and which was now clearing the way for infantry and armour on their victorious march to Berlin. Truly, artillery was the Soviet *God of War*.[41]

Notes

1. Opening quote: General Sir Robert Wilson, *Brief Remarks on the Character and Composition of the Russian Army and a Sketch of the Campaign in Poland in the Years 1806 and 1807*, (London, 1810), p. 20; origins of Russian artillery, see the author's 'The Firebird and the Bear: 600 Years of the Russian Artillery', *History Today*, (September, 1982), pp. 16–20; Lieutenant-General of Artillery V. G. Fëdorov, *K voprose o date poyavlenii artillerii na Rusi (On the Question of the Date of Artillery's Appearance in Russia)*, (Academy of Artillery Sciences, Moscow, 1949), pp. 78, 132–33; A. N. Robinson, ed. *Kulíkovskaya Bitva v Literature i iskusstve (The Battle of Kulíkovo in Literature and Art)*, (Nauka, Moscow, 1980), pp. 52–9; capture of Moscow: George Vernadsky, *A History of Russia*, Vol. III *The Mongols and Russia*, (Yale University Press, New Haven, 1953), pp. 265–67; jubilee: *VV* 8/1980, p. 69 begins a series of articles on the history of Russian and Soviet artillery running up to the Great Patriotic War (*VV* 1/1982, pp. 63–68). Pages 71–72 of the latter feature the first series of questions in the jubilee competition; 500th anniversary: A. Pozdnev, *Tvortsy otechestvennogo oruzhiya (Founders of the Nation's Armaments)*, (Moscow, 1955), pp. 37–38; General N. Brandenburg, *500 letiye russkoy artillerii (The 500th anniversary of Russian Artillery)*, (St. Petersburg, 1889).

2. Nomad defeated by gunpowder: Fernand Braudel, *The Mediterranean and the Mediterranean World in the age of Philip II*, (Collins, 1978), Vol. 1, p. 172; Friedrich Engels, cited in *VV* 8/1980, p.69; little use made by Tartars, Prince N. S. Golitsyn, *Allgemeine Kriegsgeschichte aller Völker und Zeiten (Universal Military History of all Peoples and Times)* (Cassell, 1874), Abteilung II, *Mittelalter*, Band 2 1350–1618, p. 216.

3. Exploding factory: Pozdnev, p. 153; 1408 and 1451: Brandenburg, p. 5; industry under Vassiliy, Golitsyn Abth. II Band 2 p. 216; artillery vs. small arms: L. J. D. Collins, 'The Military Organisation of the Crimean Tartars during the Sixteenth and Seventeenth

Order
Of the Supreme High Command
No. 225

19 November, 1944

Moscow, the Kremlin

Comrades, artillerymen and mortarmen, engineers and technicians, officers and generals of the Soviet artillery!

Today the Soviet people celebrate Red Army artillery day.

The whole nation acknowledges the enormous significance of artillery as the main striking force of the Red Army.

As is well known, artillery was that force, which helped the Red Army halt the advance of the enemy on the approaches to Leningrad and Moscow.

Artillery was that force, which guaranteed for the Red Army the destruction of German forces at Stalingrad and Voronezh, at Kursk and Belgorod, at Kharkov and Kiev, at Vitebsk and Bobruisk, at Leningrad and Minsk, at Yassy and Kishinëv.

With its crushing fire, artillery successfully cleared the way for infantry and tanks in the titanic battles of the Patriotic War, as a result of which the enemy was kicked out beyond the borders of our land.

Now, together with the entire Red Army, the Soviet artillery is bringing down crushing blows on personnel, materiel and fortifications of the enemy in the final decisive battles for victory over Germany.

Everybody knows, that Soviet artillery attained complete domination over the enemy artillery on the battlefield, that in numerous battles with the enemy, Soviet artillery men and mortarmen covered themselves with undying glory, showed exceptional manliness and heroism, and the commanders and senior officers evinced great skill in directing fire.

This is a success of which our nation should truly be proud.

Comrades, artillerymen and mortarmen, engineers and technicians, officers and generals of the Soviet artillery! I congratulate you on artillery day!

In recognition of the decisive successes of Red Army artillery in the Patriotic War, I COMMAND THAT:

Today, 19 November, to be known as artillery day, at 1900 hours in the capital of our nation — Moscow, in the capitals of the Union republics and in the cities of Leningrad, Stalingrad, Sevastopol, Odessa, Khabarovsk, Novosibirsk, Sverdlov, Gorkiy, Molotov and Tula, in the name of the Motherland, we honour our glorious artillerymen with a twenty gun salute.

Long may Soviet artillery live and flourish to the confusion of the enemies of our land!

Supreme High Commander,
Marshal of the Soviet Union J. STALIN
(*Pravda*, Sunday, 19 November, 1944)

Centuries' in V. J. Parry and M. E. Yapp, ed., *War, Technology and Society in the Middle East*, (Oxford University Press, 1975), pp. 270–71.

4. 'What his gunners can do': John Milton, *A Brief History of Moscovia and other less known Countries lying eastward as far as Cathay* . . . (London, 1682, limited edition reproduction, 1944), p. 44. Milton's account is based on sixteenth century sources, mainly Anthony Jenkinson; Brandenburg, p. 22; Kazan': Marshal of Artillery K. P. Kazakov, ed., *Artilleriya i rakety (Artillery and Rockets)*, (Voyenizdat, Moscow, 1965), pp. 15–16; Narva: Brandenburg, p. 26; Kobenzel: Brandenburg, pp. 10–11.

5. Foundation of pushkary: Brandenburg, p. 19; Pskov: D. Skalon, ed. *Stoletiye voyennago ministerstva (A Hundred Years of the War Ministry)*, (St. Petersburg, 1902), Vol. VI, part 1, book 1, p. 15; Petrine reforms, Brandenburg, pp. 21, 35.

6. 1687 and 1689: Golitsyn, Abth. III, *Supplement*, pp. 38, 271–74; quote: Captain A. F. Becke, *A Short Introduction to the History of Tactics, 1740–1905*, (London, 1909), p. 32.

7. Breech loaders: Colonel A. Nilus, *Istoriya material'noy chasti artillerii (History of Artillery Materiel)*, Vol. 2, *Field Artillery*, (St. Petersburg, 1904), pp. 94, 113–14. The inscription is 'aen. drs. heeren segen. ist alles', on one of the 1.7″ pieces; see also V. T. Novitsky, ed. *Voyennaya Entsiklopediya (VE)*, (*Military Encyclopedia*), (St. Petersburg, 1915), Vol. 17, p. 81: O Mikhaylov, *Ustav ratnykh pushechnykh i drugikh del, kasayushchikhsya do voynskoy nauke, sostoyashchiy v 663 ukazakh ili statyakh (Regulations on various artillery and Other Matters relating to Military Science, in 663 articles . . .)* ed. V. Ruban, published on the orders of Prince Grigoriy Aleksandrovich Potëmkin from manuscripts found in 1775, (St. Petersburg State Military College, 1781), pp. 1–2.

8. Peter: Professor K. Bazilevich, *Russia's Art of War* (Soviet War News, 1945), pp. 7–9; Zubov: Christopher Duffy, *Russia's Military Way to the West: Origins and Nature of Russian Military Power 1700–1800*, (Routledge and Kegan Paul, London, 1981), p. 199.

9. 'Arbiter of victory' . . . Kazakov, *Artilleriya* . . . p. 22; Brandenburg, pp. 33, 38–9.

10. Pozdnev, pp. 56–7; effect and distribution of shot: Major-General B. P. Hughes, *Open Fire: Artillery Tactics from Marlborough to Wellington*, (Anthony Bird, Chichester, 1983), p. 20; first production batch, Brandenburg p. 43, 1757–8, p. 49, trials, p. 50. Frederick captured 20 Secret Howitzers at Zorndorf and put them on display in Berlin under the contemptuous label 'a Russian secret'; whole platoon with a single round, Duffy, p. 71, indirect fire and Glebov, pp. 121–22; Paltzig, *Sovetskaya voyennaya entsiklopediya (Soviet Military Encyclopedia)*, (*SVE*), (Voyenizdat, Moscow, 1978), Vol. 6, p. 198 and N. M. Korobkov, ed., *Semiletnyaya voyna: materialy o deystvii russkoy armii i flota, 1756–1763gg. (The Seven Years' War: Documents relating to the Operations of the Russian Army and Fleet)*, (Voyenizdat, Moscow, 1948), diagram no. 4.

11. '*Relyatsiya P. S. Saltykova Imperatritse Elizavete o podrobnostyakh srazheniya pri Kunersdorfe*' (P. S. Saltykov's Report to the Empress Elizabeth on the events in the engagement at Kunersdorf) (9 (21) August, 1759), in Korobkov, p. 488 and plan no. 5; Rumyantsev: N. Kopylov, *Razvitiye taktiki russkoy armii s xviii do nachala xx vek (Evolution of Russian Army Tactics from the eighteenth to the beginning of the twentieth centuries)* (Moscow, 1957), p. 87; Suvorov and Ismail: Kazakov, *Artilleriya* . . . pp. 29–30.

12. Brandenburg, pp. 68–9, 75, 78–9; Nilus, Vol. II pp. 20, 21, 23, 26; Gneisenau quote; Michael Jenkins, *Arakcheyev, Grand Vizier of the Russian Empire*, (London, 1969), p. 157.

13. Lesson in technique to the French: Patrick Griffith *French Artillery* (Almark, London, 1976), p. 7; Wilson, p. 25; Visit to France *VE* Vol. 14, pp. 429–30; Kutaysov's regulations, *Obshchye pravila dlya artillerii v polevom srazhenii* in Skalon, ed. *Stoletiye* . . . Vol. 4 part 2, book 2, pp. 315–18 and commentary thereon. Speed and lightness, '*bystrotoyu i legkost 'yu*', plunging fire, '*vse pochty ikh vstrely, krome kartechnykh, sut' navesnye*'. 1840s: Hughes, pp. 92–3, 144–45; Kutaysov's death, *SVE*, Vol. 4 (1977), p. 543; General Mikhail Skobelev 'Instructions to his Artillery before the Storm of Geok Tepe in 1880'. Translations etc. supplement to *Proceedings of the Royal Artillery Institution* (PRAI), France II, (May 1882), p. 3.

14. Strength at Borodino: *SVE*, Vol. 1 (1976). p. 567; greatest killer, Brandenburg, p. 97 citing French Captain Chambrais; Lieutenant-General N. A. Okunev, 'On the new Employment of Artillery, and The Revolution it is destined to Produce in the System of Modern Tactics', *Colburn's United Service Magazine*, March, 1847 pp. 481–93 and July 1847 pp. 345–357. Grand battery, July, 1847, p. 348; swamp enemy, pp. 346–7; Okunev's other work *VE*: Vol. 17, p. 117.

15. Reforms: Skalon, *Stoletiye.* — Vol. III, section VI, p. 248; breechloaders v. smoothbores, Nilus Vol. II pp. 125, 160, 166; Royal Artillery Institution, *Professional Visits of Artillery Officers 1861–66* (1867): 1862 report, p. 24, 1866 report p. 92.

16. Use against Turkomans, Major F. V. Longstaff, *The Book of the Machine Gun* (London, 1917), p. 57; Gorlov v. Gatling: S. Kaminskiy 'Skorostrel'nye pushki nashey artillerii', *Voyenny Sbornik* (1870) Vol. 59, No. 12, pp. 363, 372–76; *VE* Vol. 8, p. 248; for an independent foreign opinion, British War Office *WO/33/24* Minute No. 30,097, p. 105. When quick firing field artillery appeared at the end of the century, the name for Gatling type guns obviously lapsed to avoid confusion. In addition, multibarrelled weapons were replaced by the true modern machine gun, a single barrelled automatic weapon, and these were called by the modern Russian name of *pulemët* (literally 'bullet thrower') (see Chapter Three).

17. *VE* Vol. 4, pp. 388–89; *SVE*, Vol. 1 (1976), p. 392.

18. Spade Brake, *VE* Vol. 14, p. 530. I am grateful to Dipl. Ing. Franz Kosar and Ian Hogg for their advice on this; Engelhardt: *Russki Invalid* extract translated in *RUSI* Vol. 43, Jan–June, 1899, p. 588. 'Really excellent gun . . .' Major J. M. Home in *Reports of British Observers Attached to the Russian and Japanese Armies in the Field*, (War Office, General Staff, 1907), Vol. 3, p. 210; 'most powerful field gun . . .' Lieutenant-Colonel H. A. Bethell RFA 'The 1903 pattern Russian QF Field Gun', *Journal of the Royal Artillery*, Vol. 33, 1906, p. 290.

19. Zasyadko: A. Sotnikov, *Voyenno-istoricheskiy muzey artillerii inzhenernykh voysk i voysk svyazi — kratkiy putevoditel' (Military historical museum of Artillery, Engineers and Signal Troops — A Short Guide)* (Leningrad, 1968), p. 175; N. V. Kartashov, *Boyevye neupravlyayemye rakety (Military Unguided Rockets)*, (Voyenizdat, Moscow, 1968), p. 4; Pozdnev, pp. 103–06; Konstantinov: Pozdnev, pp. 106–08, Sotnikov, p. 176, futuristic views *Professional Visits of Artillery Officers*, 1862 report, p. 23.

20. 4000 shots: Pozdnev p. 64; factory names *SVE* Vol. 4 (1977) pp. 188–89; tenacity of steel *Professional Visits . . .* 1866 Report. p. 71; Chernov: Pozdnev, pp. 66–67; see also pp. 71–3 for another notable metallurgist, Kalakautskiy; British report *WO/33/24*, Minute from the Secretary, Woolwich, no. 30,048 (2 April, 1872); Mendeleyev, *VE*, Vol. 15, pp. 256–57; overall industrial capacity. Lewis Siegelbaum, *The War Industries Committees and the Politics of Industrial Mobilization in Russia, 1914–17*, (D. Phil, Oxford, 1975).

21. See the author's 'The Russian Artillery and the Origins of Indirect Fire', *Army Quarterly and Defence Journal*, Vol. 112, Nos. 2 and 3 (April and July, 1982). Indirect fire in Crimea; F. Whinyates, *From Coruña to Sevastopol: A History of 'C' Battery*, (London 1891), p. 121: 'There must have been some very good system of signalling carried on by the Russians from their outlook on the Inkerman ridge or heights, for if any considerable body of troops were assembling, although they could not be seen from Sevastopol, there was certain to be a cannonade opened from the neighbourhood of the Malakhoff . . .'; Karl Georgiyevich Guk, *Zakrytaya strel'ba polevoy artillerii (Field Artillery Fire from Covered Positions)*, (St. Petersburg, 1882), pp. 11, 27–8, 56, 60; Major Keir RA 'Direct and Indirect Fire', *PRAI*, Vol. 24 (1897), pp. 231–37 and contemporary articles; sights: Captain L. R. Kenyon, RA 'Field Artillery Materiel on the Continent' *PRAI*, Vol. 29 (1902–3), p. 236 and 'O vvedenii v polevuyu artilleriyu uglomera dlya bokovoy navodki orudii', *Artilleriyskiy zhurnal (AZh)*, No. 6 (1898), Official Section, *prikaz* No. 61. The Russians had been testing the sights for 2 years. Employment in war: *Notes upon Russian Artillery Tactics in the War of 1905 with Conclusions drawn therefrom, translated from the Russian Artillery Journal* (War Office, General Staff, 1907). Extracts from articles by Lieutenant-Colonel Belyayev, p. 40

and Colonel C. V. Hume's Report in *Reports of British Observers* . . . p. 327. Sweeping like brooms: Belyayev, p. 50.

22. Seniority vs. Corps of Pages, Captain J. M. Grierson, *The Armed Strength of Russia*, (Intelligence Staff, War Office, London, 1882), pp. 244–45; 1900 opinion: Captain J. A. Douglas, Bengal Lancers, *Notes on the Russian Troops in China*, (War Office, London, 1902), p. 3; Tolstoy: S. S. Doroshenko, *Lev Tolstoy, voyn i patriot: voyennaya sluzhba in voyennaya deyatel'nost' (Leo Tolstoy, Soldier and Patriot: Military Service and Attainments)*, (Moscow, 1966); French parallels, Colonel E. L. Cordonnier, *With the Japanese in Manchuria*, translated from the French by Captain C. F. Atkinson, (London, 1914), Vol. 2 part 3, p. 258; Norman Stone, *The Eastern Front, 1914–17* (Hodder and Stoughton, London, 1975), p. 32; scarcely members of the same army: *Reorganisation of the HQ Artillery Department of the Russian War Ministry*, from *Novoye Vremya* 4 February, 1909, translated for the Chief-of-Staff, India (Simla, 1909), pp. 1–2; lack of co-operation with infantry: Colonel Knox, *Desptach Y* from Petrograd to London (8 June, 1915), *WO/106/1062*, little use of artillery: *Professional Visits* . . . 1866 Report, p. 25; disbelief in indirect fire: Belyayev, p. 43; not proper proportion of guns: Captain J. B. Jardine, *Reports of British Observers* . . . Vol. 2, p. 297; brigade of M-1900s kept back, Colonel W. H. H. Waters in *Reports of British Observers*, Vol. 3, p. 121; attempts to improve co-operation, *Reorganisation of HQ Artillery Department* . . . p. 1.

23. Gunners fighting hand to hand and casualties inflicted by artillery: *WO/33/712, Report on Certain Aspects of the Military Situation in Russia, & c.*, (1915) pp. 3, 10. Density of fire Major-General John Headlam, *Report on Visit to the Russian Front*, 12/25 February to 12/25 March, 1917, typescript in possession of Royal Artillery Institution, Woolwich, Section, 7 Effect of Fire; efficiency on South West Front, Bernard Pares' Report, *WO/106/1134* 27 January 1916.

24. V. F. Kirey, *Artilleriya ataki i oborony (Artillery in the Attack and the Defence)*, Ed. Yu. M. Sheydeman (originally two pamphlets written in 1916 and 1917, 2nd edn., Voyenizdat, Moscow, 1936). The first pamphlet, *Vyvody iz primeneniya artilleriyskikh mass pri atake (Conclusions from the employment of artillery masses in the attack)* was published on 17 September 1916 as Western Front Order No. 605, classified Secret, with an introduction by Inspector of Artillery Major-General Shikhlinskiy. Gorlitse-Tarnuv: *SVE*, Vol. 2 (1976), pp. 607–08; Ward Rutherford, *The Ally: the Russian Army in World War I*, (Gordon and Cremonesi, London, 1975, pp. 125–26; Captain J. M. House, *Towards Combined Arms Warfare: A Survey of Tactics, Doctrine and Organization in the Twentieth Century*, (Combat Studies Institute, US Army Command and General Staff College, Fort Leavenworth, 1984), p. 33; V. D. Grendal *'Ogon' artillerii (Artillery Fire)* (Voyenizdat, Moscow, 1926), p. 48; tears of blood, Kirey, *Artilleriya ataki i oborony*, p. 131; French norms, Kirey, p. 7; shells and metres of operation, Colonel A. A. Sidorenko, *The Offensive* (Moscow, 1970, translated and published under the auspices of the United States Air Force, US Government Printing Office, Washington DC, 1974), p. 16; use of mountain guns and breakthrough sector, Kirey, p. 72 and Appendix 3, keeping bombardment short, pp. 51–3; general dispositions, A. A. Strokov, *Vooruzheniye sily i voyennoye iskusstvo v pervoy mirovoy voyne (Armed Forces and Military Art in World War I)* (Voyenizdat, Moscow, 1974), pp. 393–94 Pflanzer-Baltin and thoughtful preparation, Stone, pp. 251, 252; use of AAA against tanks, Kirey, pp. 140–41.

25. Registration point: 'Did you know?' *VV* 2/1982, p. 59; Headlam's comments in his Report . . . Part III, sections 12–19; cool and competent performance, S. Mamontov, *Pokhody i kony (Raids and Riding)*, (YMCA Press, Paris, 1981), pp. 35–38. Mamontov confirms that the situation at the front was better than in the rear and that fraternisation did not begin on this front until after September, 1917. Batmen, p. 41.

26. Imperial-Soviet continuity and early Soviet organisation: Kovalenko, *Oboronnaya promyshlennost' Sovetskoy Rossii 1918–20 gg. (The Defence Industry of Soviet Russia)*, (Nauka, Moscow, 1970), pp. 98–9; 113; *Istoriya Otchestvennoy artillerii (History of the Motherland's Artillery)*, (Leningrad, 1963), pp. 94, 98, 113; I. S. Prochko, *Artilleriya v boyakh za rodinu (Artillery in Battle for the Motherland)*, (Moscow, 1957, pp. 63–4; N. D.

Yakovlev *Ob artillerii i nemnogo o sebe (On Artillery, and a Little about Myself)*, (Voyenizdat, Moscow, 1981), p. 96.

27. Beginnings of the Civil War: Peter Kenez, *Civil War in South Russia*, Vol. 1, 1918 (University of California, Berkeley, 1971), p. 65; gunnery and tactics, Mamontov, pp. 233–34; N. M. Khlebnikov, *Pod grokhot soten batarey (To the Thunder of Hundreds of Batteries)*, (Voyenizdat, Moscow, 1974), p. 50.

28. Sheydeman: see A. Raykhtsaum, '*Pervy nachal'nik artillerii*' ('The First Chief of Artillery'), *VV* 11/1967, pp. 57–60; Grendal': see Chief Marshal of Artillery N. N. Voronov, '*Vidayushchiysya Sovetskiy artillerist*' ('Outstanding Soviet Artilleryman'), *VIZh* 12/1963, pp. 57–64. The works of these officers are examined further in Chapter Two. Paris gun and influence on Russians, 'Did you know?', *VV* I/1985, p. 57; V. Vnukov, *Mozhno li strelyat' na sotnyu verst (Is it possible to fire at a range of 100 versts?)* (Gosizdat, Moscow, 1927), pp. 3, 25–6. A verst is an old Russian measure, equal to 1.06 kilometres; General N. Golovin, '*Ustroystvo artillerii*', ('The Constitution of the Artillery') in 'Thoughts on the Establishment of the Russian Armed Forces of the Future', *Voyenny Sbornik*, Vol. 7 (1925), pp. 201–18.

29. I. B. Berkhin — *Voyennaya reforma v. SSSR 1924–25 gg. (Military Reform in the USSR 1924–25)*, (Moscow, 1958), pp. 205–16.

30. V. Triandafillov, *Kharakter operatsii sovremennykh armii (Character of the Operations of Modern Armies)*, third ed. (Voyenizdat, Moscow, 1936), pp. 74–5, 80–82, 104–07, 110–13, 117.

31. 'Interesting phenomena of the past', F. O. Miksche, *Attack! A Study of Blitzkrieg Tactics*, (Random House, New York, 1942), Chapter ix 'Artillery decentralized', PU-36 cited in John Erickson, *The Soviet High Command 1917–41*, (London, 1962), pp. 438, 441; underestimation of artillery's importance and Stalin's reaffirmation of it: Yakovlev, pp. 49, 65; Internecine warfare: Yakovlev, pp. 47–8, 59; N. N. Voronov, *Na sluzhbe voyennoy (In the Service)* (Voyenizdat, Moscow, 1963), p. 165.

32. Colonel-General of Artillery L. Sapkov '*Evolyutsiya taktiki i boyevogo primeneniya artillerii*' ('Evolution of the Tactics and Military Employment of Artillery'), *VV* 4/1982, p. 65; Marshal of Artillery G. Ye Peredel'skiy, '*Boyevoye primeneniye artillerii v. armeyskikh oboronitel'nykh operatsiyakh*' ('Employment of Artillery in Army Defensive Operations') *VIZh* 11/1979, p. 17.

33. Spain and anti-tank fire: Voronov, p. 88; 9200 guns: *Militärwissenschaftliche Rundschau*, September, 1938, pp. 604–05 67,000: *SVE*, Vol. 1 (1976), p. 276; direct fire, Colonel Louis B. Ely, *The Red Army Today* (Military Services Publishing Co., Harrisburg, 1953), pp. 64, 66; Voronov, p. 165 Yakovlev, pp. 41–57.

34. Surface artillery, AAA and air: Philip Jordan, *Russian Glory*, (Cresset, London, 1942), pp. 39–40; heavy artillery: Yakovlev, pp. 94-4; PS-42; G. Ye Peredel'skiy, A. I. Tokhmakov, G. T. Khoroshilov, *Artilleriya v boyu i operatsii (po opytu Velikoy Otechestvennoy voyny) (Artillery in the Battle and Operation (According to the Experience of the Great Patriotic War))* (Voyenizdat, Moscow, 1980), p. 18.

35. German system; Khlebnikov, pp. 95–6; High Command Reserve: Sapkov, p. 66; artillery division: *SVE* Vol. 1 (1976), p. 265; AKPs, p. 269; groupings, pp. 264–65; mortars, Voronov, pp. 404–05.

36. Regroupments: Colonel V. Chernukhin and Lieutenant-Colonel V. Tarakanov '*Peregruppirovka artillerii RVGK na bol'shiye rasstoyaniya po opytu nastupatel'nykh operatsii tret'ego perioda voyny*' ('Regrouping of Supreme High Command Reserve Artillery over large Distances according to the Experience of the Third Period of the War') *VIZh* 6/1980, pp. 12, 15; percentage of targets identified; Peredel'skiy '*Bor'ba za ognevoye prevoskhodstvo v gody voyny*' ('The Struggle for Fire Superiority in the War Years') *VIZh* 11/1981, p. 21; firing on a narrow sector: Major-General F. W. von Mellenthin, *Panzer Battles*, (Futura, London, 1977), pp. 358, 359; artillery in concert with air, 70 per cent of artillery . . . mixing tanks and SPs: Lieutenant-Colonel A. Tsynkalov '*Bor'ba s protivotankovymi sredstvami protivnika v tret'em periode voyny*' ('The struggle with Enemy Anti-Tank Weapons in the

Third Period of the War') *VIZh* 7/1979, pp. 18–23; trend to sharper bombardments: Colonel-General M. Sidorov, '*Ognevoye porazheniye pri proryve oborony protivnika po opytu Velikoy Otechestvennoy voyny*' ('Fire Destruction during the Breakthrough of Enemy Defence according to the Experience of the Great Patriotic War'), *VIZh* 8/1984, pp. 18–23. ISU 122 and 152: Peredel'skiy *et al. Artilleriya v boyu* . . . p. 16.

37. Colonel-General of Artillery V. M. Mikhalkin, '*Boyevoye primeneniye artillerii v Belorusskoy operatsii*' ('The Military Employment of Artillery in the Belorussian Operation'), *VIZh*, 6/1984, pp. 25–33; Marshal of Artillery K. P. Kazakov, '*Boyevoye primeneniye artillerii pri proryve oborony v Bobruiskoy operatsii*' ('The Military Employment of Artillery in Breakthrough of the defence in the Bobruisk Operation') *VIZh* 12/1980, pp. 18–24; *SVE*, Vol. 1 (1976), pp. 431–34, 506–508.

38. *SVE* Vol. 8 (1980), pp. 674–76; Army General V. Tolubko, '*Artilleriya 3-go Ukrainskogo fronta v Yassko-Kishinëvskoy operatsii*' ('Military Employment of Artillery of 3 Ukrainian Front in the Yassy-Kishinëv Operation'), *VIZh* 8/1979, pp. 37–42.

39. *SVE*, Vol. 2 (1976), pp. 147–50; Marshal of Artillery G. Peredel'skiy, Colonel G. Khoroshilov, '*Artilleriya v srazheniyakh ot Visly do Odera*' ('Artillery in the Operational Battles from the Vistula to the Oder'), *VIZh*, 1/1985, pp. 30–34.

40. *SVE*, Vol. 1, (1976), pp. 456–61; Peredel'skiy *et al.*, *Artilleriya v boyu* . . ., pp. 49–52, 68–9; heavy howitzers in streets, Ely, p. 68; seventeen gone mad, Colonel E. Lederrey, *Germany's Defeat in the East, 1941–45*, (Official History, War Office, London, 1955), p. 219 note. Tërkin, from Aleksandr Tvardovsky's narrative poem *Vassiliy Tërkin* (1943).

41. 335,000: *SVE*, Vol. 1 (1976), p. 277; Marshal Zhukov's figure of 360,000; figures for rocket launchers Colonel V. Amelchenko, 'Legendary Katyushas', *Soviet Military Review* (*SMR*) 11/1981 p. 31; 188,000 guns and howitzers, '*Ognevoy shchit rodiny*' (Fire Shield of the Motherland'), *VIZh* 11/1978, p. 11; Peredel'skiy in *VIZh* 11/1981 gives 42,000 pieces for the Berlin Operation; *SVE*, Vol. 1 gives 45,000, which may include rocket launchers. Yakovlev gives 30,000 guns, Howitzers and mortars for the Belorussian Operation (p. 170) and 48,000 for Berlin, including rocket launchers (p. 173). Other data from *SVE*, Vol. 1, p. 279.

2.

An Arm of Service

'Leave the artillerymen alone. They are an obstinate lot'.

NAPOLEON

PLATE 2.1.   Soviet artillery officers replete with combat experience being trained for higher command during the Great Patriotic War. The young officer nearest us is a captain (one stripe, four small stars and crossed gun badge). The officer with the other *artillery board* is a lieutenant-colonel, suggesting that this is a course for artillery regiment commanders, at least.
(British Library)

Towards the end of 1917 young Second-Lieutenant Sergey Mamontov was making his way home to Moscow. He had removed his officers' shoulder boards, cap badge and spurs so as not to run the risk of being thrown in front of a train, or worse, by the crowds of rank and file who were bent on revenge against the hated former ruling class. Mamontov snuggled up in a dark corner of a railway wagon full of troops, trying to remain inconspicuous. He pretended to be asleep, one hand on the revolver hidden inside his coat. If the worst came to the worst, he thought, he could shoot and jump from the nearby door. Soon however, something about him attracted attention, and the soldiers began talking:

'Of course he's an officer. Look at his leather suitcase and breeches with red piping on them . . .'

Mamontov was poised to shoot his way out, but then he heard a friendly voice:

'Can't you see that he's an artilleryman — black collar tabs — *artillerymen all look like officers* — leave him alone . . .'[1]

The black collar tabs with crossed gun barrels are not the only thing which Mamontov would have recognised about the *Rocket Forces and Artillery of the Ground Forces* in the 1980s. He would no doubt have been gratified to see these insignia also worn by members of two of the Soviet Union's five *Armed Services*: the *Air Defence Service* and the élite *Strategic Rocket Forces*, both scions of the artillery who now enjoy an independent existence. The Armed Forces of the Soviet Union are organised differently from those of the United States, Britain and other western powers, on functional lines. Thus, the air defence of troops on the ground and of the country as a whole, whether by AAA, Surface to Air Missiles (SAMs), or fighter aircraft, is the responsibility of one organisation, the Air Defence Service. Land based strategic missiles are not manned by the Air Force: indeed, the Soviets do not have a single 'Air Force' analogous to ours, but, very sensibly, recognised as a qualitatively distinct and independent service. Although AAA is obviously closely related to surface to surface artillery technologically, the Soviets have recognised its role as being quite different and since before the Great Patriotic War, Air Defence Forces have been considered as separate from surface to surface artillery on the one hand and attack aviation on the other. AAA for strategic Air Defence (as opposed to air defence of the field forces) was made independent of the Red Army from November 1941, reporting instead to an air defence commander responsible for all Soviet territory. However, it was not until 1954 that the Strategic Air Defence force acquired the status of an independent service under a Deputy Minister of Defence of the USSR. Since then, it has been commanded by a number of Marshals of the Soviet Union, one Marshal of Aviation and one Army General, reflecting its independence from the Ground Forces and their artillery. Because of this functional and organisational distinction, they are not dealt with in detail in this book. However, some mention of them is inevitable because they inevitably interact with Army forces on the field of battle, because the technologies involved have much in common and because there has been and continues to be interaction in terms of people.

There used to be two groups of Air Defence Forces: the *Air Defence of Ground Forces* and the *Air Defence of the Homeland* responsible for operational-tactical and strategic air defence tasks respectively. However, in 1980 evidence emerged suggesting that the latter was undergoing a thorough reorganisation. At the time, both forces were headed by Marshal of Aviation A. I. Koldunov. The reorganisation probably owes a lot to changing technology: the Strategic Air Defence Force was created specifically to counter German and, later, the possibility of American strategic bombing. However, by the 1980s the distinction between operational-tactical and strategic systems had broken down: low level cruise missiles, whether air or ground launched, were best dealt with by the systems traditionally operated by the tactical Air Defence Force. At the same time, the development of the concept of Integrated Fire Destruction of the Enemy and the expansion of Soviet military thinking to recognise the concept of a single Theatre Strategic Operation (see Chapter Four) must have called the distinction between the two forces into doubt. There is little doubt that by January 1981 operational-tactical and strategic air defence had merged into a single service under Koldunov, known as the *Air Defence Forces*. As far as we know, all the AAA and SAM troops are badged as gunners. Air Defence missile troops and artillery are clearly regarded as part of a separate service from the Army's Rocket Forces and Artillery but are sometimes listed adjacent to them because of the similarity in technologies. There is also clearly some cross mobility at the higher levels, many senior officers in the artillery and rocket troops having air defence experience.

Mobility between the Army's artillery and rocket troops and the Strategic Rocket Forces (SRF) has tended to be one way — from the Army to the SRF. The first Commander-in-Chief of the SRF was Marshal of Artillery Nedelin, appointed on 17 December, 1959. By the end of the 1950s, rockets and nuclear warheads had been manufactured in such numbers as to raise the question of who would control these new weapons. One school of thought advocated dividing them between the four existing services. Army, Air Defence, Air Forces and Navy. A second advocated control by the Navy and Air Force alone (as in the United States). A third believed that a totally new service was appropriate, and Nedelin shared this view — the view that won the day. However, given the Soviet Artillery's earlier history of interest in long range surface to surface weapons and their control over multiple rocket launchers and large tactical missiles in the war and early post war years, it was only natural that they should play the leading role in the new service. Nedelin's appointment as Commander-in-Chief of the SRF was first reported to the West in the same 6 May 1960 edition of the *New York Times* that carried the news of the shooting down of Gary Powers' American U-2 reconnaissance plane by a SAM of the Strategic Air Defence Service — the latter's only battle honour, but no mean achievement, all the same. Nedelin's appointment and career are further detailed below. Similar transfers occurred at all levels: a book about *Soviet Rocket Forces* published in 1967 detailed the career of a typical *rocketeer*, Anatoliy Basyukov. This (possibly fictitious) character attended an Artillery-Mortar training school. He then served in ground units of the air forces in the Great Patriotic War, and then entered the artillery of the airborne forces. Finally it was suggested that he join the SRF, an honour he accepted. SRF troops who joined the Armed Forces after 1960 may, of course, have spent their whole careers in the missile forces. Nedelin was succeeded as chief of the SRF by three all-arms officers (Moskalenko, Biryuzov and Krylov), a former tank officer, Tolubko, and since summer 1985, by Colonel-General Yu. P. Maksimov. There remain close connections between the Army's Rocket Forces and Artillery and the SRF, however. The SRF personnel shown in published photographs wear the traditional artillery crossed gun badge on their indoor uniforms, albeit Great Patriotic War style on the shoulder board rather than on the collar as with the Army's artillery and rocket troops and enlisted personnel wear artillery black shoulder straps. The demarcation between responsibilities has been set, somewhat arbitrarily, at 1000 kilometres, missiles with less than this range being controlled by the Army. As a rule, one could say that the SRF control missile systems based inside the Soviet Union although some must have been sent to Cuba with the missiles sent there in 1962. The SS-20 missiles now deployed in Europe are operated by the SRF. The fact that a strategic missile expert is probably indistinguishable from a field gunner of course complicates matters for western intelligence. In a more philosophical sense, the elitism of the SRF is also essentially that of the old artillery: based on their technical competence and ability to deal the most powerful blows. Because of the enormous power of their terrible weapons, they have a 'heightened sense of responsibility'.[2] Not only do Strategic Rocket Forces complement and draw upon the Army's Rocket Forces and Artillery; they are the very epitome of the Russian artillery's ethos.

Turning to the Army's Rocket Troops and Artillery, who are the subject of this book, they were also affected by organisational changes in the early to mid 1980s. Most significant, apart from the command changes described later in this chapter, was the decision by the Supreme Soviet, promulgated on 26 April 1984 affecting 'The ranks of Officer Personnel of the USSR Armed Forces'. This fundamentally reorganised the all-arms ranks structure, abolishing specific to arm ranks such as Major-General of Tank Troops, Lieutenant-General of Signals Troops. The ranks of Marshal of Artillery, Marshal of Engineers and Marshal of Signals Troops have however been retained, and the artillery are accorded the unique honour of retaining the rank of Chief Marshal of Artillery, equivalent to Marshal of the Soviet Union. By contrast, the armour have been severely deflated, the rank of Marshal of Tank Troops being abolished (although those already holding it will be allowed to retain it). This reflects concern about inter-arm co-operation and the conduct of the all arms battle at the highest level, and the Soviets' realisation that in the recent past they have placed too much emphasis on pure tank forces (as have Western analysts). The fact that the rocket troops and artillery have come through unscathed is a reaffirmation of their traditional primacy within the Soviet armed forces as well as their key role in the modern all conventional quick attack doctrine. The unique retention of Chief Marshal of Artillery also affirms and enhances the prestige of the Strategic Rocket Forces.[3] General officers of all different arms will continue to wear the distinctive insignia of their arm on their gold lace shoulder board, in the case of Rocket Troops and Artillery and artillery generals serving in the Strategic Rocket Forces, crossed guns.

PLATE 2.2.   A good shot of a junior sergeant (two bars) of the Army's *Artillery and Rocket Troops* checking the accuracy of laying a BM-21 Multiple Rocket Launcher. The black tabs with crossed guns and the shield shaped badge can be seen clearly. The letters CA on the shoulder stand for Soviet Army.

Officers below general and other ranks are clearly recognisable in service dress by the crossed gun badge on the collar and, in the case of other ranks, by the shield shaped badge on the left arm. Nowadays a green and grey-white camouflage suit is generally worn in tactical conditions, which carries no insignia at all, although officers obstinately wear their Sam Browne belts over them. The standard background colour for artillery is black, as it is for armour and engineers, reflecting the common origin of the three arms. Other ranks wear black shoulder straps and collar patches with service dress: commissioned artillery officers wear drab khaki collar patches in the field but have traditional black on their full dress uniforms. The only variation from black for other ranks is for certain troops seen wearing the crossed gun badge on the red collar patches of motor rifle troops. These are the men serving in the motor rifle regiment's own organic artillery battalion. This is extremely significant for two reasons. First, it shows that the Soviets see the artillery component of the regiment as functionally somewhat different from the general support provided by divisional and higher level artillery. Second, it indicates a desire to stress that these artillery battalions are very much the regimental commander's own. The same is true for the troops who operate the regiment's 120 mm mortars, who also wear crossed guns on red.

Although tube artillery, mortars, multiple rocket launchers and large tactical rockets are all operated by the one arm of service, the individual soldiers are usually referred to according to the type of equipment they operate: *gunners* or *artillerymen*, *mortarmen* and *rocketeers*, respectively.

How to become an Officer in the Rocket Forces and Artillery

A most important point about officer selection and training, which has a major influence on the relationship of artillery and rocket troops with the other arms, is that commissioned personnel are not trained initially alongside those of other arms as at Sandhurst or West Point. They are trained at an Artillery Higher Command School (in Russian *academy* refers to a higher stage of military education, analogous to a Western Staff College, War College or General Staff College). This is similar to the way British artillery and sapper officers used to be trained separately at the 'Shop' at Woolwich. However, if the Soviet Union has scores of Sandhursts, it has dozens of 'Shops'.

As in the West, officer candidates can enter a Higher Command School either from the ranks of straight from civvy street. Candidates are advised to begin preparation *2 to 3 years* before submitting an enrolment application because entry to the officer corps of the Soviet Army is by *competitive academic examination*. There are certain exceptions such as graduates of the Suvorov military schools and those who have completed at least one term at a civilian university with good markings in the relevant specialisms. Servicemen require a confidential report from their unit commander and both servicemen and civilians need a party or Komsomol (Communist Youth League) recommendation. All candidates are medically examined before the competitive examination and civilians also have to have attained the normal national physical fitness standards for young people their age. Thus the militarised nature of Soviet society helps with much of the weeding out on physical and character grounds which in the West has to be done at the selection board or in training itself. The competitive entrance examination is very hard, especially the mathematics and physics. The Russian language and literature paper contains questions which would come in a British 'A' level paper or an American college course, for example 'The Image of Lenin in Mayakovskiy's Work' or 'Maxim Gorkiy: Stormy Petrel of the Russian Revolution'. More intimidating are the mathematics papers, written and oral, for example:

1. Simplify the expression:

$$\frac{2a^2(b + c)^{2n} - \frac{1}{2}}{an^2 - a^3 + 2a^2 - a} : \frac{2a(b + c)^n - 1}{a^2c - a(nc - c)}.$$

2. Solve the inequality:

$$\sqrt[\log_c x]{0.2^{6\log_c x - 3}} > \sqrt[3]{0.008^{2\log_c x - 1}}.$$

3. Solve the equation:

$$3^{\log_c x + \log_c x^0 + \log_c x^0 + \ldots + \log_c x^0} = 27x^{30}.$$

4. Solve the equation:

$$8 \operatorname{tg}^2 (x/2) = 1 + \sec x.$$

5. At the base of a straight prism lies a trapezium, inscribed in a semicircle with a radius R so that its larger base coincides with the diameter, while the smaller draws an arc equal to 2α. Determine the volume of the prism if the diagonal of the facet which passes through the lateral side of the base, is sloped toward the base at angle α.

These questions are of considerable mechanical difficulty involving a lot of formal algebraic manipulation, but little mathematic flair or insight. It is a type of mathematical examination which was probably universal earlier this century, in St. Petersburg, Oxford or Harvard. In present day terms a good British 'A' level mathematics student (American college student, probably) could follow the questions and a very good one might be able to do them. The Russians find that servicemen tend to do much better at these than the civilian candidates[4]. It must be stressed that this is the *general examination* for *all officer candidates*, not just those for the technical arms. This formidable base of algebra, trigonometry and geometry is of course particular power to the elbow of the artilleryman, many of whose problems are expressed in formal algebraic form (see the calculation of norms in Chapter Four). Some Western commentators believe that the Soviet military may be unsuited to assimilate and exploit the possibilities of, for example, computers on the battlefield. In the author's view, officers who are expected to master this sort of thing as a matter of course are as well able to cope with such challenges as Westerners, and probably better. They have the additional advantage of a deep understanding of mathematical principles, enabling them to do their sums even if the computer breaks down. This is a reflection of Russia's traditional strength in logic, chess-playing, mathematics and the 'hard' sciences.

The very high intellectual standard required of regular officers is evident throughout the training process. Successful candidates attend a higher command school. For all-arms cadets this is a 3 year course, but for artillery, four and for military engineering schools, five. All graduate with the rank of Lieutenant (there are three Lieutenant ranks in the Soviet Army: Junior, Plain, and Senior although the rank of Junior Lieutenant has not, apparently, been used since the 1950s), and a nationally recognised degree. Artillery officers will generally have an engineering specialisation as part of their degree. Their military education has been full, rounded and thorough.

At the time of writing the following establishments train junior officers for the artillery and rocket troops. Because there may be some cross-fertilisation, anti-aircraft missile schools are listed as well:

Artillery and Rocket Forces School	Commander (1983)
October Revolution Higher Artillery Command School (Order of Lenin) Kolomna (Moscow MD)	Lieutenant-General of Artillery A. T. Baisara (1975)
Red October Higher Artillery Command School (Order of Lenin, Red Banner), Leningrad	Major-General of Artillery V. Sergienko (1977)
M. V. Frunze Higher Artillery Command School (Order of Lenin) Odessa	Major-General of Artillery N. A. Anan'ev (1978)
M. V. Frunze Higher Artillery Command School (twice Red Banner), Sumi (Volga MD)	Major-General of Artillery A. Morozov (1976)

Tula Proletariat Higher Artillery Engineering School (Order of Lenin), Tula, (Moscow MD)	Lieutenant-General of Artillery V. Kulev (1978)
26 Baku Commissars Higher Artillery Command School (Red Banner), Tbilisi (Transcaucasus MD)	Major-General of Artillery V. G. Shuvalov (1979)
Marshal of Artillery N. D. Yakovlev Higher Artillery Command School, Khmel'nitskiy (Carpathian MD)	Major-General of Artillery B. F. Bokov (1978)
Marshal of Artillery M. N. Chistyakov Higher Military Engineering School, Kazan' (Volga MD)	Lieutenant-General of Artillery P. R. Nikitenko (1979)
Hero of the Soviet Union Major-General A. I. Lizyukov Higher Military Command School (Red Banner and Red Star), Saratov (Volga MD)	Lieutenant-General of Artillery A. S. Kobzar (1978)
Chief Marshal of Artillery N. N. Voronov Higher Military Engineering School Penza, (Volga MD)	Major-General of Artillery V. I. Zaitsev (1978)
Marshal of the Soviet Union S. S. Biryuzov Higher Military Command School (Red Banner), Riga	—
Marshal of the Soviet Union N. I. Krylov Higher Military Command School, Kharkov	—
Chief Marshal of Artillery M. I. Nedelin Higher Military Command School, Rostov	—
Lenin Komsomol Higher Military Command School, Serpukhov (Moscow MD)	—
Perm Higher Military Command School, Perm	—

Some of the schools which train artillery officers are not specifically designated artillery. The reason for this is not clear.

Anti-Aircraft Missile Schools
S. M. Kirov Higher Anti-Aircraft Missile Engineering School (order of Lenin, Red Banner), Kiev
Higher Anti-Aircraft Missile Command School Leningrad
G. K. Ordzhonikidze Higher Anti-Aircraft Missile Command School (Red Banner), Orenburg

General of the Army N. F. Vatutin Higher
Anti-Aircraft Missile Command School
(Red Banner), Poltava
*Higher Anti-Aircraft Missile Command
School*, Smolensk[4]

After graduating from a higher command school, a young officer may
well soon find himself the *battery senior officer*, who is the Gun Position
Officer and second in command of a battery. As a senior lieutenant or
captain, he will be a battery commander. Being a conscript army, the
Soviets do not have the cadre of experienced and highly qualified NCOs
and warrant officers who fill many of the key posts in the British and US
Armies. The Soviets have attempted to create a corps of highly qualified
ensigns, warrant officers just below commissioned status, who were formed
from 1 January,1972. These are particularly important in highly technical
forces such as the Strategic Rocket Troops, and certainly play a significant
role in the command of ground forces *operational-tactical rockets*. However,
the greater breadth and depth of Soviet officers' training — relative to his
subordinates' — is such that there must be a considerable gap in expertise
and authority between ensigns and even the greenest lieutenant.

After commanding a battery, an artillery officer may be sent on the
recommendation of his army and military district commanders, to the *M. I.
Kalinin Artillery Academy* in Leningrad. The full course here normally lasts
2 years, but there are accelerated courses, and also part-time correspond-
ence courses. The various courses are known as *Central Artillery Command
Courses*, although the Academy as a whole has a major role in research,
both technical and tactical. In 1985, the academy was led by Colonel-
General of Artillery A. I. Matveyev, who has commanded since 1982, with
Lieutenant-General of Artillery A. Sapozhnikov, a noted writer on artillery
matters, leading the Central Artillery Command Courses, which have
borne the name of Marshal of Artillery K. P. Kazakov since 1969. These
courses essentially train battalion commanders and above, perhaps the
cardinal point in the Soviet artillery command structure embodying liaison
with the all-arms commander on the one hand and acting as the eyes and
ears of the higher artillery commanders on the other. After graduating from
the Kalinin Academy, officers, now majors, either command artillery
battalions or become chiefs of staff of artillery regiments. The better
officers may spend only a year as chief of staff before becoming an artillery
regiment commander. At this point the whole system of appointments and
promotion becomes extremely flexible. The brightest young officers move
very fast. Lieutenant-Colonels and above who have not attended the
Kalinin Academy may attend either the M. V. Frunze General Staff
Academy in Leningrad or the F. M. Dzerzhinskiy 'Military Engineering
Academy', also in Leningrad. Normally, officers only have one bite at the

military higher education cherry. The Dzerzhinskiy is known informally as the 'rocket academy', which hints at its true role. Founded in 1820 and redesignated the Mikhail Artillery Academy in 1846, the Dzerzhinskiy Academy now plays a key role in weapons procurement and development. During the Great Patriotic War the academy, then a purely artillery establishment, was evacuated to Samarkand, and large numbers of artillery officers were put through special accelerated courses there at a location which must have been less romantic than its sounds. Over 700 major experimental artillery projects were carried out. The Academy continued to be the centre for artillery research until 1952 when, recognising that rocket missiles and nuclear warheads were creating a *Revolution in Military*

PLATE 2.3.   Dzerzhinskiy Military Academy, Leningrad. Formerly the Mikhail Artillery Academy.

Affairs, some of the conventional artillery tasks were moved to an affiliated institution which became the Kalinin Academy although the Academy continued to train engineers for work on surface and anti-aircraft artillery and tank guns, as well as providing a centre for the development of nuclear warheads and missiles. Since 1969 the Academy has been headed by Lieutenant-General F. P. Tonkikh, who has some 60 Doctors of Science and Professors and a large number of Ph.Ds and Ph.D students working under him.[5]

Graduates of these academies may come out as full Colonels or Major-Generals, depending on their performance. One can assume that Major-Generals of Artillery command Army artillery and rocket assets and, perhaps, Lieutenant-Generals at Front, although the Soviet Army is, curiously, less rank conscious than Western armies and it is the appointment which counts, not the rank, The present Chief of Artillery and Rocket Troops, Mikhalkin (see below) was a Lieutenant-General when appointed and at the time of writing is a Colonel-General.

ROCKET TROOPS AND ARTILLERY OF THE GROUND FORCES — SENIOR COMMAND 1968–1983

COMMANDER
1963–69	Marshal of Artillery K. P. KAZAKOV. Replaced Chief Marshal of Artillery S. S. VARENTSOV in May 1963. VARENTSOV was demoted in rank 'for lack of vigilance'.
1969–83	Lieutenant-General of Artillery G. E. PEREDEL'SKY (Promoted: Colonel-General of Artillery May 1970; Marshal of Artillery 5 November 1973)
1983–	Colonel-General of Artillery V. M. MIKHALIN

(FIRST) DEPUTY COMMANDER*
1965–69	Lieutenant-General of Artillery G. E. PEREDEL'SKY
1969–	Lieutenant-General of Artillery L. S. SAPKOV (Promoted: Colonel-General of Artillery in 1977)

*Post probably up-graded to that of a *First* Deputy in late 1969.

CHIEF OF STAFF
1968–69	Lieutenant-General of Artillery L. S. SAPKOV
1969–76	Lieutenant-General of Artillery M. D. SIDOROV
1960–80	Lieutenant-General of Artillery E. V. STROGANOV
1980–83	Lieutenant-General of Artillery V. M. MIKHALKIN
1983–	At present unidentified

DEPUTY OF THE COMMANDER — FOR POLITICAL AFFAIRS; HEAD OF THE POLITICAL DEPARTMENT**
1973–77	Lieutenant-General of Artillery P. M. PETRENKO
1977–	Lieutenant-General of Artillery V. A. GRISHANTSEV

**Also Head of the Political Department of the Main Missile and Artillery Directorate.

Men at the Top

Contrary to popular belief, individuals play possibly a greater role in the evolution of the Soviet military than in the West. This is a function of the long time which senior Soviet officers spend in post, and also of the high priority and status which the military enjoys in Soviet society and the economy. The careers of certain individuals are crucial to explaining the way the Soviet artillery and rocket forces have developed and are likely to develop in the future.

Lieutenant-General of Artillery of the Imperial Army
Yuri Mikhaylovich Sheydeman, 1867–1940

PLATE 2.4. Yuri Mikhaylovich Sheydeman, first Chief of Red Army Artillery. A former tsarist Lieutenant-General, Sheydeman is wearing crossed guns which were *not* an official part of the Red Army uniform at this time. (British Library)

Sheydeman graduated from the Mikhail Artillery Academy in 1877 and served in the Russo-Japanese War and World War I. From May 1917 he had been the head of the *Special Heavy Artillery* of the Imperial Army. After the Revolution, the Bolsheviks retained him in this capacity. In August, 1918 notwithstanding the difficult conditions of the Civil War, Sheydeman headed a conference to examine the lessons of the 1914–18 war. In November 1918 he was made Inspector of Artillery on the newly created Red Army General Staff and on 21 August, 1921, Chief of Red Army Artillery. With the end of the war over most Soviet territory, Sheydeman was able to concentrate on remedying the faults which had been remarked on in 1917, (see Chapter One), by using air photographs to locate unobserved targets, correcting fire from aircraft, making allowances for meteorological conditions and setting up sound ranging units. He also perceived the need for artillery ultimately to become self-propelled, but the country's industrial and technological base would not permit this for many years. From 1922 he was Editor in Chief of *Red Artillery*, as the old *Artillery Journal* had been renamed. At the end of 1922 the few Red Army tank and armoured car units were also placed under Sheydeman's jurisdiction. This is how armoured troops came to wear black facings. At the time these units were in a parlous condition and Sheydeman, recognising the tank as a wholly new and potentially decisive form of armament, set to work organising the repair and modification of the vehicles. It is highly significant that the first Red Army tank regulations went out *under the signature of an artilleryman*, another example of the pervasive role played by the artillery in the Soviet Army as a whole.

In 1923 Sheydeman summoned the first all-Army Command Conference, at which he stressed the need for close co-operation between artillery and the other arms. He was subsequently re-titled Head of Red Army Artillery and Armoured Forces. He continued to work with demonic energy organising artillery units and improving training. In 1927 he also worked with the commission studying the history of the Great War, from which the Soviets drew many lessons, as we have seen (Chapter One). He continued to guide the organisation of artillery during the artillery build up during the Second Five Year Plan, and died in 1940. He wrote or supervised a number of seminal manuals including *An Aid to the Training of the Red Army Artilleryman, The Armament of Germany and her Allies in the World War, Problems of Counter-Battery Fire, Artillery in the Defence*, and helped translate a number of foreign military works. Sheydeman was the founding father of modern Soviet artillery, especially in the emphasis he placed on counter-battery fire and complex technical gunnery problems, and was the physical embodiment of continuity between the Imperial Army and the Soviet.[6]

Colonel-General of Artillery Vladimir Davydovich Grendal', 1884–1940

Grendal' graduated from the Mikhail Artillery Academy in 1911 and served in the Great War, attaining the rank of Colonel. He joined the Red Army in 1918, serving on the Southern Front in the Civil War. He was made Inspector of Artillery for that Front and, from January to December, 1920, of the South Western. After the war he was artillery commander of Kiev and Petrograd (as it was then) military districts and in 1923–24, Head of the Red Army Artillery Academy. He was appointed deputy Inspector of Red

PLATE 2.5.   Vladimir Davydovich Grendal'. He is wearing the insignia of a
Komkor, equivalent to Lieutenant-General. (British Library)

Army Artillery and, from 1925, Inspector in Sheydeman's place. He was instrumental in getting the M-1927 infantry support gun into service and also in reorganising artillery into three gun batteries which at the time gave greater flexibility in using artillery to support forward troops. In concert with Mikhail Tukhachevsky he also had Special Signals Detachments introduced into artillery battalions, once again, to facilitate co-operation between artillery and infantry or cavalry. From 1935 to 1937 he held the Chair of Artillery Professor at the M. V. Frunze General Staff Academy, a most important appointment as this is when the Soviets are working out their very advanced ideas for the deep operation and employment of armoured formations. An officer of Grendal's ability and status would have ensured that the role of artillery was given its proper emphasis in these discussions. In 1938 Grendal' became Deputy Head of the Main Artillery Directorate and President of the Artillery Committee concerned with procurement. He drew up a plan for the armament of all land forces ranging from pistols to 305 mm guns. These plans shaped the re-equipment of the Red Army during and after the Great Patriotic War. In 1939 Grendal' went to the Karelian Isthmus on active service. The breakthrough of the strongly fortified Mannerheim line, a belt of permanent fortifications many kilometres deep, required massive and precise strikes by artillery. Voronov recalls him waiting silently for the artillery preparation to begin, quietly confident that the targets had been correctly plotted and that the fire would be effective. It was, and, as the senior officer present in the breakthrough sector Grendal' found himself in command of two rifle divisions, something that could happen to an artillery officer today. Grendal' handled this all-arms force ably, penetrating the line to a depth of 5 or 6 kilometres. The Soviet forces were re-grouped and Grendal' placed in command of the new 13 Army which penetrated the Mannerheim line in several places in February and March, 1940. Grendal' was made an Army Commander, second class, which became Colonel-General when the ranks were renamed. Far from being 'simply a mechanic', Colonel-General of Artillery Grendal' proved himself an able all-arms commander in a war where such men were evidently needed on the Soviet side. Grendal' wrote some 300 articles and books on artillery, including *More Accurate Fire* (1925), *Artillery Fire* (1926), *Field Service of Artillery Commanders and Staffs* (1927), and *Artillery in the Major Forms of Combat* (1940). His views on artillery and on the future of war in general were far-sighted and his work formed a basis for the employment of Soviet artillery on the battlefield in the Great Patriotic War. He also influenced another Head of Red Army artillery personally.[7]

Chief Marshal of Artillery Nikolay Nikolayevich Voronov, 1899–1968

Voronov graduated from the second Petrograd artillery course for Red Commanders: those who had not held commissions in the Tsarist army but were now to hold analogous positions in the Red Army. He fought against the forces of Kolchak and Denikin in the Civil War, and commanded an artillery battery and then battalion in 1923–24. He went to a higher artillery command school in 1924 and then commanded a regiment. In 1934 he was appointed head of one of the artillery command schools in Leningrad and was sent to Spain as a Soviet military adviser in 1936 under the pseudonym 'Voltaire'. Voronov's recollections of Spain are perspicacious and often amusing, showing a well developed sense of humour. In the battle for Madrid, Voronov's eye lighted on the tall building of the *Telefonica Central*, the main telephone exchange. With a Russian's instinct for centralising command and control of artillery fire, Voronov decided to use the building with its splendid view of the enemy positions outside the city as his command observation post, and relay orders to the dispersed batteries via the civilian telephone network. It worked, except that the girls who continued to operate the telephone exchange would occasionally interrupt a

PLATE 2.6.   Nikolay Voronov (left), here a Marshal of Artillery (one large star, crossed guns), receiving an award for his part in the siege and relief of Leningrad. (Newsreel film, IWM)

fire mission with 'have you finished?' On another occasion, Voronov was watching intently as Republican gun fire was adjusted on to a fascist battery, and an orange flash indicated a direct hit on one of the enemy guns. At this critical moment the Spanish commander ordered 'stop!'

'Why have you stopped?' asked Voronov,

'*Comida*,' said the Spaniard, 'lunch-time'.

'What do you mean?' said Voronov, 'They'll limber up and get away.'

'Oh no they won't,' said the Spaniard, 'they've got to have lunch, too . . .'

Of course, most of the fighting in the Spanish Civil War was not conducted with such levity and Voronov brought many hard learned lessons and real combat experience back to Russia. From 1937 to 1940 he was Head of Red Army Artillery, doing a great deal of work to improve artillery organisation and to make training more realistic. He also participated in discussions on procurement questions, and accelerated the development of mortars which he saw as a cheap and economical substitute for conventional artillery. In summer, 1939 he took part in the highly successful Soviet operation in the Khalkin-Gol region, where he gained experience in handling artillery on an Army Group (Front) wide scale. He also supervised the transfer of artillery to mechanical traction (most of it, as in the German

RGW-H

Army, was still horse drawn). Winter, 1939 saw him in the Karelian Isthmus alongside Grendal', drawing the same lessons about the need to identify targets precisely and meticulously, and seeing the value of artillery in the direct fire mode, especially against *permanent strong points*. He was temporarily assigned to head Air Defence forces (AAA and aircraft), something which did not please him at all, but when the Germans attacked in June, 1941 Stalin had the sense to put him back where his knowledge and experience could be utilised to the full, as Head of the Red Army's artillery. Perhaps his greatest personal achievement was in the Battle of Stalingrad, where massed Soviet artillery played a decisive role and Voronov reintroduced World War I Imperial artillery regulations as the most appropriate ones for positional warfare. When the Germans capitulated in February, 1943, Voronov, as representative of the Stavka of the Supreme High Command (see Chapter One) put his signature as a Colonel-General of Artillery above that of the Front Commander, Rokossovskiy. His most important contributions to the development of artillery were developing the theory and practice of the artillery offensive, anti-tank fire, creating powerful artillery formations, and the development of the Artillery Reserve of the Supreme High Command (see Chapter One). One battle he lost was to try to make the self-propelled assault guns, developed during the war, part of the artillery empire. Because the armour had the expertise and infrastructure to maintain the armoured and tracked chassis, whereas the gunners had not, these machines were placed under the command of armoured forces. Of course, assault guns had a very different role from conventional artillery, and quite different from modern self-propelled guns which are, unquestionably artillery weapons. Voronov also played a major part in the post-war development of artillery and missiles: from 1950 to 1953 he was president of the *Academy of Artillery Sciences*, a euphemistic title for the front organisation behind which strategic nuclear missiles were developed. His appointment as Chief Marshal of Artillery in 1944 reflected Stalin's delight at the performance of that arm in the war, and in 1965 he was made a Hero of the Soviet Union. He was a big man, humorous and humane, and is today buried in Red Square in the Kremlin Wall.[8]

Marshal of Artillery Nikolay Dmitrievich Yakovlev, 1898–1972

Yakovlev served briefly in the Tsarist army and was sent on a Petrograd Artillery Command Course in 1920. Between 1921 and 1930 he commanded a battery and battalion and was chief of staff of an artillery regiment, and attended a higher command course in 1924. In 1934 he commanded the artillery of the Polotsk fortified region and then a succession of Military Districts. As Head of the Main Artillery Directorate during the war he was responsible for small arms, anti-aircraft and tank guns as well as the

PLATE 2.7.   Nikolay Dmitrievich Yakovlev (right) and Peoples' Commissar for Armaments Dmitry Ustinov (left), later Minister of Defence, until his death in 1984. Yakovlev is wearing the three stars of a Colonel-General, plus crossed guns.

weapons used by the artillery alone. During the war new weapons had to be manufactured to cope with improved German armaments; for example, the 100 mm field and anti-tank gun was developed to counter the heavier armour of the German Tiger Tanks. This entailed working closely with the People's commissar for armaments, the whiz-kid civilian engineer Dmitry Ustinov, later Minister of Defence of the USSR who died in 1984. One of the most difficult tasks was keeping control over the large number of factories, dispersed across a nation covering one sixth of the land surface of the world, who were making parts for hundreds of thousands of guns and millions of shells. This was achieved by means of a strict military quality assurance standard called *military release to service* over and above the normal civilian quality control standards. The Soviets had two types of drawings, letter A and letter B. B drawings were the designs for basic weapons and components, approved by the People's Commissars for Industry and for Defence, and could not be altered without their approval and that of the Main Artillery Directorate. These guaranteed evenness of quality, standardisation and interchangeability of parts. When variants had to be produced, for example, putting rocket launchers on different chassis, or mounting them on boats, then A drawings were produced. Officers from the Main Artillery Directorate were present in the factories to ensure that standards were complied with. On one occasion a manufacturer persuaded Yakovlev that the stringent control procedure of *military release to service* could be dispensed with in his case, but the results were not good and it was applied unwaveringly thereafter.

Another problem was distinguishing between priorities during operations on widely separated fronts. On one occasion in 1945 a strong German tank formation appeared in 3 Ukrainian Front's sector. The Front's head-quarters telephoned Yakovlev with an urgent request for more armour piercing shells. Yakovlev knew that the battle for Berlin was imminent and turned the request down: he had to hold back most of these rounds for 1 Belorussian. The Front commander threatened to report Yakovlev to the Stavka, but Yakovlev held his ground. That evening Stalin whispered to Yakovlev

'Oh, by the way, did you get a call from 3 Ukrainian HQ?'

'Yes, they called . . .'

'You did right'.

Yakovlev continued to run Soviet artillery procurement until 1948, when he became a deputy minister of defence, from 1953 first deputy commander of the Soviet Armed Forces and, from January, 1955 until 1960, Commander in Chief of the Strategic Air Defence Service. He therefore presided over the development of the modern Soviet Air Defence Missile Force.[9]

Chief Marshal of Artillery Mitrofan Ivanovich Nedelin, 1902–1960, First Commander of the Strategic Rocket Forces

Nedelin joined the Red Army Artillery in 1920 at the age of seventeen. He fought in the Civil War and attended a battery commanders' course in 1928. Like Voronov, he was in a training post when the Spanish Civil War broke out and was similarly sent to be an adviser to the Republicans. He was made adviser to the artillery chief of the Madrid Army which was terribly short of ammunition, and his main task was to get ammunition production started. He was able to do some good but soon the Republicans were defeated and Nedelin was ordered back to the USSR. Between 1939 and 1941 he served as the commander of the artillery regiment of the elite Moscow Proletariat Division and then as chief of artillery of 160 Rifle Division, when he attended a ten-month course at the Dzerzhinskiy Academy (see above). Like Voronov, he applied himself to the issue of the day, underlined by German armoured successes in Poland and France, the need for effective anti-tank defence. He was asked to make a presentation to Stalin on the subject, and in March, 1941 was made commander of 4 Anti-tank Artillery Brigade of the Supreme High Command Reserve, one of ten such brigades formed at Voronov's instigation. He was lucky to escape capture when the Germans attacked in June and became head of artillery of 18 Army, then of the North Caucasus and subsequently 3

PLATE 2.8.   Chief-Marshal of Artillery Mitrofan Ivanovich Nedelin. First
Commander of the Soviet Strategic Rocket Forces. (British Library)

Ukrainian Fronts. It was as the latter that he earned his Hero of the Soviet
Union for decisive concentration of his forces (see Chapter One). Marshal
of the Soviet Union Tolbukhin, reporting on Nedelin in 1945, described him
as having 'wide operational-tactical perspectives . . . leads a modest life, has
shown personal courage in battle . . . an energetic, honourable and
thorough general. Highly disciplined, something which he demands from
his subordinates'. Nedelin's personal courage was to get him into trouble.

As we shall see in Chapter Three, by 1946 the Soviets already inclined
towards using long range surface-to-surface rockets to deliver powerful
warheads and particularly the nuclear weapon which they developed with
astonishing speed. Nedelin became Chief-of-Staff of the Soviet Army's
Artillery, and played a major role in the development of long range tactical
missiles, along with Voronov. After the launch of the first of the V2 based
Soviet missiles in 1947, Nedelin became Head of the Main Artillery
Directorate in 1948 and, in 1950, Head of Soviet Army Artillery. During

the 1950s the Soviets scored several successes with rocketry, including putting the first artificial satellite into space. All these developments took place under the auspices of the Main Artillery Directorate and the Academy of Artillery Sciences. It became apparent that this was really something quite new in warfare, and the new service was set up in December, 1959, with Nedelin in charge now referred to as 'Marshal of Rocketry'. Nedelin chose Colonel-General of Tank Forces V. F. Tolubko as his first deputy and Lieutenant-General of Artillery M. A. Nikol'skiy as his Chief-of-Staff. Another deputy was General F. P. Tonkikh, who became Head of the Dzerzhinskiy Academy in 1969.

Within a year of taking up appointment, however, Nedelin was killed. According to Soviet press announcements he died on 24 October, 1960 as a result of an aviation accident during the course of his duties. There are two versions of what happened. The first is that Khrushchev was anxious to produce a nuclear powered missile in time for the 7 November parade (somewhat unlikely, as the weight of a nuclear reactor makes it highly unsuitable for a rocket propulsion system, unless it was for use in deep space only). Dozens of nuclear scientists and government officials were on hand to watch a trial. The rocket, spacecraft, nuclear engine or whatever it was failed to fire and Nedelin left the shelter and began to walk towards it. The others obediently followed and then the motor detonated, killing 300 people, including Nedelin. The other variant is that three rockets were under test with the aim of carrying out an unmanned flight to Mars. Two failed to fire and when the third failed also, the Soviets began to extract the fuel prior to an inspection. Nedelin became impatient and decided to inspect it himself. Once again, there was an explosion and some 200 top scientists and officials and the Marshal died.[10]

Marshal of Artillery Konstantin Petrovich Kazakov, 1902–

At the age of thirteen Kazakov became an apprentice in the Tula armaments factory and, subsequently a metal worker. In 1919 he joined the Komsomol and in 1921, entered a military school, the first of our eminent artillerymen not to have served actively in the Civil War. He graduated in 1923 and commanded an artillery section, battery and battalion. In 1930 he went on a higher artillery command course and in 1936 to the M. V. Frunze General Staff Academy. He taught in one of the Moscow artillery schools before being sent abroad on various 'government assignments' in 1939–41. When the Great Patriotic War began he was commanding 331 howitzer regiment of the Supreme High Command Reserve in Kiev. He escaped the initial German assault, although his unit was down to its last rounds at one point, and was appointed head of the operational section of Voronov's department. His first task was to experiment with artillery groupings to

PLATE 2.9.   Konstantin Petrovich Kazakov, on an officers' course, 1921.
The pointed headgear was deliberately modelled on the medieval Russian
helmet, in order to avoid resemblance to pre-revolutionary uniform and
arouse deep seated patriotism. (British Library)

support counter-attacks. He then helped plan the artillery support of the
Stalingrad counter-offensive, including identifying German defensive lines
and amassing ammunition stocks. By 1944 it was obvious that Kazakov had
been a back room boy for too long and he was sent to command the artillery
of 2 Shock Army on the Leningrad front. He did well, controlling the
employment of three artillery divisions and in all 60 artillery regiments
and concentrating 220–230 artillery pieces and mortars on a kilometre of
front. In March, 1945 he commanded the artillery on the Danzig (Gdansk)
axis, as part of the East Prussian operation, and then commanded the
artillery of One Red Banner Army in Manchuria during the swift and
expansive operation to destroy the Japanese Kwantung Army. This gave
him experience in handling operational artillery formations in mountain
and *taiga*, the toilsome far eastern forest. After the war he attended the
Frunze General Staff Academy and from 1948 was artillery commander of
various Military Districts. In 1954 he was given a high post in the (then)
Strategic Air Defence Service, another example of how senior artillery
officers tend to do a tour in that organisation. Voronov had commanded it

PLATE   2.10.   Marshal   of   Artillery   Konstantin   Petrovich   Kazakov.
(British Library)

briefly and Yakovlev did so from 1955, so Kazakov must have worked closely with the latter during the late 1950s. From 1963 to 1969 Kazakov was Commander-in-Chief of the Army's Rocket Troops and Artillery. As we shall see in Chapter Three, these years were not efflorescent with tube artillery systems but saw the appearance of a number of tactical missiles and anti-tank guided missiles. Kazakov's Air Defence experience was naturally relevant here. Since then he has been employed as an inspector and adviser to the USSR Ministry of Defence.[11]

Marshal of Artillery Georgiy Yefimovich Peredel'skiy, Chief of
Rocket Forces and Artillery 1969–1983, 1913–

It is a measure of the pace of change over the past 70 years and the continuing relevance of even pre-Revolution practices that Peredel'skiy began his artillery training, on his own admission, on Tsarist artillery pieces. That was in 1934, when he was called up to serve in 73 Artillery

PLATE 2.11.   Marshal of Artillery G. Ye Peredel'skiy, Chief of Rocket
Troops and Artillery from 1969 to 1983.

Regiment in Omsk. He was quickly sent on an officers' course and by 1938 was Chief-of-Staff of an artillery battalion in 54 Artillery Regiment. He received his baptism of fire in battle against the Finns in 1939–40. In 1941 he commanded an artillery regiment and in 1942 the Reconnaissance section of 32 Army's artillery staff, a most important post as counter-battery fire and techniques for striking unobserved targets were developing rapidly at that time. At the age of thirty, he returned to command an artillery regiment once again on the northern flank in Karelia. Fate obviously intended him for far away places: after the war he was artillery commander of the White Sea and Northern Military Districts. In 1947–48 he attended the Higher Artillery Staff course, at what is now the Dzerzhinskiy Academy, and then returned to the Northern and Caucasus Military Districts. He seemed destined for a career on the wings when in 1965 he was suddenly appointed Deputy Head of Soviet Artillery and Rocket Forces. After a 4-year apprenticeship under Kazakov, he took over command in 1969.

Peredel'skiy is notable for his prolific and erudite writing on artillery matters, especially co-operation with all-arms forces. He has also proved an assiduous trainer of artillery officers, and has paid great attention to raising and maintaining standards in Artillery Higher Command Schools, and to the major campaign in the open military press to broaden officers' horizons and raise standards. He presided over the enormous artillery build up in the late 1970s and up to the time of his retirement, and this must have been planned and begun during his earlier time as Chief. As we shall see, he was closely involved in the development of the all-conventional quick attack doctrine and such concepts as Fire Strike and Integrated Fire Destruction. At the time of writing, he continues to put his name to perspicacious articles on the battlefield employment of artillery.[12]

Pavel Nikolayevich Kuleshov, Head of the Main Rocket and
Artillery Directorate from 1965–1983, 1908–

PLATE 2.12.   Pavel Nikolayevich Kuleshov, rocket expert and head of the Main Rocket and Artillery Directorate from 1965 to 1983. Large star and crossed guns indicate a Marshal of Artillery.

As head of the USSR Ministry of Defence Directorate concerned with artillery and tactical rocket procurement, Kuleshov has naturally remained a shadowy figure compared with the more prominent commanders of artillery and rocket forces. He entered the Red Army in 1926, and in 1938 entered the Dzerzhinskiy Academy. We have seen what a formidable effort the Academy made in the weapons design field during the war, and the highly qualified staff who were on hand, so it is probable that Kuleshov's ability at weapons engineering was noticed there. He then served as deputy to the head of Voronov's directorate who was, of course, Kazakov. After serving for a short while in the Rear Services Directorate he was sent to command an *Operational Group* dealing with multiple rocket launcher units. These were and are small groups of officers with signals staff, sent by the higher formation commander to control and direct units operating away from the main forces; a demanding and hazardous service. From 1943 he was deputy commander of rocket launcher units and also served as the Supreme High Command's special envoy in operational groups attached to the North Caucasus, Voronezh and Steppe Fronts. He was then deputy commander of the artillery of 1 Baltic Front and from August, 1944, Voronov's Chief-of-Staff. Once again, this was a responsible job for someone now 36 years of age. From 1946 to 1952 he was head of a faculty and then deputy head of the Dzerzhinskiy Academy, participating in the development of nuclear warheads and rockets. In 1952–57 he worked in the central administration of the Ministry of Defence, and was then appointed deputy chief of the Strategic Air Defence Force from April 1957, under Yakovlev. He did another General Staff job from 1963 to 1965, before taking up post as head of the Main Artillery Directorate, described by Yakovlev as 'operose and vast'. Kuleshov's career is clearly somewhat different from those of the commanders of artillery and rocket troops, but in his time he held command positions in rocket launcher units and air defence forces. With his experience of the central bureaucracy, which terrified Yakovlev, Kuleshov was the ideal man to control operational requirements and the procurement of artillery and missiles for 20 years from the mid 1960s until the mid 1980s. Kuleshov's experience with and liking for multiple rocket launchers and missiles may be reflected in the high priority they continue to enjoy in the pantheon of Soviet artillery equipment, but all the systems introduced recently and which may appear during the later 1980s, if not beyond, will bear the stamp of Pavel Kuleshov.[13]

Colonel-General of Artillery Vladimir Minayevich Mikhalkin
Commander of Rocket Forces and Artillery, born 1925–30

Mikhalkin remains a relatively unknown figure. He was first identified as head of artillery and rocket troops in the Belorussian Military District in late 1976. By mid 1980 he had been given a responsible post in the artillery and rocket troops' central command, possibly as Peredel'skiy's deputy or chief-of-staff, as he represented Peredel'skiy on several occasions. One of these was the main Ministry of Defence conference to mark the 600th anniversary of Russian artillery. As head of the Belorussian Military

PLATE 2.13. Vladimir Minayevich Mikhalkin, Colonel-General of Artillery, Chief of the *Artillery and Rocket Forces* of the Soviet army.

District he would have been chief artillery adviser to Colonel-General of
Tank Troops Zaytsev, who became commander of Group of Soviet Forces
Germany in 1980. He would therefore be extremely hot on the problems of
co-operating with advancing all-arms forces and clearing the way for them.
While in the Belorussian Military District, Mikhalkin appears to have
devised an experimental artillery battery and battalion organisation and to
have tried it out on students at the Kolomna Higher Artillery Command
School, although it did not meet with universal approval. In 1983, he signed
the obituary of a notable Lieutenant-General of Artillery, Parovatkin,
indicating that he had taken over from Peredel'skiy in the rank of
Lieutenant-General. By 1984 he was a Colonel-General of Artillery.
Mikhalkin is the first commander of rocket troops and artillery not to have
major experience of the Great Patriotic War or, indeed, any war. However,
he has spent the last decade and a half wrestling with the problems of
employing artillery on the high speed armoured battlefield, and particularly
training needs. It would be surprising if he did not tighten up his arm's
battlefield performance considerably.[14]

Lieutenant-General (Engineer) Yuri Mikhaylovich Lazarev,
Chief of the Main Rocket and Artillery Directorate, born
1925–30

Little is known about Lazarev, either. He graduated from the Air Defence Engineer and Radio Academy in the late 1940s and, like his predecessor, Kuleshov, has a background in Air Defence. He was a deputy chief of the Main Rocket and Artillery Directorate from about 1977, possibly with responsibility for research and production. In July 1982, he gave an address on the development of artillery material to the 600th anniversary conference.[15] It is possible that he has been replaced in the wake of the Severomorsk missile storage depot explosion in 1984. If that is so, it is a further measure of the Directorate's all pervading role, responsible for explosives storage regulations for the fleet as well as the ground forces.

Major-General of Artillery A. P. Lebedev, Deputy Chief with
Responsibility for Combat Training

Our first glimpse of Lebedev is in the mid 1960s when, as a young battery commander, he won a Red Star for proficiency and mastering new equipment. Nothing more is known until 1979 when he was identified as a Major-General of Artillery and artillery commander of the Turkestan Military District. This was an extremely important post as in December 1979 the Soviets mounted the invasion of Afghanistan through Turkestan. Lebedev would have organised artillery support for the invasion and subsequent operations. He is therefore one of the relatively few senior officers of his generation with active service experience. In 1983 he took over as deputy chief of artillery and rocket troops from I. Anashkin, who had held the post since 1969. Lebedev is particularly well qualified to direct training, and his experience in mountainous terrain is reflected by an article he wrote in 1976 about support of a motor rifle unit in the mountains.[16] He is no doubt behind the current emphasis on fighting in all types of 'special conditions' (see Chapter Four).

Many Western analysts assume that the Soviet military is a vast impersonal machine, and that the individual counts for little. In the author's view, this is wrong. All the evidence shows that Soviet officers with ability can rise very fast indeed, that their postings are carefully selected, and that their individual abilities and tastes are reflected to a surprising degree in the work that they do. Their individual identity is also projected in the way they use the open press to disseminate knowledge on the profession of arms in articles which are personally attributable. We can learn a great deal from their experience and aptitudes, and, of course, the man remains, as ever, the most important single factor in war. *Ecce homo!*

Notes

1. Obstinate lot: quote in Colonel R. B. Heinl USMC, *Dictionary of Military and Naval Quotations*, (US Naval Institute Press, Annapolis, 1984), p. 19; Mamontov, p. 46.

2. Formation of Air Defence Service: *SVE*, Vol. 2 (1976), pp. 317, 321; merging of air defense forces, David R. Jones, ed. *Soviet Armed Forces Review Annual No. 6* (1982) (Academic International, Gulf Breeze, 1982), pp. 138–40; Strategic Rocket Forces: Harriet Fast Scott 'The Strategic Rocket Forces and their Five Elites', *Air Force Magazine*, (March, 1983), pp. 58–63; 'Soviet Sets up Rocket Command: Artillery Expert named as Chief', *New York Times*, (6 May, 1960); Basyukov in P. T. Astashenkov, *Sovetskiye raketnye voyska (Soviet Rocket Forces)*, (Voyenizdat, Moscow, 1967), p. 95; 'sense of responsibility', Major-Generals of Artillery (note!) G. F. Biryukov and I. I. Arendarenko. *Sluzhu v raketnykh (I serve in the Rocket Forces)*, (DOSAAF Press, Moscow, 1980), p. 19.

3. Decree of the Supreme Soviet of the USSR, 26 April, 1984, *'O voinskikh zvaniyakh ofitserskogo sostava Vooruzhёnnykh Sil SSSR'* ('On the military ranks of the Officer Personnel of the USSR Armed Forces'), reported in *Krasnaya zvezda (KZ)* 12 June, 1984, p. 2.

4. Entry procedures and establishments, I. A. Kamkov and V. M. Konoplyanik, *Voyennye akademii i uchilishcha (Military Academies and Schools)*, (Voyenizdat, Moscow, 1974), pp. 17, 25–26, 60–65, 92.

5. Kalinin Academy: *SVE*, Vol. 2 (1976), pp. 179–80; Central Artillery Command Courses: Colonel O. Makovey *'Tsentral'nye artilleriyskiye'*, *VV* 7/1983, pp. 69–71; Dzerzhinskiy Academy: *SVE* Vol. 2 (1976), pp. 176–177; Professor Marshal of Artillery G. Odintsov and candidate of Military Sciences Colonel K. Kuznetsov, *'Stareyshaya kuznitsa artilleriyskikh kadrov'* ('The oldest forge for artillery specialists'), *VIZh* 12/1970, pp. 112–120.

6. A. Raykhtsaum' *'Pervy nachal'nik artillerii'* ('First Chief of Artillery'), *VIZh* 11/1967, pp. 57–60.

7. Chief Marshal of Artillery N. N. Voronov, *'Vydayushchiysya sovetskiy artillerist'* ('Outstanding Soviet Artilleryman') *VIZh* 12/1963, pp. 58–64; Artillery Fire is *Ogon' artillerii* (Voyenizdat, Moscow, 1926); *Artillery in the Major Forms of Combat* is *Artilleriya v osnovnykh vidakh boya (korpus, diviziya, polk)* (Voyenizdat, Moscow, 1940). The latter contains a considerable section on the Great War, and some lessons from Spain.

8. See Voronov's unusually readable memoirs, *In Military Service. Have you finished?* p. 87, Lunch, pp. 89–90. Reintroduction of Imperial regulations, John Erickson, *The Road to Stalingrad* (Harper and Row, London, 1975), p. 431; control of SPs, Voronov, pp. 364–67.

9. See Yakovlev's *On Artillery* . . . Military release to service is the author's translation of *voyennaya priyёmka*, pp. 146–150; conflict of priorities, pp. 110–11. General career and Air Defence Command, *SVE* Vol. 8 (1980), p. 658.

10. See Harriet Fast Scott's article and Colonel-General of Artillery M. Nikol'skiy and Colonel G. Ryshenkov *'Glavny Marshal Artillerii M. I. Nedelin'* ('Chief Marshal of Artillery'). *VIZh* 11/1972, pp. 78–81.

11. Colonel-General of Artillery (As he was then) G. Ye. Peredel'skiy *'Marshal Artillerii K. P. Kazakov'*, *VIZh* 12/1972, p. 126–128.

12. Army General I. Pavlovskiy *'Marshal Artillerii G. Ye. Peredel'skiy'*, *VIZh* 4/1983, pp. 95–96; guns made before the Revolution, Peredel'skiy, *'Etapyna bol'shogo puti'* ('Milestones along the highway') (On the 600th anniversary of Russian artillery), *VV* 7/1982, p. 12.

13. *SVE* Vol. 4 (1977), pp. 516–17. Kuleshov wrote the introduction to V. A. Shmakov, ed. *Vyshli na front katyushi (Katyushas to the Front)* (Moscow Workers' Press, Moscow, 1982), indicating his continued specialised interest in multiple rocket launchers; Operational Groups: *SVE* Vol. 6 (1978), p. 50.

14. *Sovetskaya Belorussia*, 20 November, 1976; *Krasnaya zvezda (KZ)* 8 October 1978, comment by Mikhalkin on criticism of 'complacency' at the Kolomna Higher Command

School; increase in training standards, Major-General of Artillery V. M. Mikhalkin and Colonel A. Sidorenko '*Kompleksnaya trenirovka*' ('Integrated training'), *VV* 3/1977, pp. 29–33.

15. Lazarev's replacement of Kuleshov, *KZ* 12 July, 1983; responsibilities, *KZ* 27 October 1977, obituary of Colonel-General Engineer A. A. Grigor'ev, formerly a senior officer in the Main Rocket and Artillery Directorate.

16. Lebedev noticed *KZ* 9 December, 1979. Appointment as Deputy Chief, *VV* 3/1983.

3.

The Deadliest Weapon

THE BREECH OF THE "NON-RECOIL" GUN, WITH ITS FUNNEL-SHAPED ATTACHMENT, IS SWUNG OPEN. IT HAS BEEN SUGGESTED THAT THE FUNNEL IS A DEVICE WHICH USES EXPLOSION-GASES ESCAPING THROUGH VENTS TO PRODUCE A FORWARD MOVEMENT AND SO NEUTRALISE THE RECOIL.

PLATE 3.1.   The M-1935 recoilless gun shortly after its capture by the Finns at the end of 1939 or beginning of 1940. The *Illustrated London News'* caption indicates that western experts did not fully understand how it worked, an indicator of how far ahead the Soviets were in this field in the 1930s. (*Illustrated London News*)

Ahead of the Times?

In the last week of 1939 and the first week of 1940, a savage battle raged around Suomossalmi, in the remote central region of Finland's frontier with the USSR. Soviet divisions, strung out along roads, were cut up into *mottis* or 'little logs of firewood', each motti then being surrounded and destroyed. Near Raate, the Finns were combing the grisly wreckage of one such formation. One young soldier, dazed from the action and the vicious white cold, was not too concerned about the mechanical and human debris strewn along the road. He would not have remembered anything special about it had he not been summoned to a debrief. 'Take a look at this' said the Captain, pointing to the back of one of the Soviet trucks; 'it's a new Russian invention – a *non-recoil gun.*'

The gun was unlike anything they had seen before. To a modern eye its appearance is familiar enough. It resembles a larger version of a Carl Gustav anti-tank weapon of the 1970s. It has the same characteristic 'venturi' at the back indicating an advanced understanding of recoilless gun design. The venturi slips away at the touch of a catch to enable the gun to be loaded. The gun's outer surface is ribbed to provide a greater surface area from which the heat of firing can be dissipated. It is mounted on a pedestal, which originally stood on the back of the truck. It was captured with a large stock of ammunition, with cardboard cartridges. It would appear to have been intended for immediate, organic defence of vehicle convoys, especially of motorised infantry. The only apparent anomaly is the date stamped on its side, on the right of the breech, just forward of the venturi; Ss-35 [1935]. Two such guns were captured; one was sent to the Germans who no doubt used it to assist their own developments. This gun subsequently disappeared. The other can still be seen in the Sotamuseo (Military Museum) in Helsinki. British experts took an interest in the gun, and it was featured in the *Illustrated London News* of 6 April, 1940. The experts consulted thought that the venturi was designed to produce a forward movement and so neutralise the recoil, which is not exactly right. The jet of gas is not to develop thrust but to act as a countershot, since the weight of the gas times its velocity balances the weight of the projectile times its velocity. Therefore, the faster the jet of gas is moving, the less gas needs to be bled off and the smaller the charge can be made. The conical 'de Laval' nozzle has the effect of accelerating the gas jet, which is why it is also employed in rocket motors. In a recoilless gun, about four fifths of the propellant gas is bled off, only one fifth pushing the projectile. The design of the Ss-35 indicates how very advanced the Soviets were in this field at the time. A Soviet engineer, L. V. Kurchevskiy, designed a *recoilless gun (DRP)* in May, 1923, in which the rate of escape of the propellant gas was regulated by a nozzle which, like that on the 1935 model gun, was in the shape of an expanding cone. Recoilless guns underwent further development at the end of the 1920s and early 1930s under the engineer V. M. Trofimov and Professor A. Berkalov and also again under Kurchevskiy in 1932–4.

A number of models of recoilless guns had been adopted for service by 1937. These included the 37 mm anti-tank rifle (RK), the 76 mm battalion gun BPK, the 76 mm 'high powered' gun, the 76 mm aircraft cannon APK-4, the 405 mm self-propelled field howitzer SPGK, and others. All these guns had rifled barrels and breech blocks with a central nozzle. The M-1935 gun captured at Raate is of 76.2 mm calibre, so it could be either the battalion gun or the 'high powered' gun. The latter is possible although Finnish/German tests found it to have a muzzle velocity of 360 metres per second — which is not particularly high by the standards of ordinary guns. The 305 mm recoilless gun could, it is said, fire a 250 kg projectile for 16 kilometres.

Recoilless guns were particularly suited to the requirement for a light and highly mobile source of fire-power for irregular or airborne troops. The Soviet army was the first in the world to employ parachute forces, with the

PLATE 3.2.   Airborne artillery with recoilless gun, 1935.

first drop in 1929. The first experimental airborne detachment of 1931 was equipped with six 76 mm DRPs. The following year a number of other airborne detachments were formed, each equipped with six such guns. The airborne DRP was mounted on a light-wheeled carriage, as the rare and extraordinary photograph from 1935 shows. This gun appears to be somewhat shorter than the gun captured by the Finns, but otherwise its design is similar although it does not have the ribbed surface to carry away heat. It may be the 76 mm 'battalion gun'. The use of such a revolutionary gun by a new arm of the forces, in the year 1935 bears witness to the Russians' extraordinary lead then as now in certain areas of military science, art and technology.[1]

The Killer

The gun and the rocket are not the artilleryman's weapons. The weapon is the shell or the rocket warhead; everything else is designed to get it to its victim. One thing to remember about the huge concentrations of artillery described in Chapter One is that many of the guns were of relatively small (76 mm) calibre and that the individual shells were light, not only by modern standards but by the standards of other armies of the time. A 76 mm *high explosive* shell weighed 6.23 kilograms and an *armour piercing* one, 6.3. Modern Soviet systems however give a throw-weight per system which compares with that of other modern armies. Although it obviously depends on the type of shell, a 122 mm projectile weighs some 22 kilograms, a 130 mm one from the obsolescent M-46, 33 and a 152 mm one, 44. The latter is roughly comparable with the 155 mm calibre which is becoming standard in Western armies. A 203 mm piece would throw a projectile weighing some 100 kilograms. These weights are consistent with Great Patriotic War equipments.

The area over which a conventional high explosive shell is able to kill or maim depends on a great many factors; an unlucky person might be hit by a splinter a long way off. Soviet figures indicate that a 122 mm round is virtually certain to destroy men or equipment (except armour) over an area of 27 square metres, that is, roughly a 6 metre diameter circle. Because of the trajectory of the shell the lethal zone is in fact an ellipse. A 152 mm shell will do the same over a 43 square metre area, equivalent to a 7.4 metre diameter circle, and a 240 mm mortar round, 125 square metres, or a 12.6 metre diameter circle. Shells break up into fragments of various sizes, the smaller ones often being nastier as they bury themselves deep in the body rather than causing large, ripping wounds.

The different types of ammunition in Soviet service are shown with their component parts. The Russian terms can be found in the glossary. Nuclear ammunition presents certain problems as the density of the fissile material and the necessary shielding makes a nuclear round much heavier for its size than a conventional one. This puts considerable extra strain on the rifling and breech of a gun. For this reason, only certain pieces are 'nuclear capable'.

The Soviets are as anxious as anyone else to improve the effectiveness of their conventional rounds. They have shown considerable interest in improved conventional munitions (ICMs) being introduced in the West, which are particularly suitable for providing destruction over a wide area without using nuclear weapons. The Russians refer to *sub-munition projectiles* as 'cassette shells'. Two articles in the popular magazine *Technology and Armament* at the beginning of 1984 devoted attention to these. The first covered tube artillery shells: the 105 mm M413 shell, the 155 mm M692, the 203 mm M404, the 155 mm M483 A1, and various individual sub-munitions. It mentioned the *Multiple Launch Rocket System (MLRS)*, and especially the AT-1 and AT-2 anti-tank mines. The second covered

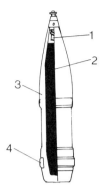

FIG. 3.1.   High explosive/fragmentation round (this one has a time fuze so it can be set for airburst). 1, fuze; 2, explosive (bursting) charge; 3, body; 4, driving band.

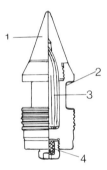

FIG. 3.2.   Sub-calibre armour-piercing round (this one is akin to the M-46's). 1, ballistic cap; 2, recess; 3, armour piercing core; 4, tracer element.

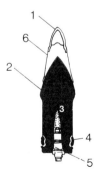

FIG. 3.3.   Full calibre armour-piercing round. 1, ballistic cap; 2, shell body; 3, bursting charge; 4, driving band; 5, fuze; 6, armour piercing cap.

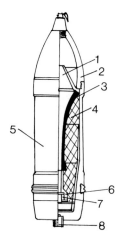

FIG. 3.4.   Shaped charge shell. 1, protective cone; 2, screw in head; 3, metal 'crater'; 4, bursting charge; 5, shell body; 6, central tube; 7, percussion cap; 8, tracer element.

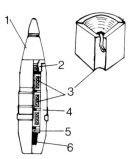

FIG. 3.5.   Incendiary shell. 1, delay fuze; 2, screw in head; 3, incendiary charges; 4, shell body; 5, diaphragm; 6, bursting charges.

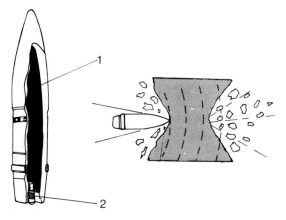

FIG. 3.6.   Concrete busting round. 1, explosive charge; 2, fuze at base.

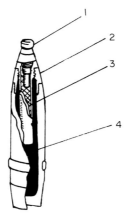

FIG. 3.7. Smoke shell (same configuration as chemical shell). 1, fuze; 2, screw in top; 3, explosive charge; 4, smoke producing (chemical) agent.

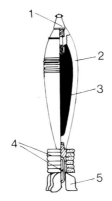

FIG. 3.8. Mortar bomb. 1, fuze; 2, body; 3, explosive charge; 4, propellant charge; 5, guidance fins.

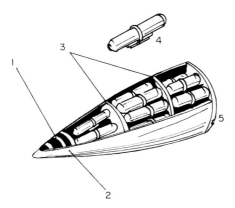

FIG. 3.9. Sub-munition rocket warhead. 1, fuze section; 2, submunition warhead body; 3, bulkheads between 'cassettes'; 4, sub munition; 5, base section.

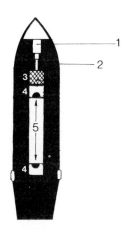

FIG. 3.10. Nuclear round. 1, detonating mechanism; 2, casing; 3, conventional explosive charge; 4, neutron reflector; 5, fissile material.

sub-munition warheads for large rockets particularly Lance. Such warheads, it said, achieved a more equable distribution of explosive over the target, and were suitable for destruction of personnel, tanks, armoured personnel carriers (APCs), and anti-aircraft sites, and for remote mining. It noted Lance's ability to deliver *sub-munitions* either over a 300 metre diameter circle or an 800 metre long ellipse to destroy vehicles moving in column. The ability to remotely deliver mines might be of particular value to the Soviets in, for example, sealing off the flanks of OMG penetration with instant minefields.

The Soviets are relatively more advanced in techniques such as fuel-air explosives. A conventional explosion releases a great deal of energy at its source, but the blast wave tails off very rapidly. By distributing droplets of a petroleum based substance over the target and then igniting them, a much more even pulse is created, which gives the desired effect over a much wider area. These have been reported used in Afghanistan, as have two other ingenious weapons. One is allegedly a bomb designed to cover a killing zone, which is exploded in the air and releases two different incendiary materials and sub-munitions. One incendiary material as a rapid effect; the other smoulders for days. The second special bomb contains rods made of a magnesium-phosphorus combination which burn fiercely with tremendous heat and suck huge amounts of oxygen from the air, creating a Hamburg-style fire storm. This would be particularly effective in built up areas, in streets and buildings. All these weapons have been deployed initially in aerial bombs, and there are problems making them work on a smaller scale. However, if it is possible to get one of these devices into an artillery shell, the Soviets might find it an attractive idea and there would be no theoretical objection to putting them into a large rocket warhead. One special munition which the Soviets have used as an artillery shell is the incendiary thermite round, designed to set fire to forests and vegetation. The Soviets share this predilection for blinding and choking the enemy with smoke with the Mongol Khans.[2] This could be very important in the heavily forested terrain of western Germany. Another improved round which the Soviets have introduced is the flechette shell. Flechettes are tiny steel needles which do horrible things to troops in the open but which rain harmlessly down on even the most lightly armoured vehicles. Soviet artillery firing flechette rounds can therefore keep up suppressive fire as motor rifle and tank troops are actually overrunning a position.

The Deliverer

The Russians talk about *active* and *reactive* systems. In the former, the explosion acts on the projectile to push it (guns, howitzers, mortars): in the latter, the projectile drives itself in the opposite direction to the thrust, as in Newton's third law of motion (rockets). The formal Russian name for rocket artillery is *reactive artillery*, and a rocket is a *reactive shell*. Rocket assisted shells, which are becoming more and more important these days, are *active-reactive shells*.

Active systems are defined as follows:

Guns give accurate long range fire and have a high *muzzle velocity*, over 650 metres per second. The length of the barrel may be up to 75 times the calibre.

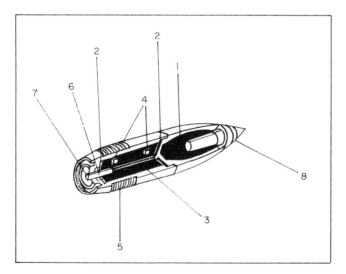

FIG. 3.11.   Rocket-assisted shell. 1, explosive charge; 2, shock absorbers; 3, propellant charge; 4, bushes holding propellant charge; 5, driving band; 6, ignition delay; 7, rocket nozzle.

Howitzers produce high trajectory fire with relatively low muzzle velocity, between 400 and 600 metres per second. They have shorter range than guns and may weigh only half as much as field guns of the same calibre. The barrel length ranges from 22 to 30 calibres.

Gun Howitzers combine the characteristics of guns and howitzers. Officially, these have a muzzle velocity of up to 700 metres per second. It does not help when the Soviets themselves do not stick rigidly to this definition: the 2S1 and 2S3 self-propelled pieces are referred to in Soviet writings as howitzers, but their barrel length (37 calibres for the 2S3) add muzzle velocity (700 metres per second for the 2S3 and 690 or 740 for the 2S1 with high explosive or anti-tank rounds respectively) are in fact appropriate to gun howitzers, if not guns.

Mortars are of lightweight construction, perhaps one ninth of the weight of a howitzer of similar calibre, and have a high angle of fire (45 to 85 degrees). Although there is no formal definition of barrel length, it is not normally much more than 20 calibres.

Combination Guns, or *Howitzer-Mortars*, are a recent development, not dissimilar to what are called gun-mortars in the West. These can fire either in a howitzer (flat trajectory) or mortar role, and are extremely versatile (see below).

Rocket Launchers are normally known as 'war machines' in Russian, which gives the initials BM. However, NATO's Multiple Launch Rocket System is referred to as a *Rocket Volley Fire System*, which abbreviates to *RSZO* in Russian.

Artillery is subdivided as follows:

Below 76 mm calibre	*light*
76–130 mm guns	*medium*
76–155 mm howitzers	
over 130 mm guns	*heavy*
over 155 mm howitzers and rocket launchers	
Anti-aircraft guns are defined as	
Below 70 mm calibre	*light*
70–100 mm	*medium*
over 100 mm	*heavy*

Two other terms encountered, particularly in historical works mean, literally, *high powered artillery* and *artillery of special power*. The former refers to artillery in the High Command Reserve (see Chapter One). It was used in the 1930s to refer to, for example, the 107 mm gun model 1877, the 120 mm French gun model 1878, and the 127 mm Armstrong gun. In the war, it referred to the 152 mm gun model 1935, the 210 mm gun model 1939, the 203 mm and 305 mm howitzers and the 280 mm mortar. It therefore refers to the general performance of the system and not just its

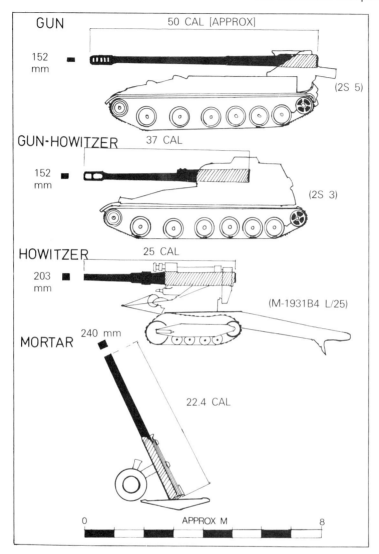

Fig. 3.12.   Types of active artillery systems.

calibre. However, for simplicity the author has translated these terms as *heavy* and *super-heavy* artillery, respectively. Finally, the very few monster guns the Soviets produced were called *super-powered*; the 356 mm gun and the 500 mm howitzer.[3] Modern Soviet military writings refer to present day Front level artillery as *high powered artillery*.

Military Doctrine, Art and Weapons Design

It is sometimes thought that the relation between *Military Doctrine, Military Art* and design in the Soviet Union is the opposite to that in the

PLATE 3.3.   Doctrine and design. The Kremlin in the background, M-1935
152 mm guns on tractor chassis in the foreground. (Terry Gander)

West: that in the latter technology has its own momentum and that people then think up ways to use it, whereas in the former all weapons development forms part of a logical plan emanating from the top. Some would see a perfect harmony in the Soviet Union between the dictates of high policy and the details of weaponry, as highlighted by the M-1935 pattern 152 mm guns before the Kremlin in the photograph. This is a gross oversimplification. In the first place, doctrine, in the Soviet sense of the word is so broad, covering the likely course and nature of a future war, that it can only exercise the most general influence on design as in, for example, the comparative neglect of conventional artillery systems during the late 1950s and 1960s when it was believed that nuclear missiles had not only become the decisive but, indeed, the overwhelmingly predominant form of weaponry. The relation between the prevailing doctrine and weapons procurement can be detected from the matrix in Fig. 3.13. However, even the Soviet system is not capable of enforcing such an omniscient scheme and the possibilities and limitations of technology and production methods constrain and influence military doctrine and military art. It was the rocket and the nuclear warhead which created the *Revolution in Military Affairs*, which the Soviets acknowledged from 1957, and this in turn led to the emphasis on the nuclear and post nuclear battlefield as the criterion for procurement decisions. Conversely, in the immediate post war period, Stalin sought to reinforce his conventional land superiority as the only possible counter-weight to the nuclear, naval and air superiority of his

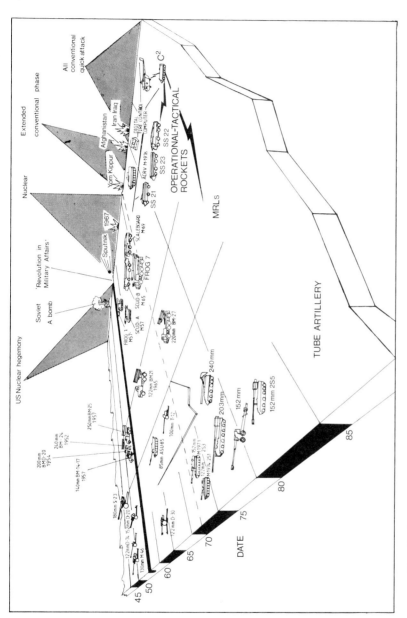

FIG. 3.13.   Rocket Forces and Artillery Procurement in relation to doctrine. Prevailing doctrine and significant events are shown on the horizon. The correlation with procurement priorities is clear: before the Revolution in Military affairs, the Soviets stressed more or less conventional systems in an effort to counterbalance US nuclear superiority with their conventional strength on land. After that Revolution, in the mid 1950s, emphasis switched to nuclear rocket systems, until the early 1970s, since when there has been a remarkable increase in the quality and quantity of conventional artillery and Multiple Rocket Launchers (MRLs). Specialised anti-tank guns, last exemplified by the T-12 introduced in about 1965, may not be seen again. The most significant future development is likely to be in the field of Command and Control (C²), a *Reconnaissance-Strike Complex* (see Chapter Four).

principal potential adversary. The relation is one of complex inter-dependence.

Special Factors which the Soviet Designer has to Consider

The most obvious of these is the varied and often unfriendly Russian environment: terrain and weather. Engelhardt, who designed the 1900 pattern gun (see Chapter One) deliberately avoided using hydraulic buffers because in the Russian winter the fluid would freeze. Instead, he used india-rubber buffers to absorb the shock. The Russian predilection for india-rubber, solid and hard wearing, is still evident today, in the rubber foam filled tyres of the S-23 180 mm and M-46 130 mm guns and the D-30 122 mm gun-howitzer. Another example of the weather being a major consideration is recorded in Voronov's memoirs. The inadequacies of the F-22 76 mm gun, model 1936, became apparent during trials in winter conditions. This led Voronov to demand its replacement with the USV, which became the model 1939, although necessity led the Soviets to procure large numbers of F-22s. The Germans captured many F-22s and thought highly of them, considering the system to be a 'fully modern weapon' with an excellent range. This is an example of how Soviet requirements were more demanding than German. A final example of General Winter's influence is in the sleek Artillery Command and Reconnaissance vehicle, known to NATO as the ACRV (see below). This is part of a family developed from the MT-L civilian arctic tractor, with a system for preheating the engine and a heated crew compartment. This is not a luxury in the Soviet Union, but a necessity.

PLATE 3.4.   'F-22' M-1936 76.2 mm field gun. (Author's photograph, with kind permission Sotamuseo)

The influence of Russian terrain is equally important. Its flatness has influenced Soviet designers in their predilection for high muzzle velocities, flat trajectories and a low silhouette. The extenuated road network and the presence of wide expanses of forest and marsh has led to what at first seems to be a paradox of Russian and Soviet artillery design and doctrine, although it is not. The Russians have always stressed the concept of *mass*, yet their individual guns have on the whole been relatively small and light. A large number of small and manoeuvrable guns can be concentrated at the decisive point more quickly and easily than a few large ones, especially if roads and railways are few and far between. Thus, in World War I the Germans were unable to bring up the massive howitzers they had used against the Belgian forts to reduce Russian fortresses, because Russian railway bridges were not strong enough to carry the heavy trains. In 1925, General Golovin (see Chapter One) confirmed that the rule laid down by Frederick the Great of Prussia in the eighteenth century, that no gun should weigh more than three tons, was still valid; men and horses could not move anything heavier over Russian roads. The state of the Russian road network partly explains why horse traction remained in use much longer in Russia than in the West, and why the Russians retained small calibre field guns (76 mm) long after they had been eschewed by the Western powers. Another factor was the continued emphasis on direct fire which further predicated lightness and mobility. The influence of terrain also partly explains why the largest calibre Russian and Soviet guns and howitzers widely deployed in both world wars were of 152 mm calibre. The Russians had a few 203 mm guns, but they do not seem to have been widely used, and fewer still 240 mm and 305 mm. They never shared the predilection of Americans, French and Germans for monster guns. The same is true for naval armaments, where the Russians preferred to have many but smaller guns on their warships, as they were more easily handled. Even quite recently, Western experts were surprised that the Soviet M-1955 gun S-23 was found to be of 180 mm calibre and not, as had been thought, 203 mm.

In endeavouring to overcome the apparent dichotomy between mass and mobility, Soviet designers in the 1920s and 30s turned to new technologies: recoilless guns, mortars and rocket launchers. This was also partly motivated by economic considerations. Mortars in particular were capable of projecting a comparatively heavy bomb from a relatively light launcher (see above), but, like recoilless guns, were handicapped by lack of range. The most promising work of all for resolving the mass-mobility problem was in the rocket field, where the Russians had a tradition of expertise (see Chapter One), and where their usefulness in mountains was particularly valued, another example of terrain considerations affecting design.

A last terrain factor is the presence of many rivers in Russia, especially western Russian and eastern Europe: usually wide and shallow, and running perpendicular to the line of advance (or retreat). The sparse road network mentioned above is reflected in the corresponding paucity of bridges, not that it is advisable to rely on existing bridges in war anyway. This has probably influenced Soviet designers who have endeavoured to make their systems amphibious as far as possible, for example in the case of the 2S1 122 mm howitzer, which is the only fully amphibious self-propelled artillery piece in the world, with its distinctively boat shaped hull.

After weather and terrain, the third special factor to be considered is the Russian soldier. Many Russians have a mechanical turn of mind, but they do tend to be careless. A top secret German report of 1938 which fell into allied hands after the war noted the 'lack of care for high quality war materiel in the Red Army . . . bringing with it an excessive rate of consumption'. Optical and precision instruments were therefore 'kept more primitive than the equivalent gear in the up-to-date armies of the Western powers'. This is not to say, of course, that the equipment did not work adequately. An example of concern for the user occurs in Yakovlev's memoirs. A suspiciously large number of direct hits seemed to be striking Russian mortars, with fatal consequences for all the detachment. Soon the true cause of the explosions was revealed: during periods of rapid fire the detachments would hurl bombs down the barrel but, in the smoke, confusion and noise of battle, could not always tell when that round was fired. Sometimes the mortars would be loaded twice and, when the lower bomb was fired the one in front of it blew up – *tochka*! The Artillery Directorate therefore developed a simple attachment to go on the muzzle which closed when the mortar was loaded, preventing a double charge, and was only opened by the departing bomb. Yakovlev noted that the Germans had no such device.

Connected with this talent for making things simple, in the Soviet period there has been a willingness to cut corners as far as the appearance and finish of equipment is concerned, provided its functioning is not affected prejudicially. Thus, Voronov records how the engineers wanted to produce beautifully finished guns, but how he persuaded them that by forsaking an elegant appearance the number of guns produced could be increased by 20 per cent.

One very important influence has been the size and shape of the Soviet army, and in particular the reliance in war on, and the consequent need to practise, the recall of large numbers of reservists, many of whom may not have seen a gun (or any other weapons system for that matter) for many years. This makes it desirable, indeed essential, to make sure that as far as possible the controls on a successor system are in exactly the same place as they were on its predecessor. In this way, a recalled reservist will be able to go straight to a gun and work it, with little if any retraining.[4]

The Unbroken Thread of Continuity

As we have seen, procurement of artillery and related systems is controlled by the GRAU, which is responsible for what we would call operational requirements and operational analysis as well. GRAU is one of the *Main and Central Directorates*, whose roles are defined as carrying out tasks connected with placing orders with industry, operating and repairing various types of armament and military equipment, working out tactical-technical requirements for the construction of new equipment and the procurement of existing types. GRAU therefore works out the *tactical-technical instruction* (*TTZ*, in Russian), which is the main document regulating weapons development. If a design is approved for series production then a *Technical Criterion (TU)* is prepared, which forms a contract between the technical administration — in the case of artillery and rockets, GRAU, and the production enterprise, and is the basis of the control exercised by the GRAU representative at the factory (see Chapter Two). The *TTZ* is worked out by GRAU in co-operation with design bureaux and other research institutions such as the military academies (see also Chapter Two), but the *TU* is given by GRAU direct to industry. *TTZs* are probably passed to research and development agencies through the General Staff. Some designs may, however, originate within these agencies on a 'private venture' basis, as they did in the Great Patriotic War.[5]

The Chief Designer is a particularly important figure in this process. This stems partly from his undoubted high technical and technological competence and from his position at the crucial interface between research and product, user and planner. The Chief Designer supplies the leadership and co-ordination which is all the more necessary in the Soviet Union because of the lack of a responsive economy. The designer is identified with the success or failure of a project and enjoys a degree of autonomy quite remarkable in that society.

A good example of the Chief Designer's role is provided by the career of the eminent artillery constructor Fëdor Fëdorovich Petrov (1902–1978). In the 1930s the Soviets had improved a number of Tsarist pieces, bringing them up to respectable contemporary standards, for example the rare 107 mm gun M-1910/30. The first artillery piece for which Petrov was responsible was the 152 mm gun-howitzer M-1937, known in Russia as the DL-20. This was developed on his own initiative. Petrov then led the design teams for the 122 mm gun M-1931–37 (A-19) (Plate 3.5), the M-1938 122 mm howitzer (Plate 3.6) still in service today, and the 107 mm gun M-1940 (M-60). Another advanced gun, not Petrov's, was the 152 mm M-1938 howitzer. The war accelerated the process of development, of course, and one day in April, 1943, Petrov received a telephone call from Dmitry Ustinov of the State Defence Committee, saying that by 1 May the

Committee required tests to be complete on five new types of 152 mm howitzer. Petrov had an idea for a new howitzer which would be markedly superior to existing designs. If it was to stand a chance, eighteen days remained. Petrov either volunteered to meet the deadline, or was ordered to.

Petrov gathered his engineers together and between them they thought up a scheme for a light howitzer, with a 152 mm barrel on the carriage of the M-1938 122 mm howitzer. The military customer in the Soviet Union is

PLATE 3.5.   122 mm gun M-1931/37 (A-19). (Steve Kimminau)

PLATE 3.6.   M-1938 122 mm howitzer, still in use today. (Author's photograph, with kind permission Sotamuseo)

apparently often dissatisifed with the conservative ideas of the designers; often revised versions of earlier products. Given the timescale to which Petrov had to work, however, it is hard to see how he had any choice in this case. On 1 May, five prototype 'D-1' howitzers were placed on rail flats and despatched to Moscow. The D-1 was put into series production soon afterwards. It proved very successful, although not all Soviet guns are cobbled together in such haste. Besides having the same carriage as the M-1938, the D-1 also has an identical screw breech system (see photograph). This system is, incidentally based on the French Schneider system from before World War I. The Russians bought a number of Schneider guns or made them under licence.

Petrov also worked on Soviet SP and tank guns during the war, and afterwards he appears to have been responsible for our first case study, the development of the 122 mm gun-howitzer D-30 (see below). He probably also influenced the design of the M-46, our second case study, which has certain similarities with the F-22 and the A-19 M 1931/37. There is therefore a direct personal link between Soviet artillery design of the late 1930s and today.

Another vital man was Vassiliy Gavrilovich Grabin (born 1899). Grabin who had graduated from the Dzerzhinskiy in 1930, was responsible for the F-22 and the much improved USV, and subsequently the ZIS-2 57 mm anti-tank gun and ZIS-3 76 mm field gun, model 1942. The latter was apparently described by Hitler as 'the most ingenious design in the entire history of gun artillery', perhaps Hitleresque hyperbole but an indicator of its high quality. Grabin also worked hard to improve the rate of production of equipment. For example, substituting stamped axles for cast ones on the ZIS-3 reduced the time taken to produce them 20 times. The total time taken to manufacture and test an artillery piece was reduced from 30 months in 1939 to between two and two and a half months in 1943.[6]

Foreign Influences

Although many writers stress the 'evolutionary' tendency of Soviet design philosophy, that is not the whole story. The path of Soviet artillery design is often twisted and deflected by extraneous influences. To give one example, it will be remembered that the Russian and Soviet artillery has always been less interested in *very* heavy guns and howitzers than other armies (see above). A good way of discovering in which areas the Soviets felt themselves to be weak in the last world war is to examine the equipment they requested from Britain, the USA and Canada, which is recorded in the various supply protocols. On the whole the Soviets did not need help with artillery, although they were desperately short of automobiles to tow it. The one exception which stands out a mile is the request in the 4th protocol for

Selected Equipments appearing in the Text, Great Patriotic War (some still in use).

	Gun M-1910/30	Gun M-1936 F-22	Gun M-1939 USV	Gun M-1942 ZIS-3	Gun M-1944 BS-3	Gun M-1931/37 A19	Howitzer M-1938 M30	Howitzer M-1938 M10	Gun Howitzer M-1937 ML20	Howitzer M-1943 D1	Howitzer M-1931 (later variants)*
Calibre, mm.	107	76	76	76	100	122	122	152	152	152	203
Length of barrel, calibres	38	51	42	42	60	46.3	22.7	24.3	29	28	21–24
Length of barrel and carriage, (m)	4.5	3.9	3.2	3.3	9.37	5.7	2.8	3.7	4.4	7.6	5.1
Length of rifling (m)	3.3	3.2	2.6	2.6	—	4.6	2.3	3.1	3.5	—	4.0
Elevation/depression (°)	−5, +37	−5, +75	−6, +45	−5, +37	−5, +45	−2, +65	−3, +64	−1, +65	−2, +65	−3, +65	0, +60
Traverse (°)	6	60	57	54	58	58	49	50	58	35	8
Weight in fire position (kg)	2,380	1,480	1,480	1,200	3,650	7,250	2,450	4,100	7,270	3,600	17,700
Weight travelling (kg)	2,580	2,500	2,300	1,850	—	7,907	2,800	4,550	7,930	3,640	19,000
Weight of round: – high explosive HE	17.2	6.23	6.23	6.23	15.6	25	21.8	40	43.6	51.1	100
– armour piercing (kg) AP		6.3	6.3	6.3	15.9						
Maximum range (metres)	16,100	13,290	13,290	13,290	20,000	20,400	11,800	12,390	17,230	12,400	18,025
Muzzle velocity (metres/sec) HE	670	706	680	680	887	800	515	508	655	508	607
AP		690	662								
Rate of fire, rds/min (where known)	5–6	15	12–15		3–4	3–4	5–6	3–4	3–4	4	1–2

	122 mm rocket launcher BM-13	Fixed 300 mm rocket launcher M-30	300 mm rocket launcher BM-31-12	160 mm mortar M-1943
Armour penetration, (where known)				130–160 mm at 500 mm; 125 mm (90°) 110 mm (60°) at 2000 m
Calibre (warhead) (mm)	122	300	300	160
Number of rockets	16	12	12	
Length of rocket minus fuze (mm)	1120	—	1760	Weight of round (kg) 40.5
Weight of total rocket (kg)	—	72	92.4	Maximum range (metres) 5,700 Weight of system (kg) 1,170
Weight of warhead (approx) (kg)	33	—	—	—
Initial velocity (metres/sec)	—	—	35	—
Maximum velocity (metres/sec)	—	—	255	—
Maximum range, metres	8,470; with improved round M-13 UK, 7900*	2,800	4,325; with improved round M-31 UK, 4000*	—

*There were some six variants of this piece. Soviet sources refer to the last three, and so does this table. *Where sources conflict, Soviet sources are taken as definitive. These are usually conservative compared with Western estimates*

*Although the range of the improved rounds was shorter, the grouping of rounds was three times tighter for the BM-13 and six times for the BM-31

Selected Modern Soviet Artillery Equipments

Ordnance type	T12 Anti-tank gun	D30 gun-howitzer	2S1 SP gun-howitzer	M46 gun	D-20 gun-howitzer	2S3 SP gun-howitzer	M1952 mortar	M-1975 SP mortar	2S5 SP gun	M-1976 S-23 gun	M-1975 SP gun
nickname	rapier	—	carnation	—	—	acacia					
calibre (mm)	100	122	122	130	152	152	240	240	152	180	203
detachment	6	8	4+2	8	10	4+2	8–9	—	—	15	—
Weight: overall (kg)	3,000	3,150	16,000	7,700	5,700	23,000	4,240	—	—	20,400	—
firing position (kg)		3,210		8,450	3,610		3,610				
length (travel)		5.4	7.3	11.73	8.14	7.8	6.51		c7.9		
width (travel)		1.5	2.85	2.45	2.35	3.2	2.21		c3.2		
height (travel)		1.4	2.4	2.55	2.46	2.7	2.49		c2.7		
ammunition: type	AP SC	HEF, SC S, I, C	HEF, SC S, I, C	HEF, APS, S, L, C	HEF, SC, AP, S, I, C In, ? RAP	HEF, SC, AP, S, I, C,? RAP ?nuke	HEF, C nuke?	HEF, C nuke? CB? ICM?	HEF, C nuke C	HEF, C nuke CB, RAP nuke	HEF, C nuke, ICM?
weight (kg)	5.5, 9.5	c22	c22	c33	c44	c44	100	c100	c44	30.4 (HEF) 43.8 (CB)	c100
elevation (°)	−10, +20, +70	−7, +70	−3, +70	−2.5, +45	−5, +63	−3, +65	+45, +70	—	—	−2, +150	—
traverse (°)	27	60	360	50	58	360	17	—	—	44	—

maximum range (metres)	8,500	15,300	15,300	27,000	17,230 (RAP 30,000)	17,230 (RAP 30,000)	9,700	12,000(?)	28,000–29,000	28,000–30,400 29,000 (43,800 RAP)	30,000	
Muzzle velocity (metres/sec)	1500 (AP) 900 (SC)	690 HEF 740 (SC)	690, 740	930 (HE, AP) 687 (I)	700	700	362	—	—	—	790 (HEF) 850 (RAP)	
Rate of fire: Max (rds/min)	10	7–8	5–8	5–6	5	4	½	1–2?	—	—	1	
sustained, one hour.	—	75	70	70	65	60	—	—	—	—	40	
Armour penetration 90° (vertical) at 1000 metres	400	460	185 (AP) 460 (SC)	240 (AP)	120 (AP) 400 (SC)	120, 400	—	—	—	—	—	
unit of fire	60	80	40	80	60	—	—	—	—	—	—	
Time into action (minutes)	—	1.5	—	4	5	—	—	—	—	—	—	
Date introduced	1965	1963	1974	1954	1955	1973	1952	1975	1981	1976	1955	1975

AP = Armour Piercing (solid), C = Chemical, CB = concrete busting, HEF = high explosive/fragmentation, I = illuminating, In = incendiary, ICM = improved conventional (minelet, bomblet, fuel-air etc.), RAP = rocket assisted, S = smoke, SC = shaped charge (armour piercing).

PLATE 3.7.   Grabin's outstanding 76 mm gun M-1942 (ZIS-3). (Author's photograph, with kind permission Sotamuseo)

two 240 mm Howitzers M-1 on carriage M-1, and for two eight-inch guns M-1 on carriage M-2. These guns were requested for the period July 1944 to June 1945, and would probably have been shipped after January, 1945. Given that the Soviets had some 107,300 guns and mortars in service against the Germans in 1945, *two* guns and *two* howitzers would hardly have made any difference. The Soviets did have 203 mm (eight-inch guns) which they could have used for special missions, and some heavier pieces. The only feasible reason for this odd request is that the Soviets wanted to examine the US guns and howitzers from a technological viewpoint. They probably felt that in this area, that of very heavy artillery, they were a little behind. Did the Soviets draw on the design features of these weapons? Maybe.

In 1955, a new Soviet heavy gun appeared, the S-23. The weapon is sometimes referred to as a 'gun-howitzer', but with a muzzle velocity of nearly 800 m/s and a barrel length of 47–49 times the calibre, the designation 'gun' is appropriate. There are similiarities with the American eight-inch gun, notably the shape of the jacket round the barrel. The S-23's most striking resemblance is in fact to the American eight-inch *howitzer* (the double wheels and the fact that the buffer and recuperator are mounted below the barrel) and to the 155 mm gun M1. The Russians did not order the latter weapons from the Americans, but they may have had access to specimens already. The Germans captured a number of 155 mm guns in North Africa and Italy, and at least a battalion of eight-inch howitzers at Bastogne. The Germans, as we have seen, used captured weapons, but not usually against their original owners, so that if they were recaptured, ammunition would not be readily available. The captured American guns and howitzers could therefore have been sent to face the Red Army, and would have fallen into Soviet hands. There can be little doubt that the Soviets examined these weapons and copied those features which they thought good. They also added various improvements of their own, such as a muzzle brake. It is impossible to categorise Soviet guns as 'evolutionary' or 'foreign influenced'; for hundreds of years, the Russians have had a record of sensible, selective adaptation. Another design trait, related to this, is their propensity for making the most of existing technology by combining parts of different designs, as in the D-1. Another example of ingenious adaptation is the 152 mm gun M-1935, which was mounted on the chassis of ordinary agricultural tractors (see plate 3.3).[7]

Case Study Number One: the D-30

The combination of evolution and innovation is most evident in the 122 mm M-1963 D-30 gun-howitzer. This gun is therefore of particular interest, and it also happens to be the numerical mainstay of the Soviet artillery's close support capability, although it is being phased out. It remains very important because it has been exported to many other European, Middle

PLATE 3.8. M 1963 D-30 122 mm gun-howitzer. In the middle of the sequence for bringing it into action. (Author's photograph)

Eastern and 'Third World' countries. The Soviets regard it as rather old hat, since fairly detailed descriptions of it have appeared in books for Soviet schoolboys. A number of specimens are available for examination in the West, as a result of the Middle East wars.

The D-30 represents what were probably the most advanced design and analysis concepts available to Petrov and his team in the early 1960s. It appears to be a descendant of the FH43 and the Bofors 105 mm L 28, in that no firing pad is used but that the stresses are transmitted directly through the *trails* to the ground. Its traditional Russian characteristics are the sleek, low silhouette, good range, the use of rubber foam in the tyres, the multi-baffle *muzzle brake*, and the ruthless exclusion of 'luxuries'.

The original version has *no* brakes, *no* applied safety and the layer has *no* seat. The muzzle brake absorbs about half the recoil, facilitating a simple and reliable *recoil system*. The penalty for this is paid in high overpressures in the crew area, about twice the standard acceptable to the US Army. Soviet pictures of the D-30 in action often show a long lanyard being used to fire it! Some would say that this makes it a 'primitive' weapon. But by economising on these desirable but, in Soviet eyes, non-essential features, it has been possible to produce a weapon that is compact and light given its calibre. It is fast into action (90 seconds), although it has to be balanced precariously on its sole plate in the process (see the photograph). It has all-round traverse, making if ideal for anti-tank fire, although its elevation is limited for 60 per cent of the total circle (known as 'top traverse'), where otherwise the breech would foul the *trails* on recoil. Specimens in the West have the elevation limited to 18 degrees over these sectors of arc although a recent Soviet publication claimed the limit was 22 degrees. The limit is imposed mechanically, by a roller on cam arrangement which actually prevents the gun from firing. It is possible that the roller on cam arrangement has been modified on more recent pieces, when it was found that the original safety limit was excessive. Other ways of increasing the elevation over the trails would be to raise the height of the *trunnions*; involving a considerable amount of redesign; or the attachment of a recoil limiting gear. The latter is fitted to the British Light Gun. The Soviets claim that the maximum range at 22 degrees elevation is 12 kilometres, which is feasible although it would require a heavy charge. For the remaining 40 degrees of the traverse, the top limit of elevation is 70 degrees, and the maximum range is 15,300 metres.

The D-30 is somewhat unstable, and in order to assist stability when firing is 'nailed' to the ground with spikes. This makes it slow out of action; a disadvantage bearing in mind the stress that the Soviet artillery is now placing on survival. Otherwise, however, the D-30 is clearly designed with survival in mind. The cradle shields the recoil system and a small shield protects all the gun's vital parts (not the gun detachment). Unlike some earlier ordnance, for example the 152 mm D-20, the D-30 does not have to be depressed to load it, improving its rate of fire. Finally, it is cheap and it is simple to operate and teach, making it good as a training gun. The D-30 has a vertically sliding, wedge shaped single thrust, surface block breech. Such breeches have been fitted to small calibre Soviet field guns such as the F-22, although larger calibre guns and howitzers have often had interrupted screw breeches.[8] Since about 1980 a modified version has been seen in Middle Eastern service, with a new double baffle muzzle brake (which does not add greatly to the efficiency), a hydraulic system for emplacing the gun, a *braking system*(!) and towing lights.

Case Study Number Two: the Mighty M-46

PLATE 3.9.   M-46 130 mm gun in travelling position. (Author's photograph)

This is a true long-barrelled gun, with exceptional power and range for its weight, calibre and vintage. Although obsolescent by European standards, it will remain a component of Soviet artillery reserves for some time, and is one of the most effective pieces fielded by the Vietnamese army, the world's third largest, and most Middle Eastern states. It is a winner because of its simplicity and mobility as well as its ballistics, a reminder that the highest tech is not necessarily the best from the soldier's point of view. An influential South Vietnamese staff officer affirmed that the enemy had 'still better weapons' than their own. 'One weapon our troops were most scared of was the 130. It can fire farther than the 105s, is very accurate and devastating in the impact area.' A Rand Corporation study into the fall of South Vietnam concurred. The enemy artillery was said to have been 'very effective, especially the Russian 130. Though its range was, at 27 kilometres, five kilometres less than the big American 175, it was simpler and more manageable, and was used to good advantage by the enemy'. Israeli soldiers who have faced the M-46 also have a high respect for this gun and the Israelis have modified captured M-46s and use them. How the Russians managed to get such range accuracy and endurance from a 130 mm barrel on a relatively light carriage and why it has this particularly nasty effect in the impact area is something of a mystery; their traditional expertise in the field of heavy metallurgy and its flat trajectory may explain it.

The M-46 was developed from the M-36 130 mm naval gun and was first seen openly at the 1954 May Day parade. According to popular Soviet open sources it appeared 'in the first half of the 1950s'. From then on it replaced the 100 mm BS-3 field and anti-tank gun. The Soviets have traditionally expected their field guns to have an anti-tank role and vice versa, and this philosophy is apparent in the M-46 also. At this time the evolution of rocketry led the Soviets to eschew the development of heavy and super heavy tube artillery, but the M-46 (usually referred to in Russian simply as the 130 mm gun), the somewhat similar looking 152 mm gun and the D-20 gun-howitzer were all introduced with a role 'in both conventional and nuclear conditions'. This does not mean that a nuclear round was developed for the M-46; its calibre is too small and the Soviets have shown little interest in nuclear shells for tube artillery. Most likely, it means that the M-46's range, high mobility and anti-tank capability made it an ideal complement to nuclear weapons on the nuclear battlefield.

On first approaching the M-46 in the travelling position it appears surprisingly chunky compared with the impression gained from published photographs. This is partly because the barrel and recuperator are drawn back in the travelling position; in the firing position they come forward. The small two-wheeled limber under the rear of the trail in the travelling position is withdrawn to the right or left rear when the gun is in the firing mode. The general arrangement of the carriage and limber is similar to that of the A19 M-1931/37 122 mm gun, while the appearance of the breech block and cradle is very reminiscent of the F-22, a reminder that the Soviets tend to retain proven design characteristics. Similarly certain of the M-46's distinctive traits are reproduced in the 152 mm 2S5 SP and the towed variant of it which are together replacing it (see below). On the M-46, the two large brackets on the trails, seen clearly in the second photograph with bollard shaped projections sticking upwards, are turned upside down when the gun is in the firing position and the bollards driven into the ground to anchor the trails and give stability.

The small shield is obviously designed to protect the working parts against back blast from the muzzle and possibly against enemy fire. It is

PLATE 3.10.   Breech of M-46 130 mm gun. (Author's photograph)

definitely not intended to protect the gun detachment from enemy fire as when you sit on the layer's seat to the left of the gun you are only half covered by the shield. Of course, on the D-30 the layer does not even get a seat.

The gun has a horizontally sliding wedge breech. The specimen here has the breech removed but the aperture is clearly visible in the second photograph. The mounting for the dial sight, is a standard Soviet type, very similar to that of the D-30, and is unremarkable. More interesting and unusual are the chain, gas cylinder and downward telescopic projections shown in the first photograph. The bicycle chain is part of the mechanism for withdrawing the gun and recoil system on to the cradle for travelling. The gas cyclinder is also part of the mechanism for pulling the gun back on to the cradle. In front of the gas bottle a collection of valves can just be seen which are used in this process. Compressed air in the cylinder is released to move the barrel and recoil mechanism and another valve is opened when the gun fires to recharge the system using the recoil energy. Given the weight of the barrel and recoil system in the pulled-back position, lifting the trail on to the small two-wheeled limber by hand would be extremely difficult and this explains the third item of interest; the telescopic rods. These are hydraulic jacks which enable the trails to be lifted sufficiently to get them on to the limber. The support they provide is clearly somewhat precarious, but adequate for the job, as in the case of the D-30. The handle socket on the right side of the box can be seen in the first photograph.

One anomaly is the perforated muzzle brake on the original M-46, which is not particularly efficient in that role. Other Soviet artillery pieces of the same vintage, for example the D-20 have double baffle muzzle brakes which are much more efficient at braking the recoil and taking some of the strain off the recoil mechanism, thus contributing to the general efficiency of the design. The perforated muzzle brake does, however, appear to be effective as a flash eliminator. This is borne out by accounts of the M-46 in Vietnam. Apparently, this made them difficult to spot, thus making them less vulnerable to counter-battery fire. The M-46s were also moved frequently to avoid counter-bombardment, and air strikes were the main device employed to catch them. From 1972 the US forces made a determined effort to root out M-46s, as one of the most dangerous weapons they faced, and the North Vietnamese responded by allocating large numbers of anti-aircraft guns and SA-7 SAMs to protect them. Large US air strikes were used to attempt to eliminate individual gun positions, a very uneconomical use of air power. Prior to 1982 the Palestinian Liberation Organisation (PLO) used M-46s to bombard Israeli towns from north of the border with Lebanon. Targets 10 kilometres and more inside Israel were hit with consistent accuracy. The fact that the PLO were able to hit targets this far inside Israel from well outside surveillance range of its borders bears witness to the gun's range and accuracy. It is possible that the PLO used forward observers deployed as undercover agents inside Israel, but the gun is sufficiently accurate to enable it to be used for predicted fire with enough precision for terror purposes at this range. One of the major problems with using an accurate long range gun of this type is, of course, precise and timely target acquisition.

The Soviets are now standardising on the 152 mm calibre, and the M-46 is being phased out of European service. This will no doubt take some time and the M-46 will remain a battle winner in Africa and Asia.[9]

Newer Active Systems

The self-propelled 122 mm 2S1 and 152 mm 2S3 appeared in the early

1970s and fulfilled the need for highly mobile artillery able to survive on the battlefield in close proximity to forward units. These are replacing the D-30 and D-20 although this is a gradual process as the sheer size of the Soviet army means that any new equipment takes a long time to percolate right through the system. Also, the Soviets never throw anything away. The 2S1 nicknamed *carnation* is larger overall than, for example, the old British 105 mm Abbot, but has the traditional very low Russian silhouette. Its gun is a modification of the D-30, although when it first appeared it was thought to be an entirely new barrel. This means that it can fire all the D-30's ammunition, as well as that of the old M-1938 howitzer. Clearly, in a fast moving and confused environment such as that expected to characterise a future war, with units cut off from higher level sources of resupply, artillery units may well feel grateful for any resupply and the greater the degree of commonality the more chance that available shells will fit. The evolutionary nature of much Soviet design of course helps in ensuring commonality. In accordance with normal Soviet practice, the 2S1 has direct fire sights and is expected to be able to operate in the direct fire role, as are all Soviet systems including the ZSU-23-4 *shilka* radar controlled anti-aircraft gun. The 2S1 does not have an automatic loader, so its rate of fire is rather slow. The 2S3, nicknamed *acacia* by Russian soldiers, is similarly larger than its Western counterpart, the 155 mm M-109 howitzer. It has a massive slab-sided turret which may contain an auto-assisted loading mechanism. In spite of its monolithic appearance, the 2S3's armour is rather thin: 15 mm on the chassis and 20 mm on the turret, but well sloped. It is of course important to remember that these self-propelled guns are not intended to charge into enemy fire head on, like tanks or Great Patriotic War assault guns, but are protected against shrapnel from indirect fire and the unlucky small arms bullet.

Since *carnation* and *acacia*, other artillery for use at Army and Front level has been introduced, and also a new regimental artillery piece which is extremely interesting from a design point of view as well as from its intended employment.

In 1975 a 203 mm self-propelled gun and a 240 mm self-propelled mortar appeared. Neither of these has a fully protected mount but the armoured chassis provides some protection for the crew and ammunition, at any rate on the move. The 240 mm mortar's chassis is similar to that of the 2S3, which is in turn similar to that of the SA-8 Gaskin surface-to-air missile, with six road wheels inside the track. The 203's is quite different, unrelated to the SA-8's, with seven road wheels, very long and low, with a low armoured cab at the front like the prow of a ship. The whole design is extremely sleek and futuristic. A 203 mm (eight-inch) gun is a very formidable piece of ordnance, and the new 203 is extremely long in the barrel. The Soviets have clearly given a lot of thought to making such a piece sufficiently mobile to be employed in modern battlefield conditions. It has an enormous crane on the right-hand side of the chassis to load the ammunition, and a spade not dissimilar to that of the later 2S5 but much bigger and with spikes which dig into the ground when in the firing position. When the first photographs appeared in 1985, Western experts were surprised at how different the gun and chassis were from their expectations. Details of the performance of this and other new systems are given in the summary tables.

PLATE 3.11.   The M-1975 203 mm (eight-inch) heavy gun. The great length of the barrel can be seen from the gun in the background. This gives it an estimated range of *at least* 30 kilometres, *without* rocket assisted, extended range or base bleed projectiles (see text).

The 240 mm self-propelled mortar has a tube very similar to the M-1952 towed 240 mm mortar. It is mounted on the back of the chassis so that it can be swung down into the firing position so that the base plate rests on the ground, to withstand the terrific shock of firing. Unlike most self-propelled systems, the mortar has to face *away* from the front of the chassis in the firing position, as with a towed piece. This, and the time taken to unfold the thing into and out of the firing position suggests that there is very little difference between this and a towed piece. Like the M-1952, the self-propelled mortar is not loaded from the muzzle, which would be impossible, but is swung upwards so that it can be loaded from the breech. Even so, on the M-1952 just lifting the round is a four or five man task. The configuration of the new 240 mm (see Fig. 3.14) suggests that the round can be pushed into the tube in the horizontal position straight from the chassis, and it is believed to have a power rammer giving a faster rate of fire, perhaps one round per minute.

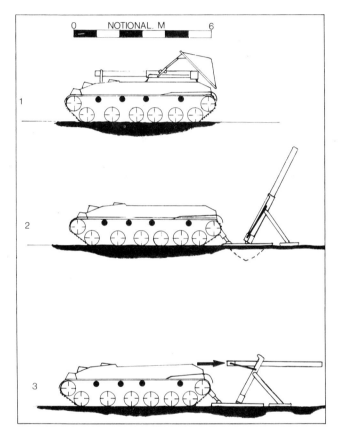

FIG. 3.14.   240 mm Self-propelled Mortar
(best available information, mid 1985).

Whereas the towed mortar is reported to have a maximum range of 9700 metres, some sources give that of the self-propelled one as 12,000. Normally, the muzzle velocity of a mortar is limited to about 310 metres per second, or just below the speed of sound, because of the ballistic performance of the mortar bomb. At the optimum elevation of 45 degrees this gives a maximum theoretical range of just under 12 kilometres in a vacuum, which is in reality less because of the loss caused by drag (see below). The 9700 metre range reported for the M-1952 is about the maximum which can be achieved unless the round is supersonic. This could mean that the new self-propelled mortar fires a supersonic round, which would entail very major improvements to the bomb design and place an enormous strain on the mortar's structure, although as we have seen with the D-30, high overpressures in the crew area are unlikely to worry the Russians. Otherwise, the bomb has to be rocket assisted or the reported range of 12 kilometres is wrong.[10]

PLATE 3.12.   M-1976 152 mm gun, first revealed publicly in the 9 May 1985 parade to celebrate the fortieth anniversary of the victory over Nazi Germany. The gun has a range of 28–29 kilometres and is nuclear capable. (Associated Press/LASERPHOTO)

In 1976 a new towed *gun* (not howitzer) appeared, the replacement for the M-46. Not surprisingly, it is mounted on a four wheeled carriage: Most towed guns of comparable calibre are and the Israelis had mounted captured M-46s on four wheeled carriages for greater efficiency. The new gun was first displayed publicly in the May 1985 parade to mark the fortieth anniversay of victory in Europe. Known provisionally as the M-1976, it has a thicker and more substantial barrel than the M-46, with the jacket extending further up the tube and a much larger and more efficient multi-baffle muzzle brake. It has brackets on the trails to anchor them which are very similar to those on the M-46 but are carried further away from the breech in the travelling position. In 1981 a self-propelled version of the same gun was seen, which we now know is called the 2S5 and is becoming standard. Once again, the completely unprotected mount looks unusual, almost a retrograde step when compared with the 2S1 and 2S3. However, the 2S5 and its towed counterpart are Army and/or Front level weapons, and would not normally be in close contact with enemy forces. The gun is for counter-battery and long range precision work. If such guns were to be caught by a MLRS or air strike light armour would be little comfort and their best protection would be their mobility. In order to provide the gun's firepower and accuracy on a mobile chassis, something from the firepower-mobility-protection triad has to be sacrificed, and the Russians have chosen to sacrifice protection.

PLATE 3.13. 2S5 gun, the self-propelled version of the M-1976 towed equipment. The chassis appears to be a variant of the 2S3 howitzer.

The 2S5 shares a common chassis with the 2S3 and new 240 mm mortar, with the three rear wheels closely spaced, not so much to support the weight of the 2S3 turret or the 2S5 breech, but to withstand the shock of firing. The 2S5 also has a recoil spade which is of an unusual ribbed design. The gun itself is new, bearing no resemblance to the M-46 and S-23 barrels. The 2S5 has the same large and effective muzzle brake as the towed variant.

There is no clearer example of the tradition of ingenuity and excellence, permeated by flashes of genius, which characterises Russian weapon design, than the new 120 mm self-propelled howitzer-mortar, called the *combination gun* by the Russians. This appeared in the early 1980s and was also first shown openly in the May 1985 fortieth anniversary parade. Based on the chassis of the BMD airborne (parachute droppable) combat vehicle, it is a traditional Russian delight in its simplicity and agility. Although the vehicle is very compact, which led many Western analysts to miss it in the parade, the howitzer mortar has a maximum range of some 10 kilometres, good enough for regimental artillery tasks, and fires a formidable range of ammunition in either the mortar or the howitzer role. The ordinary BMD chassis is lowered to the ground between the tracks to protect them when it is air dropped, and this design characteristic has been used to provide the combination gun with a stable firing platform despite the lightness of the vehicle. It is not clear whether this is essential to the operation of the system in the mortar role, the shock of the recoil passing directly through the bottom of the hull to the ground, or whether this is just to give greater stability and to reduce wear on the suspension with the barrel having a spring recoil mechanism; probably the latter. The space in the back of the BMD, originally designed for a six man section, enables the vehicle to carry masses of ammunition, especially as the mortar rounds do not require cartridge cases. The combination gun is breech loaded in the mortar role as well as the howitzer, being swung into the horizontal position for reloading. Even so, it can probably fire at a formidable rate, maybe ten rounds a minute. The combination gun shown in the photograph is in airborne service, where it is replacing the air droppable ASU-85 assault gun. Normally, the Soviets like to have supporting equipment like this on the same chassis as the elements being supported, so there is no problem for airborne forces. The question then arises whether the combination gun on the BMD-chassis could be deployed with other units such as BMP mounted motor rifle troops. If the kneeling chassis is essential to the weapon's operation, then it might be worth putting up with the logistic complications of deploying BMD based combination guns with BMP and BTR mounted troops: if not, the turret assembly, which seems a good and successful design, could be fitted to other vehicles such as the BMP, which are heavier and might not require the kneeling posture to give stability. In the long term, the combination gun could therefore supplant 120 mm towed mortars and even D-30s in motor rifle and possibly even armoured regiments and battalions.

The combination gun on the BMD chassis is obviously expensive to make, and would initially be deployed where its agility and versatility was a particular asset, particularly first echelon forces in Germany where a unit or formation may be selected to form part of an operational manoeuvre group (see Chapter Four) or a tactical ground-air strike team. It is certainly a brilliant design, ingeniously capitalising on a characteristic of an existing system, and whoever thought of it deserves to be made a hero of Socialist Labour, if he is not one already.

The new 152 and 203 mm guns and the 240 mm mortar can all fire nuclear rounds. However, the Soviets have always shown less interest than the West in atomic tube artillery, preferring rockets to deliver weapons of mass destruction. The limited range of the mortar in particular, casts doubts on whether firing nuclear rounds is one of its prime roles. In the author's

PLATE 3.14.   120 mm Howitzer-Mortar known as the 'Combination gun'.
This one is in airborne service (the officers are wearing airborne uniform with
artillery crossed guns on airborne light blue collar tabs), but these weapons
could replace 120 mm mortars and D-30s in other regimental artillery units.

opinion, it might be very suitable for fighting in built up areas, firing over
walls and buildings and possibly able to fire the 'killing zone' type bombs
used in Afghanistan. It is also possible that it fires a special concrete busting
round. The increased calibre of all these weapons also makes them suitable
for firing chemical and ICM rounds.[11]

Future Developments

   The design of the five weapons introduced most recently has been
something of a surprise, and history teaches that the Russians can be
expected to do something different from what has been predicted. As noted
above, there seems to be most scope for improvement with the ammunition. Besides making the round more lethal, it can be modified to extend
the range. An elegantly simple solution to increasing the range of tube
artillery has emerged with Extended Range sub-calibre (ERSC) and Full
Bore (ERFB) ammunition. The former is a shell which is tapered all the
way from the driving band at the back, instead of having a cylindrical centre
section, and is thinner than the bore of the gun. To impart spin and prevent
it wobbling about in the barrel there are two collars or sabots which discard
in flight. An ERSC round fired from a US 155 mm M-109 howitzer has a
range of over 22 kilometres instead of the normal 14.6: a 50 per cent
improvement. However, this is obviously wasteful in that not all the calibre
is used, and because of their shape ERSC rounds are unsuitable for high
explosive shells. Another variant of the same principle is the ERFB. This is

tapered all the way, as with ERSC, but is the full diameter of the bore at the base and is held in place at the front by blister shaped protrusions which are skewed to meet the twist of the rifling. When such shells have been fired from the Anglo-German-Italian FH 70 155 mm howitzer they have increased its range by about 8 kilometres.

Perhaps the most interesting ERFB development is the use of base bleed technology, invented by the Swedes. There is a container at the base of the shell which contains combustible material. This burns to generate oxygen deficient gases. This does *not* provide extra thrust, as in a rocket assisted projectile (RAP). What it does is to increase the pressure in the base area of the shell by about 80 per cent. Three types of drag act on a shell in flight: body drag, caused by rotation and friction, wave drag, caused by the shape of the shell, and base drag resulting from the partial vacuum formed at the base, pulling the shell back. ERSC and ERFB clearly reduces wave drag: base bleed reduces base drag only. It obviously has most effect on shells where base drag is a high proportion of the total. Base bleed can increase the range of a round by between 13 and 30 per cent compared with non-base bleed ERFB, and a correspondingly greater increase over conventional ammunition. For example, the Austrian GHN-45 155 mm howitzer will fire a non-base bleed ERFB shell to 30 kilometres. Under the same conditions, it fired a base bleed ERFB to 39 kilometres and in the rarefied air of the Middle East, 43 kilometres without loss of accuracy. The fact that the rights to this idea are held by a Belgian firm is unlikely to worry the Russians.

Looking further ahead, the Soviets are well up with the field in laser technology and possibly in the lead with charged particle beam weapons. It is significant that as long ago as 1968 Marshal of Artillery Kazakov included a section on laser damage weapons in a book on artillery. In terms of destructive power the effort required to produce a laser beam of sufficient intensity appears inordinate compared with conventional artillery systems. However, lasers have two main advantages. One is their great accuracy, something which is used in conjunction with conventional systems with laser rangefinders and laser guided projectiles. However, it may ultimately be worthwhile dispensing with one of the elements and using the laser itself as a weapon. The other advantage which Kazakov pointed out is the extreme speed with which a laser beam strikes the target: the speed of light. Anyone who has sat in an artillery observation post will recall how the seconds between the report of shot and impact drag by. With conventional artillery and rocket systems operating at any range the time of flight is very considerable. To take an extreme example, using the formula

$$vertex\ height = 4 \times time\ of\ flight^2,$$
(in feet)   (in seconds)

the M-46, firing at maximum range of 27 kilometres, has a *vertex height* (the top of its trajectory) of 11,200 metres giving a *time of flight* of some 96 seconds. In a real battle, one would not expect forward observers to have much left of their fingernails after such a shoot. On a future battlefield, the ability to achieve *instant* destruction of the target could be critical.

The Soviets will undoubtedly examine the possibilities of ERSC and ERFB to increase the range of tube artillery, if they have not done so already. They have certainly employed rocket assisted projectiles success-fully in 152 mm and 180 mm systems, which they consider can improve the maximum range by between 25 and 100 per cent.[12] However, it appears that there is a limit to the extent to which tube artillery's range can be stretched.

Reactive Systems

'On sea and land the fighting raged;
The screaming shells contested in the air.
Then from the forest little Kate would come,
To some familiar landmark, bathed in fire.
Out she creeps, her rockets loaded up
Against our homeland's dread assailant,
And screams: a company is gone,
And howls again: no regiment.'

As we have seen in Chapter One, the Russians have a tradition of expertise in rocketry which goes back long before the characteristic howling of the *katyusha* rocket launcher in the Great Patriotic War. The Russian rocket pioneer Tsiolkovskiy predicted the use of rockets powered by liquid hydrogen and liquid oxygen for space travel in the 1900s. Tsiolkovskiy was consulted by Soviet rocket engineers, although the practical development of Soviet military rocketry began in the 1920s. In 1921, N. I. Tikhomirov established a Soviet rocket research laboratory in Leningrad, which was renamed the *Gas dynamic laboratory (GDL)* in 1928. In 1931, a *Group for the study of rocket motion (GIRD)* was set up and in 1933 *GIRD* and *GDL* were amalgamated to form the *Rocket Science Research Institute (RNII)*. GDL was initially concerned with the development of plasma jet and liquid fuelled rocket engines. In 1933, GIRD-X, the first all liquid fuelled Soviet rocket, powered by liquid oxygen and alcohol, was launched, reaching a height of 5500 metres. The far-sighted and futuristic Mikhail Tukhachev-sky, the Head of Red Army Armaments Development from 1931–34, saw the military potential of large military rockets immediately. In 1932, he noted that the liquid fuelled rocket motor had special relevance to artillery and chemical troops as it would create possibilities for firing warheads 'of any power and at any range'. The Russians were working on the theoretical basis of nuclear fission in the 1930s and it is possible that Tukhachevsky foresaw the advent of the nuclear warhead.

While Tukhachevsky prophesied the V2 and the intercontinental ballistic missile, solid fuel remained more promising for immediate military applications. From 1934 to 1938, GDL was subordinated to RNII, which during that time developed 82 mm and 132 mm solid fuelled rockets. The latter of these became the legendary BM-13 *Katyusha* multiple rocket launcher projectile. In 1939 to 1940 GDL regained its independence to concentrate on longer term work and then became the *Experimental Design Bureau (OKB)*.

In 1940, GAU placed orders with industry for parts of experimental M-13 rockets, and a launcher for sixteen rockets was developed during that year. The first *katyushas* were inspected by a team including Ustinov (later Minister of Defence), Timoshenko and Zhukov on 17 June, 1941 and mass production was approved, symbolically, on 21 June, the very eve of the German attack. The *katyusha* may have been used against German troop concentrations on 7 July, but most Soviet sources agree that they were first used at the Orsha rail junction on 14 July. Captain Flërov, the battery commander, recorded that the results were 'excellent. A *solid sea of fire*.' Flërov and his battery were later surrounded and set fire to the new engines of war to prevent them falling into enemy hands, before Flërov himself was killed.[13]

The subsequent performance of Soviet multiple rocket launchers in the Great Patriotic War justified Flërov's initial enthusiasm. The 300 mm M-30 rocket, later fired from the BM-31-12 launcher was able to achieve a density of 20–25 rounds per hectare (100 metres^2). Within this, dugouts and even concrete emplacements were sometimes entirely destroyed. Even if such an emplacement survived a near miss by a 300 mm round, the shock was sufficient to kill those inside, one Soviet officer recalling seeing the dead German soldiers sitting upright, frozen in death, like 'manikins'. These weapons were still limited by their short range and wide spread of shot, and Kuleshov pointed out that a modern multiple rocket launcher, presumably the BM-21, has four times the salvo weight and eight times the *total destructive capacity* of the 132 mm Great Patriotic War BM-13 *katyusha*. The 40 barrelled BM-21 122 mm rocket launcher remains the mainstay of the Soviet Army's rocket launcher force in the mid 1980s. It was introduced in 1964 and is the most widely employed rocket launcher in the world, in service with over 30 nations. The original Soviet version is unarmoured and the rockets are loaded one at a time by hand. The Czech and East German armies have a more recent indigenous version, 1972, mounted on an armoured Tatra 813 (8 × 8) truck with an automatic reload, so that it can fire two salvos in quick succession. The Soviets had not introduced such a system in 1985, for which the reason is unclear.

A new multiple rocket launcher for Army and Front level artillery was introduced in about 1977. Given the greater hardness of individual targets,

Principal Modern *Multiple Rocket Launchers*

	BM-21	BM-27 (all data estimated)
Nickname	*Hail*	—
Launcher:		
Elevation (°)	0–+75	0–+55
Traverse (°)	180	240
Rocket:		
Calibre (mm)	122	220
Weight overall (kg)	66	300
Weight of warhead (est)	19.4	100
Length overall (m)	2.87	4.8
Method of stabilisation	initial spin and fins	initial spin
Maximum range (m)	20,380	35–40,000
Minimum range: (m)		
Direct fire	500	—
Indirect fire	1,500	5,000
Types of warhead	*HEF, C, S, In*	*HEF, C, ICM*
unit of fire	120	—
Time into action (min)	2.5	—
Time out of action (min)	½	—
Vehicle:		
Crew	5	—
Type	URAL-375D	ZIL-135
Weight with launcher and rockets (kg)	13,300	23,000
Length (travelling) (m)	7.35	9.3
Width (m)	2.69	2.8
Height (travelling)	2.89	3.2
Road range (km)	750	520

especially self-propelled guns, and the greater accuracy of individual modern rockets, it is logical that the Soviets should introduce a system with fewer but bigger rockets, concentrating in particular on the range and accuracy to hit targets in the enemy depth. This is exactly what they have done with the BM-27 with its sixteen 220 mm tubes. The Soviets managed to keep the BM-27 out of public view until the first published photographs appeared in February and March, 1985. The BM-27's sixteen tubes are arranged in two banks of six and one of four, giving good stability. The launcher is carried on the same ZIL-135 chassis as the old T-5 operational tactical rocket, known as FROG-7 (Free Flight Rocket Over Ground) to NATO. In the firing position the BM-27 has a shield over the back wheels and the cab to protect them against the back-blast and outriggers to make the chassis more stable. It antedated the Western Multiple Launch Rocket System by several years, although the latter is more technologically sophisticated. The BM-27 is primarily employed at Front level, in brigades which some reports say can number as many as 72 equipments, although that would be exceptional. The BM-27 can also be expected at Army level, but its range of 35–40 kilometres is greater than that needed by division, and, being very large and requiring massive logistic back-up, it would probably be too unwieldy for a Soviet divisional level weapon.

The launcher probably has a traverse of about 240 degrees. For reloading, the tubes are layed horizontally and swung to the side. A resupply vehicle, also a ZIL-135, then loads the rockets one at a time with the aid of a rammer. The reload time is reportedly about twenty minutes.

FIG. 3.15.   BM-27s deploying under cover of a storm.

The rockets are an entirely new design, at about 4.8 metres much longer than those of the now obsolete BM-24 240 mm rocket launcher, introduced in 1953 which has 1.25 metre rockets. Like previous Soviet multiple rocket launchers, the BM-27's rockets are solid fuelled, unguided and twist fin stabilised. It carries high explosive fragmentation, chemical and minelet (bomblet) warheads. The BM-27 is a potentially devastating weapon: if we take the Great Patriotic War norm of 20 to 25 rockets per hectare, and assume that a modern 220 mm warhead is at least as lethal as an old 300 mm, two BM-27s (32 rockets) could be fairly sure of annihilating an area 100 metres by 150 with a single salvo: a NATO headquarters, perhaps?[14] In a modern high speed battle, the ability of the multiple rocket launcher to deliver a large number of projectiles at once, rather than the constant, regular pounding of tube artillery, has acquired relatively greater significance.

Large Operational-Tactical Rockets

The Soviets had a strong scientific and technological base for post-war rocket development. Although the most important German rocket scientists, Oberth and Werner von Braun, went to work for the USA, the Soviets captured a complete German rocket factory in Thuringia in early 1945, and 200 rocket engineers were transported back to the Soviet Union. The first large post war Soviet rocket, the R-1, appeared in October, 1947, looking exactly like the German V-2 on which it was based. In the same year, the Soviets produced a rocket of entirely indigenous design the BRDD-1, the body of which was designed by S. P. Korolev and the engine by V. P. Glushko. Although the Soviets had the very advanced work of GDL-OKB to build on, which had more long term potential, exploitation of German efforts offered more immediate return. Therefore, they pursued both courses in parallel. Another reason that they were keen to build on the V-2 design was the great influence of artillerymen on rocket development: they saw it in terms of a gradual extension of artillery strikes rather than in terms of a dramatic leap. Western analysts in the late 1940s noted that the Soviets had devoted most enthusiasm to *surface-to-surface missile* developments, as opposed to surface-to-air, and assumed that this was because the Germans had been most advanced in the former field. In fact, as we have seen, the Soviets had always seen rockets primarily as a surface-to-surface weapon and regarded them as super long range artillery which could substitute for manned aircraft. Western intelligence noted that there was 'little or no return to the research and study of fundamentals but instead the Soviets seem to be engaged in a vigorous programme of getting missiles to the hardware (test vehicle) stage with a minimum of research . . . the trial and error character of such a development programme might result in considerably greater performance in shorter time than the Soviets might be able to develop by a return to research in fundamentals'. Soviet missiles of the V1 (cruise missile) and V2 (A4) (ballistic missile) types of this period had up to 25 per cent improved performance over the German originals and work was in progress on a development based on the improved German A-9. The Soviets investigated possibilities for improving the range of V2 type rockets by using different propellants, and in late 1947 they made a determined attempt to enlist Germans who were specialists in the field of nitrogen-hydrogen compounds and hydrazine hydrates. A liquid oxygen-anhydrous hydrazine combination in a V2 with an increased combustion chamber pressure might give a 70 per cent increase in range and a nitric acid-anhydrous hydrazine combination a 45 per cent increase. In 1948, it was noted that the Soviets seemed to be producing a large number of guided missiles, perhaps because they felt they needed them for extensive future testing, perhaps because to simplify targeting and control they planned to fire a lot at any one target, in the nature of an artillery barrage. By the end of 1948 a perceptible shift of production and research facilities away from East Germany and the western USSR to the more remote areas was observed. Peenemunde having been evacuated some time in 1947. The two strands of development: short term exploitation of German designs and longer term basic research continued, the latter being concentrated in the region of Chelyabinsk, Kuybyshev and the western Kazakhstan republic. Fuel research investigated such combinations as alcohol-hydrogen peroxide, hydrazine and nitric acid and hydrogen peroxide-diazomethane. Stalin prize winners in 1948 included two awards for scientific research in exterior ballistics which was believed to be connected with the development of new guided missiles. Accuracy did not seem to be a major consideration, indicating that the Soviets were confident in the ability of the nuclear warhead which they first exploded in 1949 to compensate for lack of precision. In 1949, new guided missile experimental installations were set up in the Lake Baikal region west of Snezhnaya (51.27N, 104.38E). Also, the area from Rybinsk (58.03, 38.47) to Ostashkov (57.08, 33.09) was designated for testing of missiles built in the Rybinsk area. At this time, V2 derivative ballistic missiles were estimated to have a range of up to 400 nautical miles (some 650 kilometres). As noted in Chapter Two, all these developments took place under the auspices of the Soviet Artillery. Furthermore, research was compartmentalised so that a team would work on one aspect, such as guidance for several types of missile. The development of surface-to-air missiles and surface-to-surface missiles, whether operational-tactical or strategic, was therefore inextricably entwined.[15]

The first large operational-tactical rockets which can be attributed specifically to the ground forces in a surface-to-surface role appeared in 1957, the same year as the first Sputnik. These were the unguided solid fuelled rocket known to the Soviets as the T5-B and to NATO as the FROG-1, and the liquid fuelled T7-A, known to NATO as the SCUD-A. The liquid fuelled SS-12, NATO code name Scaleboard, was introduced in the mid 1960s. There have been several versions of the T-5 the latest being nicknamed *luna* (moon) or FROG-7 to NATO and one of the T-7, known as the T-7B (SCUD-B to NATO), introduced in 1961. Liquid fuel is not particularly suitable for battlefield systems; it is dangerous and requires to be pumped into the missile just before firing, and the replacements for the T-7 and SS-12, the SS-23 and SS-22 respectively, are solid fuelled, as is the T-5's replacement the SS-21.

The SS-21 and the SS-23 both conform to the trend for much more mobile and elusive battlefield missiles. The former is mounted in a derivative of the SA-8 Gecko 6 × 6 chassis. This is standard up to about half its height, but has been completely rebuilt at the top with two doors in the roof which open to the side to allow the missile to be brought into the firing position. These can be seen clearly in the photograph. It has a very distinctive boat shape, as with the 2S1, and is fully amphibious, being propelled in the water by two

PLATE 3.15. The futuristic SS-21 artillery missile, (NATO codename SCARAB) first revealed publicly in the 9 May 1985 parade to celebrate the fortieth anniversary of the Soviet victory in the Great Patriotic War. It is mounted in an amphibious chassis based on that of the SA-8 *GECKO*. This is a highly agile battlefield system, with conventional high explosive-fragmentation, chemical, nuclear and (possibly) improved conventional warheads. (Associated Press/LASERPHOTO)

waterjets. Although initially assessed to have a range of some 120 kilometres, its range is in fact only about 100. It is a highly mobile divisional level weapon, easy to conceal. Its Russian nickname is *tochka* ('point', 'full-stop' or 'curtains'), indicating its accuracy and lethality. Unlike its predecessor the T5 E (FROG-7), it may therefore have a guidance system. Like the SS-23 and SS-22, it is considered sufficiently accurate to have an ICM warhead. As with many Soviet designs, the rocket is something of a surprise, being very curved and not predominantly cylindrical.

The SS-23, with a range of about 500 kilometres, is mounted on a derivative of the same MAZ-543 eight-wheeled chassis as the T-7 (SCUD)-B, but once again built up to cover the missile entirely. Once again, it can carry conventional, chemical, nuclear and ICM warheads. The SS-22 is also known in the West as the SS-12 (modified) at the time of writing but will be referred to as the SS-22 here. It is mounted on the same unmodified MAZ-543 chassis as the SS-12, and the two systems are very similar in appearance. It is probable that only the guidance system of the missile itself is different. The missile has about the same range as the SS-12, some 885 kilometres, but is more accurate. Soviet armies and Fronts have missile brigades equipped with from twelve to eighteen T7s (SCUDS) or SS-23s.[16] The Front commander may also have a brigade of SS-12/22. However, in the author's view, given the current emphasis on the *Theatre of Military Operations (TVD)* as the cardinal level, and given the fact that these missiles have the ability to carry a nuclear warhead half way across England from East Germany, military and political considerations would suggest that these missiles should be controlled at a higher level.

Modern Soviet Operational-Tactical Rockets (Surface-to-Surface)

	FROG-7	SCUD-B (SS-1)	Scaleboard (SS-12)	SS-21	SS-23	SS-22
NATO designation						
Soviet designation	T5-plus letter *luna*	T7-B	?	ZZ-21? *tochka*	ZZ-23?	ZZ-22?
Missile:						
Length overall (m)	9.5	11.5	12.0	—	—	—
Diameter (m)	0.55	0.9	1.0	—	—	—
Weight (kg)	2500	6300	9700	—	—	—
Type of fuel	solid	liquid	liquid	solid	solid	solid
Type of guidance	none	inertial	inertial	—	—	—
Circular error probable (CEP) (m)	400	900	750	300	350	—
Maximum range (km)	70	300	900	100	500	885
Warhead types	*HEF, C, nuke*	*HEF, C, nuke*	*nuke*	*HEF, ICM, C, nuke*	*HEF, ICM, C, nuke*	*nuke*
Time into action (min)	15–30	up to 60	up to 60			
Unit of fire	1 rocket on TEL, 3 on reload veh.	1 on TEL, 1 on reload	1 on TEL 1 on reload	1 on TEL	1 on TEL	1 on TEL

Date introduced	1968	1961	1965	1976	1979	early 1980s
Vehicle: Chassis type	ZIL-135 (8×8)	MAZ 543 (8×8)	MAZ 543 (8×8)	modified SA-8 (6×6)	modified MAZ 543 (8×8)	MAZ 543 (8×8)
Crew	4	—	—	—	—	—
Length:						
with rocket	10.8	12	13	about 9	12	—
without	9.3	12	12	about 9	12	—
Width (m)	2.8	3	3	2.9	3	3
Height (m)	3.5	2.6	2.6	about 2.4	—	—
Engine	2×90 hp V8 petrol	580 hp V12 diesel	580 hp V12 diesel	diesel	580 hp V12 diesel	580 hp V12 diesel
Road range (km)	400	550	550	500	550	550
Water crossing: depth which can be forded (m)	0.6	1	1	amphibious all over	1	1
NBC protection	none	cab filtration	cab filtration		cab filtration	cab filtration

Sources: Richard F. Arndt *Waffen und Gerät der Sowjetischen Landstreitkräfte* (Walhalla u Praetoria Verlag, Regensburg, 1971); David C. Isby *Weapons and Tactics of the Soviet Army* (Jane's, London, 1981); *FM-100-2-3.* 1984; author's deductions.

Note: CEP is the *radius* from the centre of the target within which *50 per cent* of missiles fired at it will fall.

During 1984, the Soviets sought to present the deployment of SS-21, 22
and 23 missiles as a deliberate response to NATO's deployment of cruise
and Pershing 2. In fact, the Soviet missiles are straight ground forces
artillery weapons, and not qualitatively and conceptually new like the
NATO systems. In 1985 SS-22s were reported to be based at Bautzen near
Dresden and Eberswalde, north of Berlin, but since they are mobile
battlefield systems, this information is fairly meaningless. However, the
spectre of these missiles being used in Europe is not the only thing that
makes them interesting. Syria took delivery of the latest SS-21 missiles in
1984, albeit with conventional warheads only, and in the savage Iran-Iraq
war both sides exchanged Soviet made surface-to-surface missiles on a
larger scale than at any time since World War II. These were T7 (SCUD)-B
missiles, with a maximum range of 300 kilometres (180 miles) with a
conventional warhead. These were reported to be relatively inaccurate, and
the problem for the Iranians was compounded by the inability of their air
force to mount sorties to assess their accuracy. However, large explosions in
the centre of Baghdad indicated that they could certainly hit a target the
size of a city centre or an airfield.[17] The modern Soviet missiles are much
more accurate and the Soviets have vastly superior target acquisition means
available.

Command and Reconnaissance

The equipment needed to control artillery fire and find the targets is
obviously as crucial to getting the round in the right place as the gun or
rocket launcher. Just as the requirements of the high speed battlefield
saturated with fire have forced artillery pieces under armour and on to
tracks, so they have affected command, control and reconnaissance. A most
significant development is the series of vehicles known to NATO as the
Artillery Command and Reconnaissance Vehicle (ACRV) family, based on
the successful MT-LB vehicle. There is no point having self-propelled and
armoured 2S1 and 2S3 howitzers if the vital and integral command group
cannot keep up and survive equally well, and ACRVs are part of these
sub-units. They also accompany 2S5 and can be expected to control other
self-propelled systems as well. There are three ACRV variants, known in
the West as the ACRV M-1974-1, which is the vehicle belonging to the
Battery Senior Officer, the second in command of the battery and gun
position officer, who rules the gun position (three per artillery battalion);
the ACRV M-1974-2, the vehicle housing the *battery* and *battalion
commanders*, who occupy forward *Command Observation Posts* (four per
artillery battalion), and the ACRV M-1974-3, the battalion *Chief-of-Staff's*
vehicle (one per artillery battalion). The distinctive features of the three

types are clear from the photographs (Plates 3.16–3.18): all have the long and elegant armoured hull, the characteristic bow and a turret just behind the mid-point, and all carry communications equipment and a laser rangefinder. The ACRV M-1974-3 carries the one fire control computer allocated to each battalion, consistent with the recent decision to make the battalion the *main fire unit* (see Chapter Four). The need to make the ACRV amphibious has limited the thickness of its armour, and it is extremely large. The battalion Chief-of-Staff's vehicle, with its four aerials, controlling the fire of the entire battalion, makes a particularly juicy target.

PLATE 3.16.   ACRV M-1974-1, Battery Senior Officer's *(Gun Position Officer's)* vehicle. The main distinguishing marks are the small dome on the turret and the box on the right-hand side of the hull. Like many Soviet vehicles, this is amphibious with a distinctive boat shape.

PLATE 3.17.   Battery and Battalion Commanders' vehicle (*Command Observation Post*). The fender over the front of the track is not significant for identification purposes.

PLATE 3.18.   ACRV M-1974-3. Battalion Chief of Staff's vehicle (*Battalion Fire Direction Centre*). The main distinguishing features are the absence of a box on the right hand side and the extra aerials (see the diagram of the battalion radio net in Chapter Four, Figure 4.8).

Since before the advent of indirect fire (see Chapter One), finding and watching the target has been more of a problem than making a gun that will fire that far. This is even more critical today with artillery systems like the 2S5 (range 28–29 kilometres) and the BM-27 (35–40 kilometres), not to mention large operational tactical rockets. As we have seen in Chapter One, the Soviets placed enormous emphasis in the Great Patriotic War on accurately plotting the location of targets, making extensive use of air photography and sound ranging as well as ground observation. However, in the modern battle environment the first two are often too slow and the latter does not reach far enough. Therefore, there has been increased attention to *Artillery Instrument Reconnaissance (AIR)*, in other words, *artillery and mortar locating radars*. Two old artillery locating radars still in use still bear the name *SNAR: SNAR-1* and *SNAR-2*, both known to NATO as Pork Trough. Other types are *Mobile radar (PSNR)* and *Mortar Locating Radars (ARSOM)*. *ARSOM-2P*, known in NATO as Small Yawn, is a counter-mortar or counter-battery radar with an I band frequency carried on the old AT-L artillery tractor. More modern are the radars known to NATO as small and big Fred. The former is mounted on a model 1975 BMP vehicle called the PRP-3 from the Russian for *mobile reconnaissance post*, and is found both in the observation batteries of divisional artillery groups and also in individual artillery battalions. It is believed to be a J-band radar with a detection range out to 39 kilometres but a tracking range (essential to locate a target) of only 7 kilometres. The newest Soviet artillery mortar and rocket launcher locating radar is called big Fred by NATO, and is also mounted on a variant of the MT-LB. It is believed to operate in a similar way to the British Cymbeline, measuring the slant range and bearing of two points in the shell or bomb's trajectory. The time taken between these two points is also measured and all this information is passed to the computer which works out the gun or mortar's position. Big Fred's range is unknown but it is certainly under 30 kilometres, so it cannot necessarily reach out to the maximum range of the BM-27.[18] However, it is in the attack from the standing start that hitting accurately surveyed targets in depth would be most important. As we have seen in Chapter One, as the battle becomes more fluid command and control tends to be devolved and combat becomes closer. Furthermore, given the Soviets' use of norms to ensure the destruction of unobserved targets, and the other means of target acquisition available (long range reconnaissance patrols and intercepting radio emissions, for example), the limited range of the new target acquisition radars need not be a crucial disadvantage.

Experience has shown that attempting to forecast the nature and appearance of new Soviet artillery and rocket systems is an unrewarding business: both the 2S5 and the 203 mm self-propelled gun, for example, were utterly different from what Western 'experts' had expected. The artillery equipments introduced in the 1970s are likely to remain in service for many years (thirty, if the previous generation is anything to go by). From past trends, we can expect any new ones to be original in appearance and ingenious in design, and extremely rugged. The main improvements will be in the field of command and control. In particular, the Soviets may be tempted to replace the shoe-box like ACRV with something more like a BMP-based vehicle, which is more agile, has better armour and is less readily distinguishable from neighbouring vehicles. The Soviets are showing particular interest in integrated reconnaissance-acquisition-targeting and tasking systems, which are examined further in Chapter Four. Whatever happens, equipment developments will be thoroughly consistent with the Soviet view of the nature of future land warfare, and well suited to fulfil the requirements of Soviet Military Art in accordance with Soviet Military Doctrine, whether on manoeuvres or in the most testing time of all.

Notes

1. Circumstances of capture: interview with a former member of a Finnish SS battalion; 'A Puzzling Weapon Captured by the Finns: the "Non-recoil" gun', *Illustrated London News* (6 April, 1940), pp. 446–47; Early development of recoilless guns, Tsygankov and Sosulin, pp. 32–3; *NT-23-653-71-DTI-AD 739 350* (US Army) pp. 160–61, a translation of A. N. Latukhin's *Sovremennaya Artilleriya* (Modern Artillery) (Voyenizdat, Moscow, 1970); use

by airborne troops, D. S. Sukhorukov, P. F. Pavlenko, I. N. Bliznyuk, S. M. Smirnov, eds. *Sovetskiye vozdushno-desantnye* (Soviet Airborne Forces) (Voyenizdat, Moscow, 1980), pp. 11, 14, photograph after p. 32.

2. GPW shell data from Tsygankov and Sosulin, pp. 63–68, 88–91, 93–99. Lethality circles of modern shells from Ye. K. Malakhovskiy, *Strel'ba na porazheniye opornykh punktov (Fire for the destruction of Defensive Positions)*, (Voyenizdat, Moscow, 1978), pp. 53–54; 'cassette shells', Colonel L. Zabudkin, '*Kassetnye snaryady*' *TiV*, 1/1984, pp. 36–37; Colonel V. Rokhkachev, '*Kassetnye boyevye chasti raket*' ('Sub-Munition Warheads for Rockets'), *TiV* 2/1984, pp. 8–9; incendiary devices: Yossef Bodansky 'New Weapons in Afghanistan', *Jane's Defence Weekly*, 9 March, 1985, p. 412.

3. Definitions from Tsygankov and Sosulin, pp. 31–32, Kazakov *Artilleriya* . . . pp. 107–11; high powered artillery etc.: Tikhomirov (no initial given), *Artilleriya bol'shoy moshchnosti* (Voyenizdat, Moscow, 1935), especially table on pp. 98–99 and Tsygankov and Sosulin, pp. 95–96; super powered, p. 79.

4. Revolution in military affairs: Harriet Fast Scott and William F. Scott, *The Armed Forces of the Soviet Union*, (Westview Press, Boulder, Colorado, 1979, pp. 40–41, 47; Engelhardt and rubber: *Russkiy invalid*, translated in *RUSI* Journal January–June, 1899, p. 588; Voronov, *Na sluzhbe* . . . p. 115; German opinion of F-22. Lieutenant Gabriel in *Artilleristiche Rundschau*, October, 1942, translated in *Military Review*, Vol. 23, No. 5, p. 72. The German officer made the facetious comment that his men did not like using the Russian gun's full range because they preferred to get up close and 'see the pieces fly'; weak bridges: E. Barsukov, *Russkaya artilleriya v mirovoy voyne (Russian Artillery in the World War)*, (Moscow, 1938), Vol. 1, p. 212; Golovin, '*Ustroystvo artillerii*', p. 218; naval armaments: Robert B. Bathurst, *Understanding the Soviet Navy*, (Naval War College Press, Newport, RI, 1979), p. 67; lack of care for high quality kit: Adm. 223/51, part 2, pp. 29 and 35 (British Admiralty intelligence papers); mortar safety device, Yakovlev, pp. 152–53; 20 per cent, Voronov, p. 112.

5. Main and Central Directorates, *SVE* Vol. 2 (1976), p. 565; *TTZ*, SVE Vol. 3 (1977), pp. 616–17; *TU* direct to industry, Shmakov, p. 16; private venture, A. J. Alexander, *Decision Making in Soviet Weapons Procurement*, Adelphi Paper No. 147/8, Winter, 1978–79.

6. Colonel Engineer A. Latukhin, '*Vidny artilleriskiy konstruktor*' ('Famous artillery constructor'), *VIZh* 3/1982, pp. 94–95 on Petrov and the D-1, etc.; Grabin, *SVE* Vol. 2 (1976), p. 629 and Yakovlev, pp. 116 (Hitler's view), 120 (axles).

7. *Wartime International Agreements: Soviet Supply Protocols*, (US Department of State, Washington DC), 4th Protocol, pp. 95, 99 and Annex 2.

8. Tsygankov and Sosulin, pp. 127–28; overpressures: 'Soviet Weaponry: Simple, Rugged and Redoubtable', *Army*, February, 1982, p. 22.

9. Steven T. Hosmer, Konrad Kellen, Brian M. Jenkins, *The Fall of South Vietnam: Statements by Vietnamese Military and Civilian Leaders*, (Historian, Office of the Secretary of Defense, R-2208-OSD (Hist), December, 1978), p. 67; otherwise, personal observation in Israel.

10. Mortar facts: J. W. Ryan, *Guns Mortars and Rockets*, (Brassey's Battlefield Weapons Systems and Technology, Vol. 2, 1982), pp. 36–37; other data from *FM-100-2-3: The Soviet Army: Troops, Organization and Equipment*, (Department of the Army, Washington DC, July, 1984), pp. 5–59, 5–62; *Soviet Military Power, 1985*, (Department of Defense, Washington DC, 1985), p. 68.

11. *Soviet Military Power, 1985*, p. 68.

12. ERSC and ERFB: R. D. M. Furlong, 'ERFB Munitions . . .' and 'The GHN 45 . . .', *International Defense Review*, 6/1982, pp. 755–768; Kazakov on lasers: *Artilleriya* . . ., p. 406; rocket assistance improving performance 25–100 per cent: SVE Vol. 1 (1976), p. 133.

13. Poem: Anatoliy Skoblo, cited in Voronov, *Na sluzhbe* . . . p. 231; GDL etc., V. P. Glushko, *Development of Rocketry and Space Technology in the USSR* (English edn., Novosti Press, 1973), pp. 14–15, 19 and Shmakov, pp. 9, 15. Tukhachevsky 'any power and

range', David Holloway, 'Doctrine and Technology in Soviet Armaments Policy', Derek Leebaert, ed., *Soviet Military Thinking*, (London, 1981), p. 284; Soviet nuclear research began in the 1930s, see 'When the Russians Rocked the World', *Sunday Times*, 30 August, 1984. Flërov's exploits are recorded in numerous sources: see Kazakov, pp. 76–77.

14. Densities and manikins, Shmakov, p. 19; comparison with modern systems, Kuleshov's introduction to the latter, p. 9; modern equipment, *FM-100-2-3* and numerous other open sources; first photographs of BM-27 in *JDW*, 16 February, 1985 p. 263 and *Soldat und Technik*, 3/1985, p. 117. The latter gives the figure of 72 for the Front's artillery brigade but this, like some other assertions in the article, are not verified at the time of writing.

15. Capture of German scientists and exploitation of German research: Peter Gostzony, *Die Rote Armee: Geschichte und Aufbau der Sowjetische Landstreitkräfte seit 1917 (The Red Army: History and Development of the Soviet Land Forces from 1917)*, (Fritz Molden Verlag, 1980), p. 314; BRDD-1: A. P. Romanov, *Raketam pokoryayetsya prostranstvo (Rockets Conquer Space)*, (Politizdat, Moscow, 1976), p. 52; Western intelligence, *HQ USAF Air Intelligence Reports*: 100–13/9–100 dated 4 August, 1948 (15 June report), p. 10, artillery style barrage, p. 12; 13/10–100 dated 15 November, 1948, (15 September report), p. 12; 13/11–100 dated 9 February, 1949 (15 December 1948 report), p.16.

16. FM-100-2-3, pp. 67–70; *Soviet Military Power, 1985,* pp. 67–68.

17. 'Soviet Ground Missiles Fired into Baghdad', *Daily Telegraph*, 20 March, 1985, p. 4; airport, 'Civilians in Front Line of Gulf War', *Guardian*, 21 March, 1985, and numerous contemporary articles; location of SS-22s in East Germany *Daily Express* 15 April 1985, p. 8; SS-21s and 23s: 'A Small Town in East Germany', *Observer*, 31 March, 1985, pp. 20–22; Soviet description of SS-21 units *'Nacheku!'* ('On Guard!'), *KZ*, 19 January, 1984, p. 1.

18. ACRVs: *FM-100-2-3*, pp. 5-30-5-31; *AIR, SVE* Vol. 1 (1976), p. 267–68; radars in *FM-100-2-3*, p. 5–71 and PRP-3 in 'Infantry Combat Vehicle, part 4, Command Versions', *JDW*, 24 November, 1984, p. 934; Big Fred, *JDR* 1/1982, p. 4.

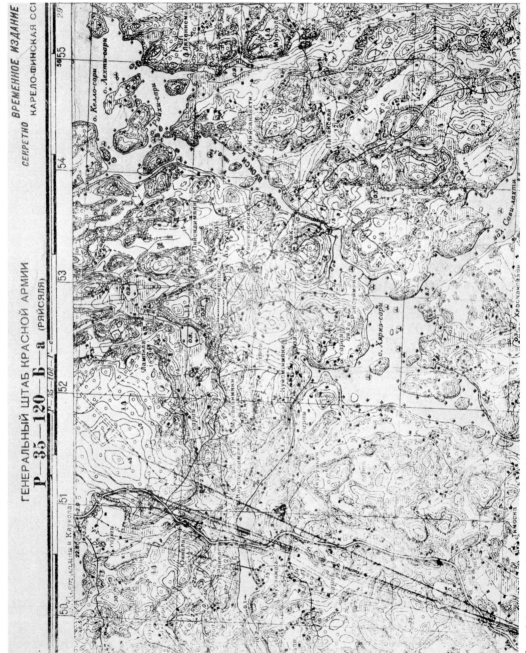

FIG. 4.1.   Map of part of the 'Karelian-Finnish Soviet Socialist Republic', found on the body of a Soviet Artillery officer, 1940. Before he was killed, he had begun to mark the bearings of reference points from his observation post south of Lake Korpi'lakhti. The map is very good, 1/25,000 scale, and is classified 'secret'. The other writing says 'General Staff of the Red Army', and 'Temporary edition'.

4.

Artillery in Modern War

'Modern battle is incredibly dynamic and fast moving. Violent and unexpected changes in the situation, the low vulnerability of armoured, highly mobile targets which are becoming more and more numerous, create new and ever more complex tasks for artillerymen. In these conditions, a high speed offensive or an effective defence is unthinkable without reliable *destruction of the enemy by fire*. To achieve this, artillery sub-units must be taught to bring down accurate, shattering fire, day and night, in any terrain and in any weather...'

Voyenny Vestnik, Leader, November 1981

The Expanding Battlefield

During this century Soviet Military Art has tended to develop as a plant grows; gradually and steadily. There are, however, three noticeable rings on the tree: the theoretical advances of Frunze and Triandafillov in the 1920s and 30s; the writings of Sokolovskiy and others on nuclear war in the 1960s, and the conceptual jump of the early 1980s associated with the name of the former Chief of the General Staff, Marshal Ogarkov. In each of these the area over which operations were envisaged was substantially increased: the time allowed was substantially shortened, and command focussed at a higher level. In the first, emphasis shifted to the Front, or Group of armies as the crucial level, after experience in having to manipulate multiple armies in the Russo-Japanese War and World War I. The second wrestled with the issues posed by the rocket and nuclear weapon and the Revolution in Military Affairs which they had created. The third marks a return, perhaps, to the main stream of Military Art, with the aim of winning a swift campaign in a major *Theatre of War* using, if possible, entirely conventional means, and a further extension of the scope of operations from the Front to the *Theatre of Military Operations*, and the possibility of defeating European NATO in a single Theatre Strategic Operation. Whereas a Front moved across a span 250 kilometres wide and penetrated perhaps 600 kilometres before pausing, a Theatre Strategic Operation might cover an area equivalent to six Fronts, 750 kilometres wide and 1200 deep. A normal Front pattern of operations, based on the most favourable Great Patriotic War conditions, might be a 600 kilometre advance in 12 days, a six day pause, and then another 600 kilometres in 12 days. A Theatre Strategic Operation might aim to cover the full 1200 kilometres in 22 days, without halt. While the Front commander clearly loses some of his authority to the TVD commander, who would control the single Strategic Operation in his theatre, a new level of command has also been created above that, the Theatre of War, embracing perhaps an entire hemisphere and extending into cosmic space. The Theatre Strategic Operation centred on the TVD, however, provides the framework for the proposed employment of artillery and rocket forces into the twenty-first century.

Although Soviet Military Doctrine in the 1960s decreed that any future war between the Warsaw Pact and NATO (or China) would most likely begin with massive nuclear missile strikes and be conducted under the constant influence of nuclear weapons, the Soviet Ground Forces did maintain the ability to conduct large operations using purely conventional means. After about 1970 there was a shift in doctrine which admitted that nuclear weapons might not be used initially, although it was still thought that they would eventually be used and would remain the decisive factor in any conflict. By the end of the 1970s the Soviets were clearly developing the ability to bring about the collapse of NATO defence on the European mainland and the conclusion of a European war using conventional (probably including chemical) weapons only. Of course, the presence of nuclear weapons in the TVD would influence the conduct of those operations. To prevent conflict going nuclear, conventional victory must be very swift indeed. It can be argued that the one thing likely to make NATO go nuclear would be rapid and spectacular advances by Warsaw Pact manoeuvre forces. However, that is clearly not the way the Russians and their allies see it. If penetration was really quick, and drove far enough into NATO territory to fragment the various countries and polarise their interests, a decision to use nuclear weapons would come too late to have any purpose. The Russians would hope to occupy key political and economic centres, paralysing political control, and to get themselves tight up against NATO forces and centres of population, thus making it impossible for NATO to use nuclear weapons against them without killing more of their own people. They would also aim to destroy or paralyse NATO's tactical nuclear weapons themselves, which tend to be located further back in the NATO area. All this requires the Russians to get very deep into NATO territory very quickly, and shift the centre of gravity of the conflict to the enemy rear.

The overall Theatre Strategic Operation would comprise four overlapping and concurrent Strategic Operations: an Air Operation, an Anti-Air Operation, a Theatre Land Operation and a Naval or Coastal Operation. The emphasis is on the interlinked nature of all these and of the use of different types of weaponry within them. Thus the Air Operation would use not only aircraft but also artillery and missiles to suppress enemy air defences and radars. This will be conducted under a single command and in accordance with a single concept and plan, to destroy enemy air and missile forces. Similarly, the anti-air operation uses missile troops and artillery, for example, to suppress NATO forward airfields as well as anti-aircraft artillery and missiles and air defence aircraft to engage them when airborne. The creation of a single *Air Defence Service* (see Chapter Two) embracing all air defence assets, tactical, operational and strategic throughout the whole depth of any Theatre of Operations is probably connected with this requirement.[1]

In connection with expanding operational concepts, a new phase of artillery and air activity has been added to the traditional three phases which have characterised Russian artillery and, later, air support since the last century. There are now four phases, of which the first is new. The new phase relates to covering the move forward for a breakthrough, and is thus rather distinct from the second and third which relate to the attack alone. The last phase is different again, and merges with the extension of the battle into the enemy operational depth:

concept is not really new, the scope might be new but concept used in WW I

Pre-emptive
    New phase 1: Fire *protection* of forces moving up for the attack.

The breakthrough
    Phase 2: Fire *preparation* of the attack, commencing twenty to thirty minutes before the FLOT is reached,
    Phase 3: Fire *support* of the attack, as the enemy positions are penetrated, usually with a moving curtain of fire,

The breakout
    Phase 4: Fire *accompaniment* of the battle in the enemy tactical depth, leading to the battle in the enemy *deep rear*.

The new first phase was initially mentioned in the context of amphibious landings and *Operational Manoeuvre Groups* (OMGs) (see below), but is clearly acknowledged as a new phase in the definitive 1984 edition of Reznichenko's *Tactics*. It involves suppressing those enemy systems which are capable of conducting Deep Battle against Soviet forces before the latter have made contact, and blinding the enemy as to Soviet movements. Its introduction is uncannily timely, as striking at the Soviet follow on forces and second echelon as they move up is the main innovation in the 1982 version of the United States manual *FM-100-5*, and had been much discussed in the West's open military press during 1981. It is unlikely to be coincidence that a new fire protection phase was first openly mooted by a Polish Colonel in 1982. Generally speaking, the progression is from carefully pre-planned fire to fluid and flexible artillery combat.[2]

Nuclear, Biological and Chemical Conditions

Although the grand design described above would ideally be executed without the use of nuclear weapons, the threat of their use remains a constant and all-pervading factor in any Soviet planning at any level. This involves defensive measures, massive and terrible retribution if nuclear weapons were to be used against Soviet forces, and possibly a massive pre-emptive strike if hard information were received that NATO was about to go nuclear. Even if the Soviets regard the nuclear option as undesirable, the chemical one looks very attractive for them, not least because of NATO's lack of an equivalent. Although the Soviets obviously also continue to develop biological weapons, they are still so unreliable and capricious in their effects that they are hardly a rational option for the Soviet High Command and the slowness of their effects makes them even less suitable as a battlefield system. They will therefore not be considered further. The Soviets talk about *Defence against weapons of mass destruction*, in their orders, by which they usually mean nuclear, chemical and incendiary weapons. The effects of these highly potent weapons is inextricably entwined with the environment as a whole: there would be 'vast zones of contamination, destruction, fires and floods'. In the artillery context, Colonel Litvinov confirmed in 1984 that artillerymen might have to fight under conditions of 'radio interference, massive destruction and conflagrations in huge zones of contamination'. In an exercise setting, for example, even a straightforward conventional action by an artillery battalion (see below) takes place when the enemy *have already used* nuclear, chemical and incendiary weapons and a 10 kilometre section of the route is contaminated with radiation.[3] It is clear that the Soviet artillery and rocket troops are well prepared for warfare in chemical and nuclear conditions should it be necessary.

We have seen how Soviet artillerymen played the key role in the development of nuclear tipped missiles of all types (see Chapter Three). In response to NATO's adoption of the idea of 'flexible response' the Soviets sought more flexible options at all levels, and this included firing small-yield weapons from tube artillery. One of the factors influencing Soviet thinking was technological progress which made it possible to manufacture nuclear shells of smaller size. However, the Soviets continued to assign atomic artillery to very limited and particular roles, in contradistinction to NATO's philosophy. The Soviets recognised the difficulties and dangers of concentrating conventional artillery in the face of an opponent who might go nuclear at any stage (so Doctrine taught). Some form of short range battlefield nuclear weapon bridging the gap between conventional artillery and large nuclear tipped missiles (even the short range FROG) might be appropriate. Articles published in 1972 and 1973 suggested renewed Soviet interest in atomic cannon, especially for use against enemy nuclear capable artillery. This accounts for the small number of Soviet atomic artillery systems; only one fifth as many systems as NATO in Europe. In 1975, Marshal Peredel'skiy suggested a set of specialised missions for Soviet atomic artillery: firstly, counter-battery operations against enemy atomic artillery and tactical missiles; second, strikes on the forward edge of enemy positions (that is, very close to Soviet troops), to facilitate breakthrough operations; thirdly, the destruction of surrounded enemy forces.

The comparatively few atomic cannon available to the Soviets reflect this specialised role. Another piece of evidence supporting this view is the similarity between the tasks of atomic artillery, above, and the roles of the *Artillery Reserve of the Supreme High Command* (*RVGK*) in the Great Patriotic War. *RVGK* units were attached to critical Fronts. In any future European war, atomic artillery might be assigned where the achievement of a breakthrough (or the breaking up of a large attacking concentration, for that matter) was critical, where the ability of massed conventional artillery to achieve this was in doubt, or where such a concentration might be nuked by NATO.

Another reason for increased interest in atomic artillery, which chronology certainly supports, may have been concern about China. Sino-Soviet tensions were very prominent in the late 1960s. Atomic artillery would help overcome the Chinese Army's numerical superiority. The Chinese have also evinced a particular aptitude for constructing robust fortifications (especially in Korea). The ability of atomic cannon to deliver nuclear weapons with great accuracy makes them particularly useful against deep, hardened installations.

There is a tendency in Western circles to stress the nuclear capabilities of Soviet tube artillery in order to make a political point. As we have seen, the new 203 mm self-propelled gun, 240 mm mortar and possibly the 152 mm 2S5 are believed to be nuclear capable. However, the Soviets do not envisage deploying nuclear artillery as a mirror image of NATO practice. Tactical rockets, also under the command of the Soviet Ground Forces' Artillery and Rocket Troops, remain the principal means of delivering nuclear weapons, and the main significance of tube artillery and multiple rocket launchers remains their ability to deliver conventional and chemical ordnance.

The SS-21 and SS-23, particularly, are ideal battlefield nuclear weapons, because of their range combined with relative invulnerability and manoeuvrability. The SS-23 is reported to have a range of 500 kilometres and to be deployed at Front and, possibly, Army level. The Soviets are no more likely to allow an Army commander the right to decide whether to go nuclear or not than any other state: probably less so. Any decision to use nuclear weapons would in the first instance be taken at the very highest level. However, the presence of these highly mobile systems capable of being controlled further down the chain of command does give the Soviet military great redundancy and resilience in the event of an all out nuclear conflict. Nevertheless, why is it thought better to have these systems controlled by the Army, rather than the strategic rocket forces, and does an Army or Front commander need systems like SS-23 and SS-22 with 500 or 885 kilometre range respectively? Once again, common sense indicates that these systems may have more of a conventional role than Western propagandists tend to admit.

This brings us to chemical ammunition for artillery and rockets. Western commentary shies away from this, partly no doubt because the West has no real retaliatory capability. Chemical weapons have also been used on a large scale on the battlefield, unlike nuclear ones, whether in the Great War or very recently in the Iran-Iraq conflict. The Soviet army has always had a large chemical arsenal, although they were not, perhaps surprisingly, deployed in the last war. The Soviets know that NATO's ability to wage chemical warfare is very limited, and this is the area where the Soviet Army has its greatest advantage. At the moment, NATO's only deterrent to the large scale use of chemical weapons by the Soviets would be the threat of nuclear retaliation. However, the Soviets probably do not believe that NATO would really respond in this way. It would be seen as a significant (perhaps the most significant) jump on the ladder of escalation, as nuclear weapons would be used in response to a lower form of killing. The Soviets might well play their unique chemical card in order to accelerate their advance. Soviet writings on the subject are couched in terms which suggest that in a future war against NATO (or China) chemical weapons could well be used. In Soviet terminology, chemical weapons are '*weapons of mass destruction*', the same term as that applied to nuclear weapons. However, the Soviets probably regard chemical weapons as being part of their arsenal for 'conventional' war.

The principal means of delivering chemical munitions are artillery (with more than usual emphasis on multiple rocket launchers) and air. All artillery weapons over 100 mm calibre are capable of firing chemical ammunition. The most suitable pieces of tube artillery are the M-46 with its 27 kilometre range, the 2S5 and its towed version with ranges in the order of 28 kilometres, and the 2S3 with its shorter range of 24 kilometres. Only about 5 per cent of the weight of a 'chemical' shell is actually chemical filling: it also contains a good deal of explosive to make it burst and give some explosive effect (see Chapter Three). This is a drawback in using tube artillery to deliver chemical. Even so, a salvo from a battalion of 152 mm weapons followed by a minute's intense fire could deliver in excess of 270 kilogrammes of chemical with 18 pieces or, with eight gun batteries, 360 kilogrammes from 24 pieces. This could be a significant quantity of chemical. Mortar bombs have a higher payload; ten per cent of their weight is chemical. These also have the advantage that they do not burrow so deeply into the ground as shells, so less of the chemical is lost.

The ideal artillery system for delivering chemical munitions is the multiple rocket launcher. About 15 per cent of the weight of rocket warheads is chemical agent, and large numbers of rounds can be delivered in a matter of seconds. This enables a critical concentration to be built up very quickly. For longer range tasks, the large tactical rockets are good chemical delivery systems: the chemical warhead of the FROG-7 rocket contains about 220 kilogrammes of agent. The effectiveness of chemical warheads increases logarithmically with the calibre, and this is one argument in favour of the BM-27, with its large calibre rockets.

The effects of chemical weapons are difficult to assess and depend very much on, for example, weather. However, if surprise is achieved and the right agent used 10 to 30 per cent casualties could be inflicted even on well-equipped troops. Although this level of casualties would not necessarily render a NATO unit ineffective, it would be a major blow and render them more susceptible to an ensuing bombardment with high-explosive and fragmentation rounds.

Chemical munitions could be used against airfields in conjunction with conventional attacks, hindering repair work and complicating the operation of aircraft. Chemical rounds might also be mixed with high explosive for counter-battery missions. This would be particularly effective against towed artillery, but would also complicate the work of self-propelled batteries, forcing guns and command posts to operate closed down and ensuring that any penetration of their armour would probably be fatal for the crew.

The longest range weapon available to Soviet gunners, the SS-22 is not known to have a chemical warhead, but the SS-23 probably does, and fired from just inside East Germany with its 500 kilometre range could saturate areas such as the Channel ports with persistent chemical agents, interrupting NATO's reinforcement plans very severely. Thus, chemical weapons in the hands of Soviet gunners could not only influence the *battle* and *operation*, but *strategy* as well.[4]

The Classification of Soviet Firepower

Fire is the decisive factor in achieving victory over the enemy. Concepts of fire are developing in parallel with the expanding battlefield. The Soviets classify firepower in a variety of ways in deciding what they need and how to use it. Let us therefore look at the various ways in which they classify and organise it before going on to see how it would actually be used in practice. Some of these refer exclusively to conventional fire: others can embrace nuclear and chemical as well.

General Notions of Firepower

Fire destruction is the general term used by the Russians to refer to the action of all fire weapons, including tank armament and air as well as artillery and rocket forces. As noted, the artillery and rocket troops provide 80 per cent of the Ground Forces' firepower. *Fire destruction* is in part analogous to our term fire support, but the Russian word means, literally, paralysis or stroke (in the medical sense). It is therefore a much more positive and aggressive belief in the killing and stunning power of all fire weapons. A recent definitive Soviet manual described the aim of fire destruction as 'inflicting such damage on the enemy, that he is incapable of making organised resistance'. The crushing effect of artillery fire on morale is therefore as much a part of fire destruction as its physical effect on people, in destroying equipment, cutting communications and blinding target acquisition.

Integrated Fire Destruction of the Enemy is the philosophy of integrating the fire effect of all weapons, including tube artillery, multiple rocket launchers and operational-tactical missiles to achieve maximum overall efficiency, exemplified in the air and anti-air operations. This is not just a loose phrase but refers to a specific concept which was first enunciated in Polish and Russian sources in 1982. The use of *integrated* is new and significant.[5] The development of the high speed offensive and more flexible tactics have made it very difficult for the artillery to cope with fire support tasks alone. This is because of the difficulty of target acquisition at ranges over about 10 kilometres, or at any range once battle is joined, the enormous ammunition requirements to guarantee effective suppression by indirect fire (see norms, below) and the reduced time available to move and shoot. The Russians and their allies have therefore put much more stress on direct fire from aircraft and particularly the armed helicopter. Control of helicopters has been decentralised; each motor rifle division now has a helicopter squadron of its own and forward air controllers (FACs) are provided more frequently, sometimes down to battalion level. They are generally co-located with the artillery commander. One example of integrated fire destruction might be the use of artillery and missiles to neutralise enemy anti-aircraft weapons while using armed helicopters to attack enemy artillery positions, which are difficult for Soviet artillery to locate and damage. This is shown clearly in Figures 4.2 and 4.3, which is based on a Soviet article of May, 1980. The article describes how it had become standard practice for artillery to switch fire to a safe area before helicopters overflew the combat zone, or to limit its fire to targets on the flanks of the helicopters' sectors. This meant that neither artillery nor helicopters could utilise their full potential, and the author suggested a solution using details of trajectories taken from a recent exercise.

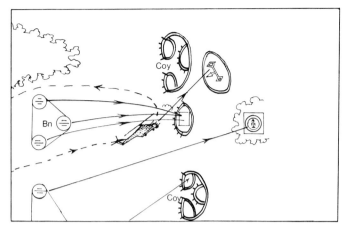

Fig. 4.2.   Hind assault helicopters engaging armoured forces with lateral separation of artillery fire and helicopters. This is an example of Integrated Fire Destruction of the Enemy: artillery is used against softer targets such as the infantry companies and anti-aircraft weapon in the forest, while the direct fire helicopters take on the tanks. (Source: Dabolin's article of May, 1980).

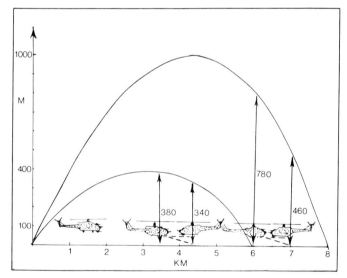

Fig. 4.3.   Vertical separation of artillery fire and helicopters. Artillery fires on targets at 6000 metres range while helicopters take on those at 4500: in the second example, artillery fires on those at 8000 while the helicopters attack those at 7000. (Source: Dabolin's article of May, 1980).

The Fire Strike is the last new concept. In Russian as in English the word strike has been used until recently to refer to a nuclear blow. Its application to powerful, paralysing blows by artillery, rockets and air clearly reflects the Soviets' intention to substitute conventional for nuclear fire if possible. It is fully consistent with new technology which is becoming available, such as the improved conventional munition (see Chapter Three) and laser designation and guidance systems, which enable conventional munitions to be delivered with sufficient accuracy or have such wide area coverage that they can substitute for nuclear. It also implies a massive, surgical strike to excise one element of the enemy defence, like that carried out by 1 Ukrainian Front's artillery in the Vistula Oder operation (see Chapter Three). When the term first appeared, it referred only to a new type of artillery fire support, not that dissimilar to the existing form of *concentrated fire*. However, in 1980 Marshal Peredel'skiy weighed in and said that there was no need for a new type of fire in that context, and that fire strike should be used to refer to the operational level employment of artillery. The definitive comment appeared in the Soviet Army newspaper *Red Star* in 1982. The combat potential of artillery and rocket forces was summarised in terms of fire strikes and that of tank and motor rifle troops as troop strikes. A fire strike might be pre-emptive, meeting or retaliatory, and is clearly a very large, operational level act, but one which, by definition, uses conventional weapons only.[6]

How Firepower is Allocated

As we have seen in Chapter One, the Soviets would allocate artillery from higher levels to lower ones in accordance with the opposition, task, terrain, logistic considerations and a host of other imponderables. Soviet artillery and rocket forces are classified in four ways in relation to the unit or formation they are helping:

Organic artillery is very much a part of the all-arms unit and, in the case of motor rifle units wears its distinctive colour (see Chapter Two).

Supporting artillery (usually a battalion) remains under the command of the *senior artillery commander* of the all-arms regiment or division, but at certain stages in the fight carries out fire missions laid down by the commander of the all-arms battalion or regiment which it is supporting.

Allocated artillery is placed under full command of the all-arms unit or sub-unit commander and carries out fire missions determined by him. However, in critical circumstances, such as repelling a determined counter-attack by the enemy, allocated artillery may revert to the control of the senior artillery commander.

Artillery under Command remains fully subordinated to the commander of the artillery group of the regiment, division or higher formation to which it belongs although it conducts fire missions 'in the interests of' the lower formation, unit or sub-unit to which it is assigned.

Classification by Strength and Intensity

Artillery and rocket fire, however allocated, is also classified according to its strength:

Fire for annihilation destroys the enemy's combat capability completely and requires a kill probability of 70 to 90 per cent, or a 50 or 60 per cent probability of destroying all of a group of targets.

Fire for demolition involves the physical destruction of installations or works.

Fire for suppression temporarily removes the enemy's ability to fight and inhibits his ability manoeuvre, and requires 30 per cent destruction of targets.

Harassing fire requires relatively modest expenditure of ammunition and effort, but is demoralising, keeps the enemy from concentrating on the task in hand and forces him to take counter-measures which consume time and effort.

The first three types of fire are referred to collectively as *destruction* (see above).

The degree of destruction which is required often influences the decision on shell expenditure, but equally often whether a target is annihilated or merely suppressed will depend on the amount of ammunition available and the time in which to fire it. Because the terms are universally understood, they are a useful form of shorthand for the Soviet artillery commander giving orders, as we shall see in the example of a battalion supporting an attack. Soviet officers have tables of the *norms* necessary to achieve a given level of damage. One of the main problems which the Soviet artillery faces is the need for what it calls *distsiplina* which does not mean discipline in the English sense so much as the all-arms commander being able to rely on the fact that if he says something should be done, it will be. He does not want to worry about whether the artillery will be able to achieve its assigned task: he must be able to rely on it totally. Norms practically guarantee the destruction of a target of a given size at a given range with a given type of weapon. The norms necessary to destroy unobserved targets are much higher than for those where observation is possible. This is particularly important where observation is not possible, as in a counter-battery mission. Examples of the norms are given in the box, which also shows how they are calculated. They take account of two sets of errors: the accuracy with which the locations of the guns and targets can be plotted, and the variation in shell distribution inherent in the guns. The system is highly mechanistic, but the Soviets place great emphasis on it and it works. In battle, of course, it is not always possible to fire the full norm before the all-arms force reaches the target or the situation changes, and Soviet officers often have to be satisfied with firing 70 or 80 per cent of the norm or even only half.[7]

Death by Numbers

How norms are calculated

The expenditure of shells, necessary for the destruction of grouped targets, depends on the task [that is, the degree of destruction required], the dimensions of the grouped target (defensive position), the accuracy of the means of establishing the co-ordinates and the destructive action of the shells. The analytical dependence . . . is expressed by the following formula:

$$N = k \frac{Ed'_0 \, En'_0}{Sp^t} \qquad\qquad \text{[formula 1.]}$$

Where: k — is the coefficient, relating to the task, that is the mathematical probability relating to the percentage of targets destroyed [see Appendix 1]
Appendix 1:

Mathematical probability	20	25	30	35	40	45	50	55	60
Value of k	0.61	0.71	0.81	0.90	1.01	1.12	1.23	1.35	1.48

Where: Ed'_0 and En'_0 are the average errors of the means for establishing the *settings for firing* and the dimensions of grouped targets (defensive position) in breadth and depth. S_p is the area of the zone of destruction of the shot, that is, its destructive action against *personnel*

t is the coefficient linking the distribution of shells and their destructive action; for high explosive-fragmentation and fragmentation fire by ground artillery the value of t is very close to unity and can be dropped without significant error, that is, taken equal to one.
The average errors Ed'_0 and En'_0 are calculated according to the formula:

$$Ed'_0 = Ed_0 \sqrt{1 + 0.152 \left(\frac{0.5 \, G_{ts}}{Ed_0}\right)^2} \qquad\qquad \text{[formula 2]}$$

$$En'_0 = En_0 \sqrt{1 + 0.152 \left(\frac{0.5 \, F_{ts}}{En_0}\right)^2} \qquad\qquad \text{[formula 3]}$$

Where Ed_0 and En_0 are the average errors of range and direction of the means for setting the gun for Fire For Effect and depending on the number of batteries and guns involved. G_{ts} and F_{ts} are the measurements of the grouped targets (of a defensive position), both depth and breadth.
For ease of calculating Ed'_0 and En'_0 a table has been drawn up (Appendix 2) which gives the depth of the target G_{ts} (Breadth F_{ts}) expressed as Ed_0 (En_0);

The use of this table can be seen in the following example:
Establish the value of Ed_0 and En_0 for the fire of a *battalion* of 122 mm howitzers firing on a platoon defensive position of dimensions 300 m (breadth) by 200 m (depth). Range 12 km. All preparations have been completed.
Solution. 1. We express the depth and breadth of the defensive position in measurements corresponding to Ed_0 and En_0.

Appendix 2.   Table for establishing Ed$'_0$ and En$'_0$ according to known measurements of group targets . . . for depth G$_{ts}$ and breadth F$_{ts}$ and the values of the average errors Ed$_0$ and En$_0$.

G$_{ts}$ into Ed$_0$ (F$_{ts}$ into En$_0$)	Ed$'_0$ into Ed$'_0$ (En$_0$ into En$_0$)	G$_{ts}$ into Ed$_0$ (F$_{ts}$ into En$_0$)	Ed$'_0$ into Ed$'_0$ (En$_0$ into En$_0$)	G$_{ts}$ into Ed$_0$ (F$_{ts}$ into En$_0$)	Ed$'_0$ into Ed$'_0$ (En$_0$ into En$_0$)
0.0	1.000	5.0	1.40	16.0	3.28
0.4	1.005	6.0	1.54	17.0	3.46
0.8	1.015	7.0	1.70	18.0	3.65
1.2	1.028	8.0	1.86	19.0	3.86
1.6	1.048	9.0	2.02	20.0	4.03
2.0	1.075	10.0	2.19	22.0	4.41
2.4	1.105	11.0	2.36	24.0	4.79
2.8	1.140	12.0	2.55	26.0	5.17
3.2	1.180	13.0	2.73	28.0	5.56
3.6	1.224	14.0	2.91	30.0	5.94
4.0	1.270	15.0	3.09	35.0	6.90
				40.0	8.15
				50.0	10.00

$$G_{ts}:Ed_0 = 200:81 = 2.5 \text{ or } G_{ts} = 2.5 \text{ Ed}_0$$

$$F_{ts}:En_0 = 300:81 = 6.5 \text{ or } F_{ts} = 6.5 \text{ En}_0$$

2. From the table for establishing Ed$'_0$ and En$'_0$, (Appendix 2), according to the values G$_{ts}$ = 2.5 Ed$_0$, F$_{ts}$ = 6.5 En$_0$, by means of interpolation [2.5 comes between 2.4 and 2.8, etc. — alternatively use the formulae 2 and 3 above], we find that Ed$'_0$ = 1.11 Ed$_0$ and En$'_0$ = 1.62 En$_0$. These values expressed in metres are Ed$'_0$ = 90 m, En$'_0$ = 74.5 m.

Having learned how to calculate the errors, it is possible to put all the calculations together and work out the expenditure of shell necessary to fulfil a given task. The method for doing this is shown in the example below. '. . . calculate the required expenditure of shell for the *suppression* of a platoon position, hastily occupied [i.e., no overhead protection] for a *battalion* of 122 mm howitzers . . . preparations are complete. [This probably means that the guns have been surveyed in with a high degree of precision and that they have been put on line with the director rather than hastily, with a compass]. Range, 4 km, required degree of *suppression* 30 per cent. Trenches and dugouts without overhead protection. (S$_p$ = 300 m). Dimensions of the defended position F$_{ts}$ = 300 m, G$_{ts}$ = 200 m. Correction of fire during the mission does *not* take place.

Soviet calculations usually give the value V$_d$ and V$_b$ to 'consistency' errors of range and traverse (line) respectively 'Accuracy' errors are given values E$_d$ and E$_n$. The types of error are shown in the diagram below.
Where:
x$_p$ and z$_p$ are accuracy errors for range and line.
x$_{ri}$ and z$_{ri}$ are consistency errors (errors of dispersal).
x$_i$ and z$_i$ are variance in point of impact of 1 shell from the target for range and line.
S$_0$ is the centre of dispersal of the shells
S$_1$, S$_2$, . . . are the points of impact of the shells for the first, second and third shots.

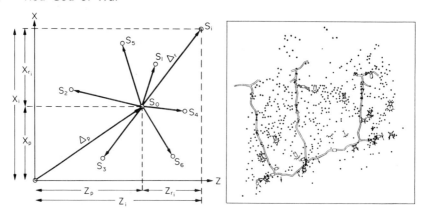

FIG. 4.4.   Errors affecting fall of shot and distribution of craters for fire for the destruction of an observed platoon position by a battalion of 122 mm howitzers bringing fire on groups of targets.

Type of target	Qty	Destroyed From covered position	By direct fire	% destruction
Tanks	2	1	1	100
APCs	1	1	—	100
ATGM launchers	4	1	1	50
Covered fire points	3	—	2	67
Grenade launchers and MGs	8	3	—	38
Dummy riflemen	55	17	—	30

Solution:

1. From the table of average errors for conducting the fire of a *battalion* (Appendix 3), we find that for fire at a range of 4000 m the average errors equal $Ed_0 = 41$ m, $En_0 = 34$ m.

Appendix 3.

Characteristics of two sets of errors (in metres) for fire brought down on a target by the first and third batteries, all preparations complete.

Range, km.	Errors of Accuracy (repeating errors)					Errors of Consistency (Non-repeating)			
	For the fire of one bty		For the fire of 3 btys.			For the fire of one bty.		For the fire of 3 btys.	
	Ed_{01}	En_{01}	Ed_{03}	En_{03}		Vd_{01}	Vb_{01}	Vd_{03}	Vb_{03}
				122 mm howitzer					
4	50	40	42	34		25	4	37	20
6	57	41	51	35		25	5	37	21
8	70	43	64	38		26	7	37	23
10	78	48	72	42		31	8	43	24
12	88	52	81	46		33	9	48	26
14	106	60	99	54		35	11	52	28

152 mm howitzer and gun-howitzer

4	51	40	43	34	22	3	35	20
6	58	41	52	35	25	4	37	21
8	68	42	62	36	28	6	40	22
10	74	45	67	39	38	7	49	24
12	87	48	75	42	52	8	68	25
14	101	53	89	47	56	10	73	28
16	118	60	106	54	66	12	84	30

160 mm mortar

4	43	28	40	26	19	13	24	16
6	56	33	53	31	29	17	34	20
8	71	34	68	32	36	18	42	21

2. We determine the average errors Ed'_0 and En'_0, taking into account the errors of accuracy ('preparation') and the dimensions of the defensive position. For this we take the breadth and depth of the defensive position as values corresponding to Ed_0 and En_0;

G_{ts} = 200:41 m = 4.9 Ed_0 and F_{ts} = 300:34 = 8.8 En_0 Then, from the table for establishing Ed'_0 and En'_0 (Appendix 2), G_{ts} = 5Ed_0 and F_{ts} = 8.8 En_0, we find that Ed'_0 = 1.40 Ed_0 or Ed'_0 = 57.4 and En'_0 = 1.99 En_0 = 67.7 m.

3. According to formula 1 we work out the expenditure of shells N, which is necessary for the destruction of a defensive position with a desired degree of destruction of 30 per cent (from Appendix 1, if M = 30 per cent, then k = 8.37.)

'In the conditions used in the previous example calculate the required expenditure of shells for the suppression of a platoon defensive position if Fire For Effect is conducted with the division of the batteries' fire into groups of targets; for the first and second batteries, on the forward edge of every target, the dimensions F_{ts} = 150 m and G_{ts} = 50 m, for the third battery, on the rear of the defensive position, the dimensions are F_{ts} = 200 m and G_{ts} = 100 m . . .'

[The expenditure of shells is calculated as 697 shells for the first and second batteries and 823 for the third — 2217 in all.]

With Observation and Adjustment

'. . . In the conditions of the previous example, determine the required expenditure of shell for suppression of a platoon defensive position, if simultaneously with the dividing up of the batteries' fire according to groups of targets [i.e. each battery has a separate target to fire at], adjustment takes place with observation of shell bursts and with the aid of the range finder.

1. From the table we find that the average errors of preparation (accuracy) in this case are Ed = 1.2 Vd and En = 0.01. Therefore, with fire at a range of 4000 metres Vd = 17 m then Ed = 20 m, En = 40 m.

2. With the aid of Appendix 2 we calculate the average error $E'd$ and $E'n$
— for the first and second batteries G_{ts} = 50 ÷ 20 = 2.5 Ed, we find that $E'd$ = 1.11 Ed = 22.2 m, and for F_{ts} = 150 ÷ 4 = 37.5 En, we find that En' = 7.2 En = 28.8 m.

— for the third battery G_{ts} = 100 ÷ 20 = 5 Ed, we find $E'd$ = 1.4 Ed = 28 m and F_{ts} = 200 ÷ 4 = 50 En, we find $E'n$ = 10 En = 40 m.

3. According to formula 1, N = k (Ed'_0 En'_0) /Sp_t, we calculate the required expenditure of shells for the destruction of each of the groups of targets

— for batteries one and two $N_{1,2}$ = 8.37 $\dfrac{22.2 \times 28.8}{30.1}$ = 179 shells

— for battery three $N_3 = 8.37 \dfrac{28.40}{30.1} = 312$ shells.

The overall expenditure of shells for the suppression of the platoon defensive position is $N = 2N_{1,2} + N_3 = 2 \times 179 + 312 = 670$ shells, that is three times *less* than in the previous example where adjustment was not carried out.'

From the calculations, norms can be obtained which will practically guarantee the destruction of any target if the rules are followed. The norms are initially calculated with great precision, for example;

Expenditure of shells per hectare of defensive position when firing with a *divizion* of 152 mm gun-howitzers (all preparations complete).

Dimensions of defensive position $F_{ts} \times G_{ts}$	Expenditure of shells for fire at a given range, km.			
	6	8	10	12
200×200	165	188	208	230
200×300	132	146	159	173
300×200	143	164	166	197
400×200	135	152	165	183
200×400	118	129	138	147
300×300	115	126	136	148
Average Value	135	151	162	180
Norm	150	150	150	180

These tables are too complicated for use in the field and a quick and easy guide is extracted from them. The figure of 180 appears as one entry in the summary table below:

Working norms for suppression of a battery of towed guns, ranges up to 10 km.

	Rifled weapons			Mortars			Rocket Launchers	
Calibre, mm	122	130	152	120	160	240	Medium	Heavy
No. of rounds	220	200	180	200	120	100	400	170

Working norms for suppression of a battery of SP guns, ranges up to 10 km.

	Rifled weapons			Mortars			Rocket Launchers	
Calibre, mm	122	130	152	120	160	240	Medium	Heavy
No. of rounds	380	260	290	300	290	175	440	210

Roughly 50 per cent more ammunition is required, therefore, when engaging an armoured battery.

Classification by Type of Target and the Way Fire is Carried Out

Fire at an individual (point) target is carried out by individual batteries, platoons or even single guns against small, isolated targets such as, for example, a dug in observation post. It is often carried out by guns or even rocket launchers using *direct fire* (see below).

Barrage fire is a dense curtain of high explosive and steel either on a single line, known as a *stationary barrage (NZO)*, or on successive lines, a *mobile barrage (PZO)*. It is essentially the same as *a fire curtain (rolling barrage)* (see below), but is used defensively rather than offensively. The last line is usually about 400 metres from the troops being protected. Orders to move on to the next line usually take the form of predators' names: lion, tiger, and so on. The edges of a stationary barrage are marked with the names of trees.

Concentrated fire (SO) involves the concentration of several batteries or battalions on a single, usually very important target, such as a nuclear weapon or higher command post. The batteries can either fire *all as one* or different target co-ordinates can be given to each. Where all the artillery is firing on the same co-ordinates, it can be ordered to fire with sights adjusted by one stop either way, to achieve complete coverage of the target, thus:

Order of settings

Number of battery in battalion	1	2	3
1		− one stop	+ one stop
2			+ one stop	− one stop
3		+ one stop	− one stop

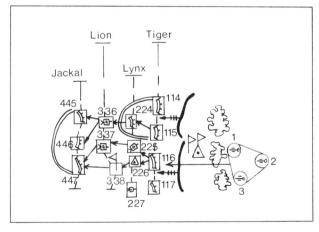

FIG. 4.5.   Successive concentrations of aimed fire (PSO). Triangle and dot with flag: artillery battalion command observation post. Plain flag: all-arms battalion commander.

Successive concentrations of aimed fire (PSO) are used to support forward moving motor rifle or tank troops in the offensive. They are delivered on the flanks of the advancing troops as well as in front. As with barrages, each line is referred to by a predator's name, but the individual targets are also plotted and numbered (see diagram).

A battalion's individual target should not be more than 9 hectares in area. As in the Great Patriotic War, the first line of targets is in fact engaged simultaneously with the last fire blow of the preparation phase. Because of the range of modern anti-tank systems, the Soviets advocate double or even treble concentrations, so that targets further back are suppressed simultaneously with those immediately in front of advancing troops.

A *fire curtain or rolling barrage (OV)* can be single or double, with between 300 and 1000 metres between main lines, with intermediate lines between 100 and 300 metres apart. The width that can be covered is determined by the number of pieces available, normally 25 metres for each piece over 100 mm calibre. As with successive concentrations, the signal to switch to the next line is given by the all-arms battalion or regimental commander (not usually by an artillery commander). The latter's responsibilities involve the planning of the barrage and any major changes necessary once the advance begins, although the scope for this is very limited. He is advised to avoid mixing types of shell or using different charges, which gives scope for confusion, and to watch the fall of shot intently at all times so that he can make any necessary corrections. The safety distances for unobserved targets are 500 metres for artillery firing at up to 10 kilometres range and 700 over that, and 1000 for rocket launchers. When observation is possible,

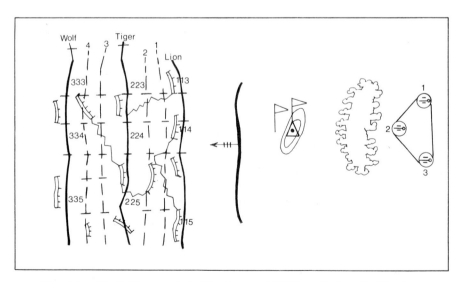

Fig. 4.6.   Single fire curtain (rolling barrage) (OV) symbols as for Fig. 4.5.

the distances are 400 metres for troops on foot, 300 for armoured personnel carriers and 200 for tanks.[8]

Different methods of Laying

Last but not least is the relatively straightforward technical difference between methods of laying (aiming the weapon). The Soviet definitions in fact highlight a key difference from Western attitudes and underline the emphasis which the Russians place on close artillery combat. They divide what Western gunners would call *direct fire* into two categories:

Direct fire, to a Soviet is when the gun or rocket launcher is layed vertically and horizontally by direct observation of the target, just like a rifle. There may be graticules on the sight to approximately compensate for range, but it is different from:

Semi-direct fire, where the piece is layed for line by direct observation but the range is calculated or estimated and the elevating drum is used to set the barrel at the correct elevation, as with *indirect fire*.[9] *Indirect fire* uses data computed from the map, as explained in Chapter One, when the layer cannot see the target.

All these different terms are used as circumstances require, and are not mutually exclusive. How they are used can be seen in the examples of artillery in action, but first we need to acquaint ourselves with the way artillery is organised and deployed.

The Artillery Battalion: the Main Fire Unit

Current Soviet estimates suggest that 55 to 60 per cent of fire missions in war would be battalion sized, 25 per cent by artillery groups of various sizes and 15 to 20 per cent by batteries. In 1980, a conference of artillery officers convened at Peredel'skiy's command to discuss the level at which fire control should normally be vested. Making the battalion the main fire unit had been under discussion for some time, for three main reasons. Firstly, the proliferation of armoured targets means that heavier concentrations of fire are needed to destroy them. Secondly, the fact that these targets are also highly mobile means that the necessary number of rounds has to be fired in less time, as modern mechanised forces can get out of the way extremely quickly once rounds start falling. This applies particularly to NATO self-propelled artillery which, in the Soviet view, can move out of one gun position and occupy another in a space of two or three minutes. It is therefore necessary to put down the norm of shell to disable it in this time. In fact, as the article pointed out, even a battalion could not do this, but would take five minutes to fire the norm. This may well be the reason why the Soviets have also adopted eight gun batteries at Army and Front level, for these are the artillery forces which would be used primarily for counter-battery fire. This increases the weight of a battalion salvo by the necessary amount.

The Russians' continued emphasis on multiple rocket launchers, which can bring down a huge weight of fire in one blow, also makes sense in this context. A third trend is the increase in the number of heavy weapons organic to motor rifle units, which enable them to deal with smaller targets themselves whereas in the last war these would have been suitable targets for an artillery battery. By making the battalion the main unit, but at the same time giving its commander more authority and perhaps independence, the Soviets have created a unit which achieves the right balance between power and manageability. The battalion is a self-contained entity which may be allocated to the support of one of the motor rifle or tank battalions of the first echelon or in other special circumstances (see below) or, alternatively, may be kept under the command of the all-arms division's artillery commander. A battalion commander is responsible both for fire planning and commanding his subunit and also for maintaining close co-operation with the all-arms commander.

A typical artillery battalion deployment is shown in Fig. 4.7. The main *Command Observation Post* (COP, or *KNP* in Russian) of 2 battalion, 5 artillery regiment is just on the reverse slope of the hill, with the three

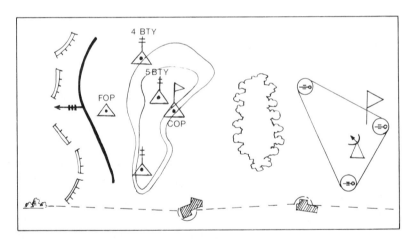

FIG. 4.7. Battalion deployment. 4 BTY = 4 Battery commmander's Command Observation Post, etc. BN COP = Battalion Command Observation Post (KNP). FOP = Forward Observation Post (PNP).

A radar. As this is located behind a feature and a wood, it is almost certainly an Artillery reconnaissance radar (SNAR), and not a ground surveillance radar; Battalion Fire Direction Centre (PUOD); All arms force, battalion strength (three cross bars).

battery commanders forming auxiliary observation posts. One of these may be a *flanking observation post (BNP)*, designed to keep an eye on terrain not visible from the COP. There is also a *forward observation post (PNP)*. The three batteries are deployed some way back. The flag indicates the *battalion fire direction centre*, where the battalion chief of staff is located. He effectively controls the battalion's fire as the battalion commander is forward at the COP, and is usually located near one of the battery positions, but up to 500 metres behind it. Considerations of dispersion to reduce the effects of counter-battery fire obviously militate against those of local defence. Similarly, the individual battery positions are commanded by the *Battery Senior Officers (Gun Position Officers) (SOBs)*. The radio links between the various commanders are shown in Fig. 4.8. Thus, the COP has links with the senior artillery commander, his own battalion chief-of-staff, the all-arms commander alongside whom he is fighting, his three battery commanders, and a helicopter controller. He does not have a link with the gun positions but the battalion chief-of-staff does. The chief-of-staff is also linked to the senior artillery commander, the meteorological station and (probably) logistic support units. Whenever possible, these links are duplicated by land line.

When it was first announced that the battalion was now officially the main fire unit, there was discussion about the battery commander's role. Although artillery battalion COPs had target acquisition radars, the battery commanders' limited assets — compass, binoculars and the mark one eyeball — meant that they were pretty redundant as far as controlling fire was concerned on the modern deep battlefield. It was suggested that they might therefore be brought back to the fire position where their experience and training would improve their batteries' accuracy and response time. This was also connected with the need to improve the batteries' chances of survival; in order to disperse the guns somewhat whilst retaining control, it was suggested that batteries be split into two sections deployed some distance apart, with the battery senior officer commanding one and the battery commander the other. However, at the end of 1982 a Lieutenant-Colonel Zirka argued persuasively that the battalion commander and a single reserve post could not effectively survey all the ground, especially given the proliferation of highly mobile targets, and that battery commanders were needed up front to ensure proper co-ordination with the all-arms forces. Judging by Peredel'skiy's book *The Artillery Battalion in Combat*, published in 1984, this view has prevailed.

Although there has been discussion about deploying batteries as two widely separated sections, most still seem to be deployed on one gun position. In the West, much play is made of the fact that batteries are often shown deployed in line, and that this makes them particularly vulnerable. Soviet analysis during the late 1970s did investigate the effect of deploying

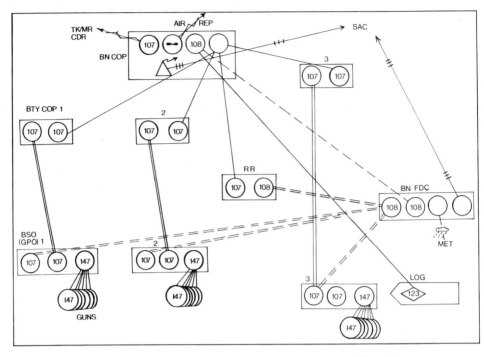

FIG. 4.8.   Artillery battalion radio net. SAC = Senior Artillery Commander; BSO (GPO) = Battery Senior Officer (Gun Position Officer/2 i/c); RR
= Radio Relay; LOG = Logistics organisation (fuel, ammunition). Battalion
Command Net. ——————— Numbers are types of radio. Battery Commander to Gun Position Officer Net (Battery Command Net)═══════. Fire
Direction   Centre   Net = = = = = = .   Senior   artillery   commander's
net —⧎———⧎—. Battalion Staff Net/Fireplanning Net – – – – – – –. Note: 1.
The battery commander apparently cannot talk to the supported arm
directly, and can only talk to the FDC via the Battalion commander. 2. The
battalion commander can only conduct fire missions via the FDC or the
battery commanders (not direct to the gun positions). 3. The air controller is
collocated with the artillery battalion commander, and is apparently not
connected directly to the supported arm. This may be to simplify the
diagram, but if it is as it appears it means that the artillery commander is
indeed the principal point of contact between the manoeuvre forces and all
other support. Source: Peredel'skiy, Artillery Battalion in Combat.

guns in different patterns, but in fact the final conclusion was that it is the
overall dispersion of the guns or rocket launchers rather than the shape that
matters, although non-linear deployments may be preferable in certain
circumstances. As Fig. 4.9 shows, the Soviets do use them, but they are not
convinced that they are a panacea. The Russians place great stress on
redundancy to help survival: alternative command posts should be
established in separate locations, and land-line duplicates radio links. In the
Great Patriotic War the katyusha rocket launchers were able to survive in
spite of their fragility and short range, because they could fire one salvo and

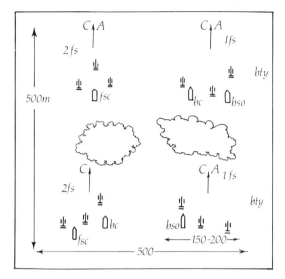

FIG. 4.9.   Deployment of batteries in split positions. Two possible variants are shown. CA, Centre of Arc; bc, Battery commander; bso, battery senior officer (gun position officer); fs, fire section; fsc, fire section commander; —≡⊣ heavy towed field gun; ⬭ command vehicle.

then move fast. The 2S5 is clearly a product of the same philosophy. Dispersing the guns or launchers not only reduces the chance of each taking a hit, but also makes it more difficult for enemy target acquisition to plot the centre of the battery. Finally, the move to eight-gun batteries at higher level may be partly to ensure some redundancy.[10]

The battalion is therefore the main building block of Soviet artillery formations. The way a battalion operates is cardinal to understanding the way Soviet artillery and rocket forces are manipulated in all phases and conditions of war, and we shall therefore look at an example here, showing how the various classifications of fire are used.

The battalion in question is supporting the attack of 2 battalion 10 motor rifle regiment, in an attack against a reinforced motor rifle company. It is probable that this occurs during the more fluid breakout phase, but the mode of operation is fairly representative of the artillery battalion commander's thought process.

'To *support* first echelon, 4 battery to the right of 4 motor rifle company, 6 battery, to the left of 5 company, 5 battery: *held under command*.

Fire missions by battery and order of execution:

First fire blow — *suppress* target 79 with three batteries firing *all as one*

Second fire blow — *suppress* target 112 with three batteries *all as one*

Third fire blow — *suppress* target 53 with three batteries *all as one* . . .

During the *support* of the attack 4 and 6 batteries will be used to *suppress* targets 112 and 224 *all as one*; after the fire blow on target 79, 5 battery to be ready to fire on newly discovered targets;

To support the committal to battle of 6 motor rifle company, the battalion will execute *concentrated fire* on target 43. . . .'

In concert with these orders, which are very lengthy and include logistics, nuclear and chemical defence and political work, the battalion commander would draw up a detailed fireplan as shown in the table below and in Fig. 4.10.

To the commander, 2 battalion 20 artillery regiment Regimental Artillery Group 10 in the Offensive. Command Post — Wood (3597). Map 1/50,000 scale, 1978 edition.

Action of all arms subunits	Phase of fire destruction	Battalion tasks and timings	Signal for opening fire	Target number of rounds
Moving out of department area. At H-47, begin to deploy into battalion columns		From H-47 to H-44 (3 min fire blow) suppress mortar platoon	'storm' red flares	no. 79 220
Successive deployment into company and platoon columns		From H-44 to H-31 (13 min fire blow) Suppress defended position on forward edge of enemy position	'lightning'	no. 112 440
	PREPARATION	From H-31 to H-17 (14 min fire blow) Suppress troops and equipment in depth of enemy defence	'hail'	no. 53 550
		From H-31 to H-37		no. 79 70
Deploys into battle order and moves to final assault position		Suppress mortar platoon. From H-17 to H-7 (10 min fire blow) Suppress defensive position on forward edge of enemy defence.	'blizzard'	no. 112 360
		From H-9 to H+3 (12 min fire blow) Suppress mortar platoon	'rain'	no. 79 160
At H-7 goes into the attack. At H+1 completes defeat of battalions in enemy first echelon	SUPPORT	Supports attack with PSO 1 line (3 min)	'lion'	no. 112 108
		2 line (6 min)	'tiger'	no. 224 96

Beats off brigade reserve counter-attack from crossroads, altitude 84.2	Suppresses enemy reserves moving up, beats off counter-attack. On call to fire on targets as follows	no. 54, 55, stationary barrage 'A'
	10 min fire blow to suppress enemy personnel and equipment. Suppress newly detected artillery and mortar batteries	no. 63, 108

ACCOMPANIMENT

Overrun brigade reserve positions from the march	Suppress personnel and equipment on brigade reserve position. On call.	no. 64
Beat off enemy brigade reserve counter-attack from lake Khor, altitude 96.7	Suppress enemy reserves moving up, beat off counter-attack. On call	no. 74, 75 mobile barrage lynx-1 lynx-2

Signals:
Call for fire — green flares
Stop — red flares
Attack — yellow flares
Own troops — three starred flares

Ammunition expenditure:
2.45 units of fire of which:
Preparation of the attack — 1.25
Support of the attack — 0.3
Accompaniment — 0.9

Chief-of-Staff, Regimental
Artillery Group 10,
Lieutenant-Colonel Petrov[11]

The Course of an Artillery Battle

Having seen how the basic artillery building block works, we can now follow an artillery battle through the phases outlined at the beginning of this chapter. Throughout, the aim of the artillery is to *guarantee* the success of the high speed offensive in the above context. The fact that the Russians say guarantee, in their language, and not support, is once again an indicator of the more active role of artillery as a means of actually destroying the enemy in their way of thinking. This involves two different and contradictory activities. The first is blasting a hole through the enemy defence, a defence that might be very deep and well prepared (all the better if it is not), using huge quantities of ammunition with meticulous planning and preparation. Then, as Soviet forces break out into the enemy depth, much more flexible support of mobile formations is required as they exploit success and press on in that most demanding phase of war, *pursuit*. Command and control are developed as the battle becomes more fluid and special considerations affect the employment of artillery with the forward elements.

The pre-emptive *fire protection* phase, covering the movement of breakthrough forces up to their assault positions, would concentrate on suppressing and destroying those enemy weapons and other assets which could interfere with it: counter-battery fire against enemy artillery,

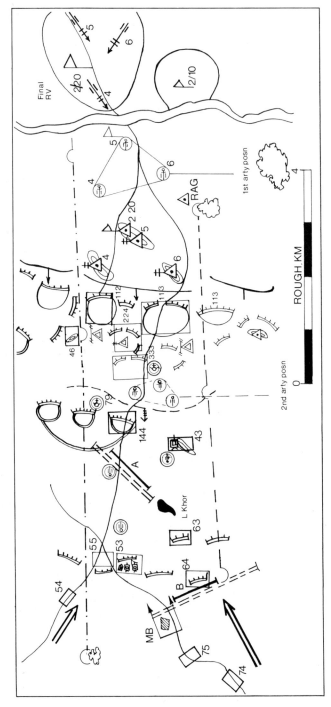

Fig. 4.10. 2 battalion, 20 artillery regiment with 2 battalion, 10 motor rifle regiment in the attack (simplified). Although no scale is shown on the original, the artillery's move is said to be 4 kilometres, which gives a general idea. A box indicates a target. All target numbers in the fireplan are shown except 108, which is reserved for targets only revealed during the course of the attack. RAG, Regimental Artillery Group (PAG); MB, Mobile Barrage; A and B indicate stationary barrages; 152 mm howitzers (Soviet)   ; 155 mm howitzers (enemy)   ; Anti-tank missile (enemy)   ; Likely directions of counter attack   ; Mortar (enemy)   ; Radar (enemy)   ; Company Observation post (enemy)   ; battalion boundary ── ─ ──   Regimental Boundary ── · ── .

suppression of enemy airfields and helicopter sites, radars and other reconnaissance equipment. The fact that this new phase is not mentioned in the battalion orders above is significant: it is a high level, operational plan conducted by Army and Front artillery according to a highly centralised plan. It would also include fire to mislead the enemy into thinking that the main concentrations were elsewhere.

The Breakthrough

The protection phase would defend and screen the massing of huge quantities of artillery and rockets close to the breakthrough sector. Great Patriotic War experience suggests that they will be good at doing this in secret but if massive artillery movements are detected it is probably the most reliable indicator of all of the imminence and direction of a major thrust. *The breakthrough* is defined formally as the defeat of the enemy in the tactical zone of defence and the development of the offensive in depth. Soviet priorities are the destruction of enemy nuclear delivery means — long range missiles and artillery, and *reconnaissance strike complexes* (see below). Other priorities, in order, are anti-tank, anti-personnel and anti-air

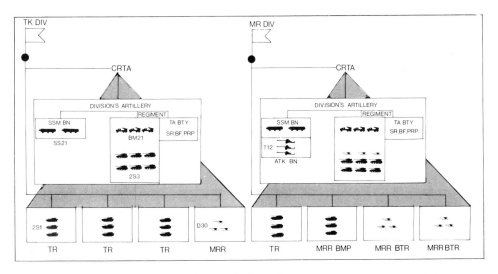

Fig. 4.11.   Divisional artillery. Each outline represents a battery of six equipments, except for SS-21s (batteries of two). D-30 battalions are being replaced by 2S1s, and the calculation in the text assumes all have been. The shaded area indicates the extent of the CRTA's overall control, although the regimental artillery is highly independent (see text) CRTA, Commander of Rocket Troops and Artillery; MRR, Motor Rifle Regiment; TR, Tank Regiment; TA, Target Acquisition. BMP and BTR indicate Regiments equipped with the BMP and BTR series armoured personnel carriers, respectively. BF, Big Fred; PRP, Forward Radar Post (Small Fred); SR, Sound Ranging.

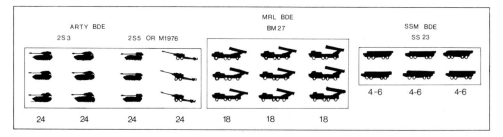

F<small>IG</small>. 4.12.   Army level artillery, mid-1980s. Each outline represents a battery, of eight guns or howitzers or six multiple rocket launchers. Vertical lines represent battalions. The two gun battalions may be either 2S5 or M-1976, replacing the old M-46.

weapons. The aim is to destroy the coherence of the defence and render it incapable of organised resistance.

As we have seen, predicting the amount of artillery that would be fired at a series of targets is virtually impossible because there is no set pattern or amount: artillery from all levels would be used in any way the Soviets felt appropriate. If we take the lead division of a Soviet army, advancing along a main axis, we can be fairly sure at least that it would have all its own artillery, as in Fig. 4.11, although we cannot be sure how much delegation to regiments the division's artillery commander (CRTA) would allow. In a major breakthrough, he would probably keep tight control of all the divisional artillery. A division advancing along an Army or Front main axis would probably also have Army and perhaps Front artillery allocated to it, supporting it or held under command of the higher artillery commander with its best interests at heart. Let us take the example of a hypothetical division advancing on an Army's main axis from Helmstedt on the East-West German border towards Hildesheim, south of Hannover. The division has all the artillery of its subordinate regiments, its own artillery regiment, plus two battalions (that is, 48 in all), 2S5s or M-1976 152 mm towed guns from Army, and from Front, three battalions of 2S3s making 72, 12 × 240 mm self-propelled mortars, 12 × 203 mm self-propelled guns and 18 BM-27 heavy rocket launchers. This gives the number of equipments shown in the table below. In addition, there would of course be the division's four FROGs or SS-21s, or any of the Army's 12 Scuds or SS-23s, or the Front's possible 24 Scuds or SS-23s, and 12 Scaleboards or SS-22s. These are not included in the table, nor does it include the division's 36 × 120 mm mortars, which are regarded as an artillery weapon but, it can be argued, are not sufficiently long ranged to form a very important part of an artillery fire plan, or the direct fire anti-tank guns.

Even if we disregard the ability of the new long range operational-tactical rockets to conduct precise and devastating strikes with improved conventional or chemical munitions against particular targets, this gives a total of

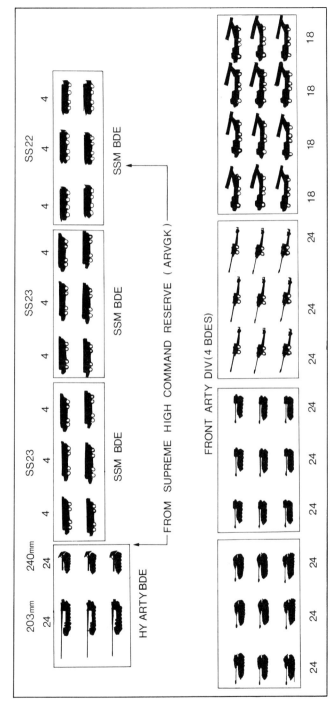

Fig. 4.13. Front level artillery, mid-1980s. Each outline represents a battery, vertical lines represent battalions. This organisation is tentative and is certainly not fixed. Although the Heavy Artillery and SSM Brigades may be located within Front boundaries, they belong to the Supreme High Command Reserve (ARVGK).

Unit to which organic	M-1975 240 mm mor	M-1975 203 mm gun	2S5/ M-1976	2S3/ D20	2S1/ D-30	BM-21	BM-27
GTR					18		
GTR					18		
GTR					18		
GMRR					18		
Division arty regt				18	36	18	
Army arty bde: 2 × bn			48				
Front: 3 × bn				72			
1 × bn							18
half assets	12	12					
Total	12	12	48	90	108	18	18

GTR = Guards Tank Regiment
GMRR = Guards Motor Rifle Regiment

306 equipments, or 342 if the mortars are included. If we take each barrel of a multiple rocket launcher separately, this gives 1278 barrels without the 120 mm mortars or 1314 with. If we are thinking of the immediate effect of a single salvo, then it makes sense to consider each multiple rocket launcher barrel separately. This would give a weight of shot, high explosive and steel, of 56.2 tonnes without mortars for a single salvo. The guns and howitzers can of course re-load much more quickly than the rocket launchers; therefore, over a long period it makes sense to treat each rocket launcher as one equipment giving 302 equipments. In a 30 min fire preparation for an assault on this axis we might assume two salvos by the rocket launchers, plus other systems firing at the hourly rate (see the table in Chapter Three), which gives some 10,760 rounds, weighing some 420 tonnes. This is using the rates of fire for the self-propelled equipments, which are slower than the towed ones they are replacing, and is if anything, conservative. These rounds are distributed much more equitably across the target than aerial bombs or missiles, and penetrate to far greater depth than the direct fire weapons of armour and motor rifle troops, up to perhaps 25 kilometres behind the NATO FLOT for the 2S5 and 203 mm gun and 30 kilometres for the BM-27, striking at previously located and known positions of headquarters, artillery and missiles positions, air defence sites and other

relatively soft locations. Another way of gauging the effect of fire is to compare the firepower used to blast the way for this formation with that used in the terrible battle of Verdun in 1916. The Germans assembled 1220 guns and howitzers on a 12 kilometre front, with an average calibre of about 122 mm, or roughly 26 tonnes per salvo. The Soviets would bring down 56 per salvo, as we have seen, but on a much narrower sector, perhaps only 4 kilometres. Therefore, the bombardment in support of a Soviet division breaking through on a main axis might be some six times as intense as the initial German bombardment at Verdun. Even very well dug in infantry, and armoured personnel carriers in the open, would take terrible punishment from such a pounding. Only the deepest dugouts and heavily armoured tanks could expect to survive if the Soviet artillery chose to give them their attention.

One of the main objectives in the breakthrough phase would be the suppression of enemy *anti-tank guided weapons (PTURS)*. By the late 1960s the Soviets clearly recognised the threat which these weapons posed to their large tank formations. The 1973 Middle East War reinforce this belief, although the Soviets did not espouse the hasty and ill considered view that the tank might have become obsolete which gained some ground in the West. Nevertheless, the 1984 edition of *Tactics* stated that over half the tanks lost in that war fell to anti-tank missiles, 22 per cent to other tanks and 28 to other means. These figures are highly dubious: the Israelis inflicted over half of tank casualties on their enemies with tank fire. Nevertheless, they have appeared in a seminal Soviet work and suppressing anti-tank missiles was, of course, a prudent thing for an army as armour oriented as the Soviet to concentrate on especially as NATO puts so much emphasis on them as the antidote to armour. This was also consistent with their views dating back to the 1930s. In 1975, a very thorough report appeared which demanded the destruction of anti-tank guided weapons not only directly in front of the tank assault, but also on either side of it. Smoke was particularly useful to blind anti-tank weapons which required to be guided visually throughout their flight. Successive concentrations of aimed fire were recommended with a mixture of high explosive and smoke rounds. One method of bringing fire to bear on an anti-tank guided weapon very quickly (fire on a single target) is to load five guns with high explosive rounds and one with smoke. The smoke round is fired in the general direction of the target and the others adjusted off it. Even if the five explosive rounds do not destroy the anti-tank weapon, the smoke usually blinds it. The report also covered anti-tank helicopters, a new anti-armour weapon, and laid down that artillery should hit their landing sites, which observers should be trained to spot. From this and other Russian reports, it is clear that suppressing anti-tank weapons and clearing the way for the tanks is a cardinal task for Soviet artillery and rocket forces, and that, in the breakthrough at least, the tank advance must be secured by organised artillery fire and cannot proceed without it, as it was in the 1930s.[12]

Inserting the Operational Manoeuvre Group (OMG)

If a cut is made deep into the enemy tactical zone, which is about 30 kilometres deep, favourable circumstances may exist for the insertion of the OMG, descendant of the Great Patriotic War Mobile Group (see Chapter One). The aim of this is to thrust fast into the enemy operational depth, and thus shift the focus of combat to the enemy rear and accelerate the advance of the main forces. The OMG is extremely vulnerable during its passage through the gap and, as in the last war, would be given massive artillery and air support. Because of the difficulty of resupplying it once in the enemy depth, and to conceal it, it is unlikely that its own artillery and rockets would fire prior to insertion. Instead, long range artillery from the main forces would fire through the gap. As the diagram (Fig. 4.14) shows, the BM-27, new 203 mm gun and possibly the 2S5 have the range to do this for all or most of the way. Priorities would be the suppression of enemy artillery, particularly MLRS which could make life very difficult for the OMG by putting down instant minefields, and of attack helicopter sites which could otherwise mount rapid counter-attacks against the OMG. The Soviet artillery might also put down its own instant minefields and probably smoke to seal the flanks of the OMG penetration. As the OMG pushed through the gap, it might be able to report back to the artillery of the main forces giving the location of newly discerned targets, thus itself solving the target acquisition problem that bedevils long range artillery. Alternatively, the OMG could preserve total radio silence, which would be in keeping with traditional Soviet march discipline. An OMG would probably be based on a tank division, but might have extra assets attached, particularly engineers and air. In the case of artillery, one obvious candidate would be the new 240 mm self-propelled mortar. One of the problems of deep penetration forces is that they get held up by strongpoints which they lack the heavy weapons to destroy. This happened, for example, in Mishchenko's raid in the Russo-Japanese War. The 240 mm mortar could be relied on to deal with local resistance very quickly, in circumstances where its limited range was not a handicap.

In these circumstances liaison with Soviet air forces is particularly important. Using artillery to blast a corridor for helicopters allowing the helicopters to penetrate and deal with targets in depth which are difficult to locate is an obvious example of integrated fire destruction. The OMG would be able to call on extra helicopters and fixed wing aircraft support to deal with unexpected opposition or counter-attacks, and would also be heavily dependent on air for resupply.[13]

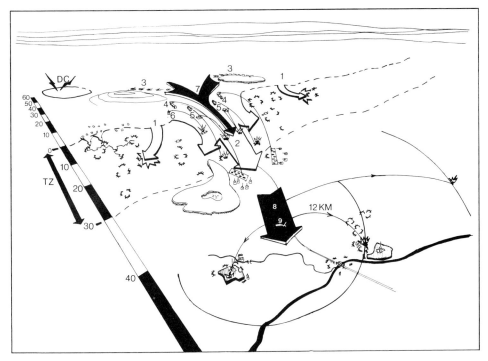

Fig. 4.14.   Artillery support for OMG insertion (postulated). DC, Dummy
Concentration; TZ, Tactical Zone, up to 30 kilometres wide. 1. Several
probing attacks to discover weak points in enemy defence; 2. Main forces
punch hole through tactical zone; 3. OMG waiting silently in concentration
areas up to 50 kilometres behind Soviet FLOT; 4. BM27s put down remote
minefield to protect flanks of penetration; 5. 2S5s (range up to 28–29
kilometres) and 203 mm gun (up to 30 kilometres) fire at targets throughout
gap; 6. Other Army and Front artillery engages other targets such as
anti-tank weapons likely to threaten flanks of penetration; 7. OMG inserted
with massive artillery and air support; 8. The OMG has now moved into the
enemy operational depth: Based on a tank division, the maximum range of
its own artillery (2S3s) is some 24 kilometres; 9. 240 mm self-propelled
mortars attached to OMG smash difficult targets close to and threatening it,
up to their maximum range of 12 kilometres.

The Breakout

Following the breakthrough, the OMG would break out and then main
forces would follow. As we have seen from Great Patriotic War examples,
control of artillery would probably be devolved as the battle became more
fluid. During the breakthrough artillery fire, particularly counter-battery
fire, would be controlled at the highest possible level, at least the divisional
artillery group and with constant reference to higher artillery commanders.
Now, battalions of artillery would be allocated to forward motor rifle and
tank battalions pressing into the enemy depth. It is here that the artillery

battalion commander, as controller of the main sub-division of artillery forces, comes into his own. Soviet writings recently have placed particular stress on the artillery battalion in support of a forward battalion in the *vanguard* and the *forward march security element, (GPZ)* which is a peculiarly Soviet device lying between the forward *recce patrols* and the vanguard, and the *meeting engagement*. As Soviet forces carry out parallel *pursuit*, or elements of shattered enemy formations counter-attack, such opportunities are much more likely, and Soviet sources have recently stressed that individual batteries may also be allocated to individual companies. This is an exception to the rule that the battalion is the main fire unit, and underlines the special nature of what the Russians call the pursuit phase.[14]

The Meeting Engagement

In the meeting engagement an artillery battalion may support an all-arms battalion in the first echelon or be allocated to it. It may move in the battalion column as one or as separate batteries. Its missions are: to prevent enemy units deploying in the encounter battle, and to cover the deployment of friendly troops, to protect the open flanks of fast moving units and to prevent the withdrawal of enemy units or their deployment into good defensive positions. Because it is likely to be operating deep in the enemy rear, such an artillery battalion needs to keep a special eye out for nuclear and chemical delivery systems, command, control and electronic installations. The correct position of the battalion in the order of march and quick reaction to a threat are particularly important. A battery belonging to the battalion attached to the vanguard of the main force is usually told off to reinforce (not support, reinforce in Soviet parlance) the company forming the forward march security element or GPZ. On coming into contact with the enemy the battery will deploy at the order of the GPZ commander, although the battery commander will give precise orders to the Gun Position Officer as to where he should take up position. In the march, the battery commander is usually with the GPZ commander near the front, with the battery under the Gun Position Officer near the back (see Fig. 4.15). The gun sections will deploy very close to the axis of advance. Fire may be directed either by the battery commander or by the GPZ commander himself. One Soviet exercise recently had a battery fighting a series of small actions along a 120 kilometre stretch along which the enemy was withdrawing, for example, capturing bridges, using both direct and indirect fire. On occasions the battery commander would control one section and the Gun Position Officer the other. In this situation, artillery is particularly likely to face minor counter-attacks by tanks, and it is envisaged

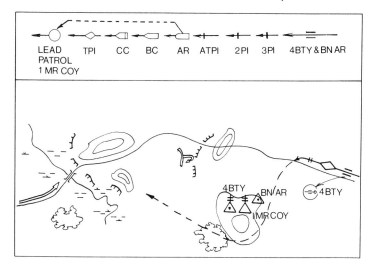

FIG. 4.15. 4 Battery with 1 Motor Rifle Company in the forward march security element. TPl, Tank Platoon; CC, Company Commander; BC, Battery Commander; AR, Artillery Reconnaissance (of battery) (may be forward with lead patrol); ATPl, Anti-tank platoon; Bn AR, Artillery Reconnaissance of artillery battalion.

that artillery batteries in the GPZ will engage them with direct fire as a matter of course.

The aim of this is to cover the deployment of the main body of the vanguard. As soon as the GPZ reports contact, the battalion *head of reconnaissance* selects a position for the battalion COP. The commander of the vanguard (a reinforced battalion) does his appreciation and the artillery battalion commander draws up a fireplan, very much on the advice of the GPZ commander. The other (two) artillery batteries are deployed as fast as possible, and cover the deployment of the main forces of the vanguard for the attack (see Fig. 4.16). Fire is brought down exclusively on observed targets, and the artillery battalion commander also prepares stationary barrage fires to prevent the enemy withdrawing. Communications with the all-arms force, speed and initiative are obviously of heightened significance in this type of engagement.[15]

Feeding the Inferno

With the Soviet forces now well into the enemy depth, we will leave them there and return to general considerations. We have seen the intensity of bombardment that Soviet artillery can put down to expedite a divisional attack, and Army and Front assets would be at work as part of a grander design as well. The good news is that the Soviets cannot, obviously, sustain bombardments of this intensity everywhere or for very long. In particular,

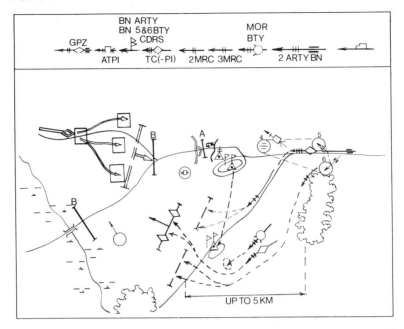

FIG. 4.16. Main forces of the *vanguard* unfolding into battle. A and B indicate barrages. GPZ is the forward march security element. TC (- Pl), Yank Company, minus the platoon in the GPZ; MRC, Motor Rifle Company. Note that the all-arms battalion, artillery battalion and two battery commanders remaining in the main body are all together just behind the head of the column.

such large expenditures of ammunition seem to militate against their requirement for a very high speed of advance. Keeping a fast moving force supplied at these rates of expenditure would be very difficult. However, the Soviets' record in the last war suggests that they have been able to overcome vast logistic problems. Furthermore, of course, it is only when the advance has slowed and stiff opposition encountered that such heavy expenditures of ammunition are required. The rate of ammunition expenditure is inversely proportional to the daily rate of advance. However, the Soviet army and particularly the artillery are facing problems. In about the middle of 1980 the logistic system at artillery *section* level was completely reorganised. Artillery ammunition and rockets are now supplied on a strictly 'to arm' basis, separately from other kinds of resupply. This means that if, for example, two artillery battalions are brought forward from divisional resources to reinforce a motor rifle or tank regiment's own artillery battalion, this does not put an intolerable strain on the supported arm unit's own resupply system. Even so, the sheer volume of ammunition (2000 rounds for a single battalion attack) means that the artillery support for the attack may take an hour to organise.

It is generally believed that artillery in forward units or units operating independently cannot be resupplied (but, see the OMG above). An artillery battalion in this role receives extra trucks with trailers filled with ammunition. Nevertheless, such battalions would have to careful about ammunition expenditure, imposing a limit on the scale of support which they could provide. Until recently, the Soviets did not have an armoured resupply vehicle and they still rely overwhelmingly on road bound trucks. The BM-27 and operational tactical missiles have a resupply vehicle, and towed T-12s have their MT-LB tractor which doubles as one. It is probable that the 2S5 and 203 mm gun, at least, have one also. However, the paucity of agile and resilient resupply vehicles must be a weakness and even if they were to decide to supply this deficiency it would take many years to do so.

Warfare in Special Conditions

Although this book has focussed on the European context, the Soviet Union covers a large part of the world's land surface and its borders manifest as wide a variety of terrain as any nation on earth. Four categories of special conditions are terrain related: mountains, forests, deserts, and the arctic. The other two are winter and night. Some of these affect the way the artillery offensive would be conducted. Another special case is fighting in large urban areas, and although this is not formally classified as *special conditions* by the Russians, they obviously regard it as a distinct case and in view of its relevance to any European conflict it is examined here first.

Artillery in Big City Fighting

Soviet practices here are based very much on Great Patriotic War experience, especially the Battle for Berlin (see Chapter One). Enemy forces make extensive use of cellars and the ground floors of buildings, linked by communication trenches or routes running behind fences and garden walls, which compounds the problems of spotting enemy positions, even from very close. Concrete beams and other debris can be used to build exceptionally strong defended points. High buildings and factory chimneys provide numerous excellent observation posts, while artillery is often deployed in parks and squares. Mortars can be fired from behind garden walls, or sited in special pits. The cushioning effect of buildings complicates sound ranging and the short distance from which it is possible to see combined with the dispersion of shell bursts makes plotting the fall of shot difficult. The centre of the city is likely to be ablaze, further confusing artillery's observation. In these circumstances, air reconnaissance has been found to be particularly effective.

Fighting in city streets and buildings tends to devolve on small sub-units, and artillery fighting is no exception. The Soviets believe that decentralisation would be the norm. Artillery batteries would act as part of 'storm groups' ordered to take buildings or city blocks. Because of the close range and the difficulty of observation, much combat would be in the direct fire mode, and this particularly applies to batteries in the first echelon and storm groups, and goes for heavy artillery as well as that normally assigned for close support. In the Great Patriotic War, between 40 and 80 per cent of gun artillery was used for direct fire, including 152 mm and above and multiple rocket launchers were also used. As we have seen, the Soviets developed special drills for dealing with obstinate buildings during the battle for Berlin: heavy artillery would open fire from as little as 150 metres away, and whole batteries would conduct *demolition fire* with concrete busting rounds at point blank range.

Artillery commanders have to pay particular attention to selecting fire positions. Crest clearance and the minimum range of artillery weapons are particularly critical when surrounded by tall buildings. The possibility of firing direct at the upper storeys of tall structures should be borne in mind. Because good fire positions are so hard to come by artillery commanders are recommended to select those which will enable them to go on firing for as long as possible without moving. Direct fire guns have to be very carefully camouflaged because of the close ranges and this includes muffling the sound of their movement. It is difficult to fix the positions of gun and observation posts accurately because of the built up nature of the ground, and as we have all noticed, one tends to be oblivious to relief in a town. This is another reason why direct fire is favoured. One technique developed during the war was to adjust fire from aerial registration points, using airburst shells. This was particularly useful when engaging very close targets or bringing down fire *on one's own position*, which often happens in the bitter hand-to-hand fighting in cities.

Because all-arms troops will not always have the opportunity to clear captured buildings completely before moving on, artillery officers and men have to defend themselves against remnants of enemy forces, to pay special attention to the local defence of the gun position, and should be specially trained in close combat techniques. Finally, it will be exceptionally difficult to deliver ammunition to a city gun position in the normal way, and gun detachments may have to go some way to pick it up themselves. All-arms troops may also be enlisted to help shift artillery ammunition, probably not a very popular task!

A number of recent articles have stressed the need for special training areas with mock ups of city conditions in which to train artillery in urban fighting. Whereas we tend to think of street fighting as very much an infantryman's battle, or one for other arms acting as infantry, the Russian artillery will have its guns at the front, as always. In extremis, they will use self-propelled guns, especially the 2S1 and 2S3, as assault guns.[16]

Night

The offensive must be prosecuted at night with the same untiring energy as by day. Although observation is made more difficult, night enhances the moral and surprise effect of artillery fire. One of artillery's missions is to fire illuminating rounds to aid the all-arms advance and also simultaneously with its own adjustment and fire, so that the fall of shot can be seen. Directions from the observation post are marked with white or, in winter, black stakes or marks on trees, or tall thin lights facing into the post dug-out. Dark natural features such as woods, marshes, bushes or plough appear smaller and further away. White dusty roads, hedges and the edges of trenches appear more distinct. More use is made of *SNAR* and *ARSOM* radars and sound ranging than by day, and Soviet observation posts are also equipped with *night vision devices*. Sometimes, artillery preparation of the attack is not carried out, to maximise the potential of night time surprise. Artillery sub-units may be devolved to lower levels of all-arms command than would normally be the case, to facilitate co-operation and gun positions further forward. The Soviets consider illuminating shells particularly useful for blinding enemy laser rangefinders in the preparation phase, but the main use of artillery by night is in support of the attack itself. The first line of a barrage or successive concentrations is usually 2 to 3 kilometres from the Soviet FLOT, and when the troops reach one and a half or two kilometres from it the artillery battalion commander shifts fire into the enemy depth. There are clear tactical advantages in night operations, but the organisation and conduct of accurate artillery fire is correspondingly more difficult.

Mountains

The Soviet military press has featured many articles in the last few years dealing with combat in mountainous areas, including artillery and rocket units. This is clearly inspired partly by operations in Afghanistan, but the Soviet Union has large mountainous areas on its borders, from the Carpathians in the west where there was so much fighting in the Great Patriotic War to the mighty Tian-Shan in the east. Special features of mountain terrain are the rapid changes in weather, mists, low cloud, the difficulty of establishing one's position, the steep rocky ground, the lack of suitable sites for gun positions which are, ideally, smooth and flat, few and poor roads and fast flowing moutain rivers with steep banks. Main observation posts are deployed at different heights to get a full perspective on the terrain in front, but linked observation posts are located on the same level. It is recommended that officers draw artillery panoramas, which seems to be becoming a lost art in the Soviet Army as in the West. This is a pity as a panorama sketch is an excellent way of recording target data

permanently and clearly. Observation post officers are warned against
setting up in dry mountain river beds, for obvious reasons. Gun positions
are often located near roads to expedite the movement of ammunition and
withdrawal, but this has penalties in making them more vulnerable to
location and air attack. Steep slopes and scarps present a problem, and it
may be necessary to cut slits or platforms for command personnel and guns
or launchers.

Howitzers and mortars are particularly useful for high angle fire against
enemy forces on reverse slopes, in valleys and ravines. When engaging an
enemy defensive position deployed up a mountain side in terraces or steps,
the artillery normally open fire on the lower levels first. In mountain
warfare, as in many other special circumstances, the battery is far more
likely to operate independently, especially against targets on narrow
mountain roads, bridges, or in gorges. The rocky terrain enhances the effect
of artillery fire terribly, giving none of the absorption provided by soft
earth, adding sharp splinters of rock to those of the shells and trapping the
blast in deep gulleys. Direct fire may also be used from one mountain height
to another. In one example from Afghanistan, a heavy anti-aircraft machine
gun was detected on an opposing height. The Russians fired rockets from
two BM-21 launchers at it at a range of 8300 metres from across the valley
— direct fire. This gives a maximum of 80 rockets, although they may not
have fired them all. One may assume not much was left when the smoke
cleared, and Soviet helicopter borne troops went into the attack.

Desert

Sharp changes in temperature during the day, sandstorms, the constant
difficulty of finding water, heat stroke and the bright desert sun which
blinds observers: these are some of the problems encountered in the deserts
which lie to the south and east, and in neighbouring countries in western
Asia where it is not inconceivable that Soviet troops may have to fight.
Soviet artillery equipment has certainly been used in these conditions
recently, notably in the Iran-Iraq war. The flat, monotonous terrain makes
navigation and position plotting very difficult with map and compass, but on
the other hand facilitates air and electronic surveillance. Observed targets
are best located by intersection. Gun positions are located between
sand-dunes and other mounds, and sometimes in dried up river beds
(wadis). Command observation posts are located on the slopes of sand
dunes, and in thickets of desert scrub. Because of the lack of natural cover
and the clear air, assets are much more widely dispersed in the desert than
elsewhere and gun positions are placed farther behind the front line. Desert
sand makes the construction of revetments particularly difficult, and the
Iraqis have devoted enormous resources to sandbagging and fortifying their

gun positions. We could expect the Russians to do the same. Finally, the hot desert sun can alter the temperature of charges considerably, thus affecting accuracy, and ammunition has to be protected from its direct rays.

The Arctic

Although the Russians have a natural genius for fighting in winter conditions, they regard the arctic as a different and special proposition. Across the north of the country and on its frontiers lie huge stretches of tundra, terrain intersected by innumerable lakes, or wide stretches of boulders and scree. Apart from the low temperature which, in addition to the human problems it poses often causes guns to freeze to the ground, making it impossible to get them out of position, the main problem for artillery is navigation. In blizzards and the long arctic winter night normal navigation is naturally very difficult, and even in summer the dense ionosphere and proximity to the magnetic pole throws compasses off line. Special stress is placed on navigation by heavenly bodies and establishing a system of known visible reference points. The offensive is normally conducted along roads or other good going. An enemy defence tends to have a focal nature, because of the need to establish positions on firm ground between marsh and lakes, and the most normal mode of operation for artillery is therefore concentrated fire or fire at individual targets.[17]

Inter-arm Co-operation: the Major Problem

One major problem pervades the employment of Soviet artillery on the battlefield, whether in the breakthrough, the exploitation and pursuit and in all types of conditions. This is the lack of inter-arm co-operation, which emanates either from artillery officers' lack of tactical 'maturity', as one Soviet article on the subject put it, or from all-arms commanders' lack of understanding of what artillery can — and cannot — do. This has caused Soviet comment rising to a crescendo in recent years. It is understandable in the light of the Russian artillery's technocratic tradition, and if the realities of war broke down the barriers in 1941–45, the long years of peace and the problems of assimilating new weaponry and techniques have pushed tactics into the background. Conversely, the Soviet armour has been very much an elite as well, and the administrative edict of April 1984 (see Chapter Two) is a clear attempt to cut them down to size. In February, 1984 an Artillery Major-General serving in the *Group of Soviet Forces, Germany* blamed the lack of understanding and interoperability on certain all-arms commanders whose knowledge of artillery's fighting abilities and potential was acquired only 'in passing'. On the other hand, it was up to artillery officers to impress all-arms commanders with their abilities. Another officer from the *Northern*

Group of Forces (Poland) thought that junior artillery officers were to blame because they 'knew little of the nature of modern all-arms combat and did not understand the objectives of the all-arms force sufficiently well'. Briefing the all-arms and artillery commanders together and gaining a superficial rapport before the operation was not enough, since the enemy would 'try with every means at his disposal to delude the opposition, use disinformation, manoeuvre secretly and unexpectedly'. Naturally combat would not always proceed according to plan. Therefore, 'artillery and all-arms commanders must be able to ensure co-operation throughout the entire duration of combat. Artillerymen should be taught more about all-arms commanders' work and vice versa. This should be done, not only during career service, but also in military educational establishments and staff colleges'. This was a clear reference to the fact that the problem began with the Russians' specific to arm system of officer training which, as we have seen, may be changing. The problem was particularly acute in the fast moving parallel pursuit where artillery and tanks were operating together in changing circumstances. The artillery officer had to be filled '*with the soul of the tanks*'. At the same time, other officers stressed the need for all-arms commanders to receive artillery training. In July 1984 Commander of Artillery and Rocket Troops Mikhalkin added his authority in an article on the all-arms training of artillery commanders. They needed 'not only to solve problems relating to the reconnaissance and destruction of targets but also to retain unbroken communication with the all-arms commanders and to exchange information and receive target co-ordinates from the commanders of motor rifle and tank sub-units'. This may all sound obvious, but coming from the head of the Soviet Army's quarter to half million serving artillerymen, it is a clear admission of a major weakness. Artillerymen have an enormous responsibility in the Soviet order of battle, for '*the connecting link between all-arms commanders and other arms of service are the artillery officers and representatives of aviation and special forces*'. The price may be high: artillerymen are exhorted to remember Suvorov's principle *sam pogibay, a tovarishch vyruchay*: 'perish yourself, but get your comrade out of trouble'. It is the spirit of service which has characterised the best Russian artillerymen from Kutaysov through Kirey to the present, but in these highly technological times it is easier than ever to forget it.

This is also the key to Soviet artillery and rocket forces' greatest weakness in a future conflict. The points where it is in contact with the other arms are few, and in the case of the artillery and all-arms battalion commanders being co-located, offer very high value targets. Break these points, unhinge them, and the contact between manoeuvre forces and the very powerful artillery force will be lost. Even quite high ranking artillery officers are clearly still quite ignorant of all-arms battle, in spite of their thorough training, and their subordinates may well be helpless without them.[18]

Future Developments

The Soviets have fairly effective ground radars for target acquisition and their artillery observation post vehicles, with inertial navigation systems, direction finding and laser rangefinder equipment are as advanced as any in the world. The main development in the employment of Soviet artillery in the next 15 years or so is likely to be the introduction of a *reconnaissance-destruction complex* which means an automated system for locating and plotting targets, allocating priorities, computing firing data and norms, and bringing fire down. Such a system would be similar to the American Stand-Off Target Acquisition System (SOTAS). SOTAS detects and tracks the movement, build up and withdrawal of enemy forces beyond the limit of a forward observer's vision. It operates at night and in adverse weather giving a moving picture of moving targets in real time. The information is provided with sufficient accuracy to allow target engagement with artillery, aircraft and other long range weapons. SOTAS has an airborne element, in a Black Hawk helicopter and a processing element in a vehicle on the ground. A Soviet real time target acquisition, processing and engagement system would operate on similar lines, probably based on the Hip helicopter. Although wary of attempts to predict what the Russians may do, the author has allowed himself one piece of artistic licence and an impression is shown in Fig. 4.17. Of course it is arguable that NATO needs this sort of automated control to squeeze the last drop out of its meagre artillery resources, while the Soviets have enough artillery and therefore do not. However, the Soviets have shown great interest in such systems, and are clearly working on their own. The need to respond quickly and accurately to enemy long range artillery and MLRS batteries and the difficulty of target acquisition are painfully obvious to the Soviet artillery, and such a system would increase the effectiveness of their very considerable artillery force logarithmically. The Soviets define these systems as *reconnaissance fire complexes*, which are essentially tactical and designed to take out tube artillery, MLRS and all-arms subunits, and *reconnaissance strike complexes*, which are operational level and would also target tactical aviation and nuclear delivery means. Soviet impressions of the Western 'Assault Breaker' and 'PLSS' systems have been illustrated in their military press recently. Both these schemes depend on air reconnaissance and a Soviet one would too, since the only way of reaching far behind the enemy FLOT is to get up high. As manned aircraft become inordinately expensive, too much so to risk overflying targets in the inferno of a central European war, the aircraft is more rationally employed spying from a great altitude, and transmitting the information back to surface-to-surface systems to do the damage. The Soviets, who have never espoused the idea of an independent air force in the way that Western powers have, could be expected to have less resistance to this shift in role. It would simply be an extension of the traditional role of artillery and rocket forces.[19]

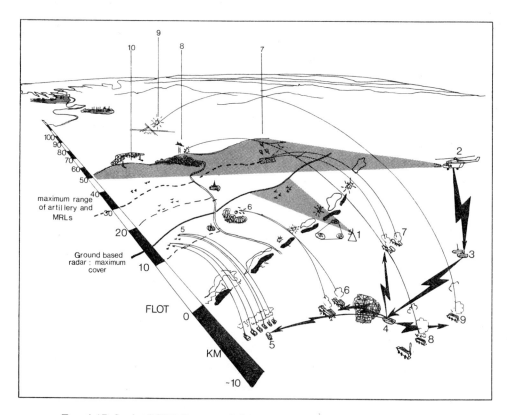

FIG. 4.17. Soviet SOTAS type real time target acquisition, targetting and fire control system (Reconnaissance-fire complex). 1. Current ground based artillery associated radar with maximum range of *c.* 20 kilometres. 2. Postulated Soviet SOTAS type system: air element mounted in HIP helicopter. 3. Helicopter signals targets to ground station. 4. Ground station signals targets and priorities to army artillery. 5. Divisional artillery engages enemy close support battery. 6. BM-27s engage enemy divisional head-quarters hidden in wood. 7. BM-27s put down remote minefield in front of enemy tank formation moving in to counter-attack. 8. SS-21 engages STOVL aircraft landing site in forest. 9. SS-21 engages airfield with Improved Conventional Warhead. 10. Lance type missiles are detected moving out of forest. Priorities are immediately reallocated to deal with enemy nuclear delivery means (priority number one) at once.

Notes

1. Opening quotation, leader *VV* 11/1981, p. 2; different types of operation: Colonel Pilot Alexander Musial, '*Charakter i znaczenie operacji powietrznych we współczesnych działaniach wojennych*' ('The Character and Importance of Air Operations in Modern War'), *Przeglad Wojsk Lotniczych i Wojsk Obrony Kraju (PWL i WOPK) (Polish Air and Air Defence Force Review)*, March, 1982, pp. 10–11; Colonel Dr. Witold Pokruszynski '*Operacja przeciwpowietrzna Wojsk OPK*' ('An Anti-Air Operation by the Strategic Air Defence Forces') *PWL i WOPK*, May, 1982, pp. 5,7; one view, Viktor Suvorov 'Strategic Command and Control: the Soviet Approach', *International Defense Review*, 12/1984, pp. 1813–20; Theatre of War, Lieutenant Commander Zygmunt Binięda, '*Geografia wojenna: ogólne pojecie teatru działań wojennych*' ('Military Geography, The General Concept of a Theatre of Military Operations'), *Przegląd Morski (Naval Review)*, 12/1981; pp. 3–4; Military Doctrine changes: maintenance of conventional capability, Colonel P. Shkarubskiy, 'Artillery Before and Now', *Voyennaya Mysl' (Military Thought)*, 2/1966, p. 57; A Khamarchuk, '*Pochemu taktika?*' ('Why tactics?'), *VV* 8/1968, p. 44; 1970s, V. Ye. Savkin, *Basic Principles* . . . pp. 167–74; single air defence service, see Chapter Two.

2. New first phase: Lieutenant-General V. G. Reznichenko, *Taktika (Tactics)*, (Voyenizdat, Moscow, 1984), p. 111, reveals its Russian name as *prikritiye*. It is also referred to in Major Wojciech Michalak '*Lotnictwo w działaniach rajdowomanewrowych wojsk ladowych*' ('Aviation in raid Manoeuvre Operations of the Ground Forces'), *PWL i WOPK*, February, 1982, pp. 5–9: 'cover . . . against detection and strikes by enemy air' and in Musial, '*Rola lotnictwa uderzeniowego w zabezpieczeniu działán desantów morskikh*' ('The role of Strike Aviation in Support of Sea Assault Landings'), *PWL i WOPK* May, 1982, pp. 11–12.

3. 'Vast zones of destruction . . .' Colonel A. A. Sidorenko, *The Offensive* (Voyenizdat, Moscow, 1970, translated under the auspices of the US Air Force, US Government Printing Office, Washington DC, 1976), p. 61; artillery context: Lieutenant-Colonel B. Litvinov, '*Takticheskaya zrelost' komandira-artillerista*' ('Tactical Maturity of the Artillery Commander') *VV* 11/1984, p. 53.

4. D. M. Hart and E. M. Gormley, 'The Evolution of Soviet Interest in Atomic Artillery', *RUSI Journal*, June, 1983, pp. 27–32; Charles Dick, 'Soviet Chemical Warfare Capabilities', *IDR* 1/1981, pp. 31–38;

5. Definitive manual is Reznichenko *Tactics*, pp. 106–07 *integrated* destruction: Musial, '*Działanie bojowe lotnictwa na korzyść operacyjnych grup manewrowych*' ('Aviation Combat Operations on Behalf of OMGs'), *PWL i WOPK* 7–8, 1982, p. 13.

6. Colonel Ye. Dabolin '*Reshaya sovmestnuyu zadachu*' ('Tackling a Joint Task), *VV* 5/1980, pp. 74–5, for liaison of artillery and helicopters.; Fire strike: Lieutenant-General of Artillery Ye. V Stroganov, '*Ognevoy udar*', *VV* 11/1980, pp. 67–71, esp. p. 71; Marshal of Artillery Peredel'skiy '*O role i mesto artilleriyskogo diviziona v boyu*' ('On the role and Place of the Artillery Battalion in Combat'), *VV* 12/1980, p. 64. Final comment, Major-General I. Vorob' ëv '*Oruzhiye i taktika: komandir i sovremenny boy*' ('Weapons and Tactics: the Commander and Modern Combat') *KZ*, 12 January, 1982, p. 2.

7. Definitions in G. Ye. Peredel'skiy, '*Artilleriyskiy divizion v boyu*' *(The artillery battalion in combat)* (Voyenizdat, Moscow, 1984), artillery subordination, etc., pp. 12–13; see also Colonel V. Pogonin '*Vzaymodeystviye pri ognevom porazhenii*' ('Interworking in Fire Destruction'), *VV* 10/1984, p. 51; strength and intensity, pp. 18–19; not the full norm, p. 11, *distsiplina* . . . Colonel M. Avdeyev, '*Distsiplina v boyu*' ('Discipline in Combat'), *VV* 11/1984, pp. 54–55; norms, Ye. K Malakhovskiy *Strel'ba na porazheniye opornykh punktov (Fire for the Destruction of Defensive Positions)*, (Voyenizdat, Moscow, 1978); less than the full norm, Peredel'skiy, *Artilleriyskiy divizion* . . . p. 11.

8. Peredel'skiy, *Artilleriyskiy divizion*, pp. 19–29.

9. Direct and semi-direct fire: Lieutenant-General of Artillery I. Anashkin and Colonel V. Kolesov, '*S otkritoy ognevoy pozitsii po bol'shiye dal'nosti*' ('From an open fire position at long ranges'); *VV* 1982, pp. 61–62.

10. Main fire unit debate; Lieutenant-General of Artillery A. Sapozhnikov, '*Divizion: osnovnaya ognevaya yedinitsa artillerii*' ('Battalion: Main Artillery Fire Unit') *VV* 10/1981, pp. 54–59; Lieutenant-General of Artillery Ye. Stroganov, '*Osnovnoye ognevoye podrazdeleniye artillerii*' ('Main Fire Sub-unit of Artillery'), *VV* 8/1979, pp. 55–60; Survival: Colonel V. Ivanov, '*Obespechit' zhivuchest' batarey*' ('Guaranteeing the Survivability of Batteries'), *VV* 11/1972, pp. 60–63; Colonel V. Ivanov and Lieutenant-Colonel V. Nesterov, '*K voprosu o zhivuchesti artilleriyskikh podrazdeleniy*' ('On the question of the survivability of Artillery Subunits'), *VV* 10/1975, pp. 71–83; Lieutenant-Colonel I. Yepifanov, article with same title, *VV* 1/1976, p. 83; shape of deployment, Captain N. Kikishev, '*Nuzhna prakticheskaya proverka*' ('Practical checking is needed'), VV 4/1976, p. 72 and Colonel N. Shibayev, '*Problemu reshat' kompleksno*' (To solve the problem in an all-embracing way'), *VV* 6/1976, pp. 71–2; Lieutenant-General of Artillery I. Anashkin *Za kompleksnoye resheniye problemy*' ('For a Comprehensive Solution of the Problem'), *VV* 10/1976, pp. 72–74; General disposition of artillery battalion, Peredel'skiy, *Artilleriyskiy divizion* . . . p. 9 (percentage of fire missions), p. 14 (diagram showing positions of various OPs); what to do with the battery commander; Senior Lieutenant A. Glushakov, '*Batareya na dvukh ognevykh*' ('The Battery in two Fire Positions'), *VV* 12/1981, pp. 62–64; Stroganov, '*Mesto komandira batarei v boyu*' ('The place of the Battery Commander in Combat'), *VV* 5/1982, pp. 64–65; Colonel L. Zirka '*Mesto komandira batarei v boyu — komandno nablyudatel'ny punkt*' ('The place of the Battery Commander in Combat — the Command Observation Post'), VV 12/1982, pp. 64–65; Rocket launchers in the war: Colonel-General Popov's opinion cited in Yepifanov '*K voprosu* . . .' p. 83 also difficulty of plotting centre of widely dispersed battery.

11. Initial orders: Peredel'skiy, *Artilleriyskiy divizion* . . . pp. 79–80, fireplan, pp. 86–88.

12. Definition of the breakthrough phase in Reznichenko, p. 117, suppression of anti-tank weapons and statistics, p. 107; Israeli figures General Yisrael Tal, 'Armour, Myth and Reality', *Ha'aretz*, 20 October, 1974, and personal conversation; Soviet debate on suppressing anti-tank weapons; S. Dudarev '*Artilleriya v bor'be s protivotankovymi sredstvami*' ('Artillery in Battle against Anti-tank Weapons') VV 5(1968), pp. 40–43; Lieutenant-General of Artillery A. V. Koritchuk, '*Bor'ba s protivotankovymi sredstvami v nastuplenii*' ('Struggle with Anti-tank Weapons in the Offensive *VV* 6/1975, pp. 67–70 Smoke and Helicopters on p. 70; A. V. Tonkikh *Preodoleniye protivotankovoy oborony (Overcoming Anti-tank Defence)* (Voyenizdat, Moscow, 1978), esp. pp. 16, 66–67. Soviet organisation from *FM-100-2-3*, allocation of assets to division is imaginary. Verdun: *SVE* Vol. 2 (1976), pp. 99–100.

13. OMGs: Christopher Donnelly 'The Soviet Operational Manoeuvre Group: A New Challenge for NATO', *IDR* 9/1982, pp. 1177–86; Charles Dick 'Soviet Operational Manoeuvre Groups: A Closer Look' *IDR* 6/1983, pp. 769–76; Philip a Petersen and John G. Hines 'Military Power in Soviet Strategy against NATO', *RUSI Journal*, December 1983, pp. 50–56, Musial and Michalak, see notes 2 and 3 above. See also the author's 'Antecedents of the Modern Soviet Operational Manoeuvre Group (OMG)' *RUSI Journal*, September, 1984, for a historical perspective.

14. Major N. Strelkov, '*Podderzhka nastupleniya tankistov*' ('Supporting the Tanks' Advance'), *VV* 3/1984, pp. 60–63; Colonel V. Vyshnevskiy '*Batareya na Marshe i vo vstrechnom boyu*' ('The Battery on the March and in the Meeting Engagement'), *VV* 8/1984, pp. 56–58; Peredel'skiy, *Artilleriyskiy divizion* . . . pp. 150–160.

15. Peredel'skiy *Artilleriyskiy divizion* . . . pp. 150–60; Vyshnevskiy, p. 58.

16. City warfare: Lieutenant-Colonel A. Novikov, Colonel L. Sebyakin, '*Deystviya artillerii*' ('The Action of Artillery') in a section '*Boy v krupnom gorode*' ('Combat in big cities') *VV* 10/1982, pp. 34–38; an elaborate complex for training artillerymen in urban warfare is advocated in Litvinov, p. 53, and in Colonel A. Kielczunski and Major W. Kawalec, '*Szkolenie w Osrodku Zurbanizowany*' ('Training in Urban Centres'), three-parts, *Przegląd Wojsk Lądowych (Polish Ground Forces Review)*, June–August, 1983.

17. Special conditions; Peredel'skiy, *Artilleriyskiy divizion* . . . pp. 132–49; Major S.

Kravchenko '*Artilleristy v zapolyar'e*' ('*Artillerymen in the arctic*'), *VV* 12/1983, pp. 28–31; some technical problems for artillery in mountains are in Colonel M. Karabanov '*Uchet meteousloviy pri strel'be v gorakh*' ('The Study of Meteorological Conditions when firing in Mountains'), *VV* 2/1984, pp. 62–3; direct fire rocket launcher: Lieutenant-General of Artillery I. Anashkin and Colonel V. Kolesov, '*S otkritoy ognevoy pozitsii po bol'shiye dal'nosti*' ('From an open fire Position at Long Ranges'), *VV* 11/1982, pp. 60–63. This is described as an 'exercise' but it has the ring of truth about it.

18. 'Tactical maturity' from Litvinov '*Takticheskaya zrelost*'. . . 'GSFG and Northern Group officers' opinions in '*Polneye ispol'zovat' vozmozhnosti polokovoy i batal'onnoy artillerii*' ('To utilise the Potential of Regimental and Battalion Artillery more fully'), *VV* 2/1984, pp. 68–69; also that things will not go according to plan and the need for training to remedy this. Soul of the tanks . . . Strelkov in *VV* 3/1984, pp. 61–62; Colonel-General V. M. Mikhalkin '*Takticheskoy podgotovke artilleristov — obshchevoyskovuyu napravlennost*' ('Giving an All-arms Emphasis to the Tactical Training of Artillerymen') *VV* 7/1984, pp. 62–65, quote from p. 64; connecting link and Suvorov's exhortation, Pogonin, '*Vzamodeystviye . . .*' p. 52; for the other side of the coin, Major-General of Artillery K. Konyushko, Major A. Bondarenko, '*Artilleriyskaya podgotovka obshchevoyskovogo ofitsera*' ('The Artillery Training of the All-arms Officer'), *VV* 4/1984, pp. 54–57.

19. On SOTAS, see the entry in *Jane's Weapon Systems 1982–83*, p. 266. On Soviet interest see Major-General M. Belov and Lieutenant-Colonel V. Shchukin '*Razvedyvatel'no-porazhayushchiye kompleksy armii SShA*' ('Reconnaissance-Destruction Complexes of the US Army'), *VV* 1/1985, pp. 86–89.

Conclusion

What is Different about Soviet Rocket Troops and Artillery?

Artillery is used more aggressively by the Russians. If a good direct fire position can be found, it will be used. Soviet gunners are not and never have been afraid to lose a gun or rocket launcher if it rips an arm off the enemy in the process. The fact that the Soviets talk about *fire destruction* or *paralysis* and not support does not mean, of course, that their artillery is any more effective, round for round or individual battery for battery, than ours, but their emphasis on direct fire and, conversely, their very efficient control of artillery at the highest possible level as well, means that in these two circumstances it may be.

It therefore helps us to envisage the Russians as having two artillery forces. The first is de-centralised, organic to motor rifle and, now, tank regiments, and may be devolved further. It is the close support, often direct fire force. It does many of the jobs for which Western armies have to rely on other heavy weapons organic to infantry and armour. This is physically manifested in the way regimental gunners wear the collar tabs of the arm with which they are fighting.

The second is the centralised artillery force at the disposal of the formation or higher formation commander. This force has always been regarded as more effective the higher the level at which it is controlled. In the West a forward observation officer can in theory bring down the fire of the entire divisional or corps artillery. A Soviet battalion COP cannot do this. So what? A Soviet battalion or regimental commander has a very sizeable artillery force allocated to him to augment his own considerable firepower. Meanwhile, at the higher tactical (division) and operational levels artillery is deployed to best effect as part of a master plan, without requests from frightened junior officers getting in the way. If the Soviet Army or Front artillery commander, and the all-arms formation commander, go up front and plan the fireplan themselves, this is an admirable example of a large formation being controlled from the front. It is risky, but war is risky and it is part of the Soviet style of war.

The Soviets do certain things which puzzle Western observers. They still employ towed anti-tank guns, towed by MT-LB tractors. Surely this is out of date? Surely it is excessively vulnerable on the modern battlefield? But a towed gun pulled by an armoured carrier is no more vulnerable than an unprotected self-propelled weapon like the American M-107 or the Soviets' own 2S5. Also, losing the tractor does not mean that the gun itself cannot move. Small towed equipments can be manhandled into position, and the Russians have always been very good at camouflaging them. They continue to introduce towed equipments alongside self-propelled ones, partly, no doubt, for economy's sake, but also because they have certain advantages. Another case is the linear deployment. As we have seen, the Soviets do not believe that the shape itself makes that much difference, certainly not enough to outweigh the advantages which a straight line gives in terms of time into action and fire control. On the other hand they are very interested in Western developments where it suits them. For example, they have enthusiastically followed the foreign military press's coverage of submunition warheads, which have obvious uses for them. They have also, it is true, followed the development of copperhead, the terminally guided artillery round (Cannon-Launched Guided Projectile). Yet it is hard to see them going for that in the same way, as copperhead is primarily a long range anti-armour weapon and they have less requirement to invest resources in that than the West do. Nevertheless, precision guided munitions may have certain attractions for special missions by Army and Front level artillery against key targets.

Mirror imaging is a great problem in analysing the Soviet military and Western analysts get very exasperated when the Russians do not behave as they are expected to. The Russian artillery has a longer tradition of uniqueness and idiosyncracy than any other arm of the Russian armed forces. After all, as Tvardovskiy pointed out with a wink acknowledging the perverseness of gunners, and Russian gunners in particular, artillery (towed artillery, at any rate), is the only arm which goes into battle facing backwards.

It is still often asserted that the Soviets' quantitative superiority on land may be outweighed by qualitative factors, by which equipment, training and battle experience are usually meant. The Russian artillery has always had equipment as good as any, and often better. It has always been an extremely professional organisation: sometimes, however, this has actually been counter-productive in terms of all-arms co-operation, and the spectre of this exists today. This book has shown that Russian artillerymen are intelligent, often innovative, and take their profession extremely seriously. They are pragmatic and cynical about their arm's ability to bring its full potential to bear on the battlefield, and are constantly trying to improve it. Today, the artillery's prime aim is to guarantee a swift victory in the context of the huge Theatre Strategic Operation. If nuclear weapons are not used, so much the better. The ability of the Artillery and Rocket Troops to conduct precise but massive conventional fires is part of this process of refinement.

The Soviets will undoubtedly continue to place great emphasis on this arm, more so than in the West. There are perhaps three core reasons for this. The first is that, although the Soviets make very good guns, this side of the arm is not at the very forefront of technological development. It is in clever use of existing technology that the Russians excel; systems like artillery that are tried and true if not exactly cheap. Computers and data processing for fire control, laser rangefinders and inertial guidance systems for pinpointing targets will all enhance its performance, and the Soviets will exploit them where they can, but *it will work without them*. Secondly, artillery is reliable, methodical, mechanical. If a target is plotted and a given number of rounds are fired at it, even by guns which cannot see the target and possibly without an observer either, it will be destroyed. Artillery operations contain less of the element of chance, luck and instinct that characterise armoured or mechanised infantry combat. Artillery is precise and scientific, and does what it is told. It therefore appeals to the Russian mind. It is consequently the arm in which they should invest their strength, in the future as in the past.

The third reason, as we have seen, is that bitter historical experience has caused the Russians to revere the long range destructive power of rockets and artillery. In the last war the Red Army played the overwhelming part in defeating the Germans on land, and the artillery was without question its best arm. From their point of view, it is vital that everybody understands that it is never again going to be worthwhile making war on Russia, and her traditional strength in firepower is a very important part of that. As Khrushchev said, history has shown that turning the other cheek does not work in international politics. 'We had shown', said Khrushchev, talking about the U2 affair, 'that anyone who slapped *us* on our cheek would get his head kicked off'. He had a point. *Tochka, kayuk!*

Note

Guns going into battle backwards, from Tvardovskiy, *Vassiliy Tërkin*, the section '*ot avtora*' (later in poem), '*pushki k boyu yedut zadom*'. Khrushchëv, from Strobe Talbott, trans. and ed., *Khrushchev remembers*, Volume 2 (Penguin, Harmondsworth, 1974), p. 510.

English–Russian Glossary of Russian Artillery and other Military Terms Appearing in this Book

Russian letter '*ë*' is pronounced '*o*' or '*yo*' as in Mr. *Gorbachëv*

English	**Russian**
Acacia (2S3)	*Akatsiya*
Academy (Staff or War college, not *basic officer training)*	*Akademiya*
Academy of Artillery Sciences	*Akademiya artilleriyskikh nauk*
Accompaniment (phase of fire support)	*Soprovozhdeniye*
Active system (Gun, etc.)	*Activny sistem*
Adjusting gun	*Osnovnoye orudiye*
Aerial registration point	*Vozdushny reper*
Aiming point	*Tockha navodki*
Air balloon observation battalion	*Vozdukhoplavatel'ny divizion aerostatov nablyudeniya (VDAN)*
Air Defence Service, embracing:	*Protivovozdushnye voyska (PVO voyska)*
Air Defence of the Ground Forces, and	*Protivovozdushnaya oborona sukhoputnykh voysk (PVO SV)*
Air Defence of the Homeland (Strategic Air Defence Service)	*Protivivozdushnaya oborona strany (PVO Strany)*
Allocated (subordination of artillery)	*Pridanny*
All as one	*Vnakladku (used of drinking tea with sugar stirred in it, and of an artillery battalion firing all as one rather than having a separate target for each battery)*
Anti-aircraft artillery	*Zenitnaya artilleriya*
Anti-tank artillery	*Protivotankovaya artilleriya*
Anti-tank artillery brigade	*Istrebitel'naya protivotankovaya artilleriy skaya brigada (IPTABr) — the 'Istrebitel'naya', meaning 'destroyer is redundant in English.*
Anti-tank artillery regiment	*Istrebitel'niy protivotankovy artilleriysky polk (IPTAP)*
Anti-tank Guided Weapon (Missile)	*Protivotankovy upravlyayemy reaktivny snaryad (PTURS)*
Arm of Service	*Rod voysk*
Armed services	*Vooruzhënnye sily*

219

Armour piercing	Broneboyny
Armour piercing cap	broneboyny nakonechnik
Armour piercing core	broneboyny serdechnik
Army Artillery Group	Armeyskaya artilleriyskaya gruppa (AAG)
Army Anti-aircraft artillery Group	Armeyskaya zenitnaya artilleriyskaya gruppa (AZAG)
Army General	General armii
Army Gun Artillery Brigade	Armeyskaya pushechnaya artilleriyskaya brigada (Apabr)
Artillery battalion	Divizion
Artillery battalion commander	Komandir diviziona
Artillery board	Planshet
Artillery division	Artilleriyskaya diviziya (a large formation, not to be confused with the divizion or battalion)
Artillery instrument reconnaissance	Artilleriyskaya instrumental'naya razvedka (AIR)
Artillery Journal	Artilleriyskiy zhurnal
Artillery locating radar	Stantsiya nazemnoy artelleriyskoy razvedki (SNAR)
Artillery offensive	Artilleriyskoye nastupleniye
Artillery Reserve of the High Command (Front reserve)	Artilleriya rezerva glavnokomandovaniya (ARGK)
Artillery Reserve of the Supreme High Command (Strategic)	Artilleriya rezerva verkhovnogo glavnokomandovaniya (ARVGK)
Artillery of Special Power	Artilleriya osoboy moshchnosti
Artilleryman	Pushkar, artillerist (artillerist is used when stressing professionalism, usually of an officer)
Barrage fire (see also mobile and stationary)	Zagraditel'ny ogon' (ZO)
Barrel	Stvol
Ballistic cap (of shell)	Ballisticheskiy nakonechnik
Base section	Donnaya chast'
Battalion (all-arms)	Batal'on
Battalion chief-of-staff (of artillery battalion)	Nachal'nik shtaba diviziona
Battalion Fire Direction Centre	Punkt upravleniya ognya diviziona (PUOD)
Battery commander	Komandir batareya
Battery Senior Officer (Gun Position Officer)	Starshiy ofitser batareya (SOB)
Breakthrough	Proryv
Breakthrough Artillery Corps	Artilleriyskiy korpus proryva (AKP)
Breakthrough Artillery Division	Artilleriyskaya diviziya proryva (ADP)
Breech	Zatvor
Bulkhead (in rocket warhead)	Diafragma
Bursting charge	Razryvnoy snaryad, vzryvchatoye veshchestvo
Bushes holding propellant charge	Vkladyshi toplivogo zaryada
Carnation (2Sl)	Gvozdika
Casing (of nuclear round)	Obolochka
Cavalry-mechanized group	Konno-mekhanizirovannaya gruppa (KMG)
Central tube (of shell)	Tsentral'naya trubka

Centre of Arc	Osnovnoye napravleniye (ON)
Charge	Zaryad
Chemical shell	Chimicheskiy snaryad
Chief Marshal of Artillery	Glavny Marshal Artillerii
Close support artillery (to move with infantry)	Artilleriya podderzhki pekhoty (PP)
Combination Gun (Howitzer-Mortar)	Kombinirovannoye orudiye
Command Observation Post	Komandno-nablyudatel'ny punky (KNP)
Commission for Special Artillery Experiments	Komissiya osobykh artilleriyskikh opytov (KOSARTOP)
Concentrated fire	sosredotochenny ogon' (SO)
Concrete busting round	Betonoboyny snaryad
Conventional explosive charge (in nuke)	Zaryad vzryvchatogo veshchestva
Corps	Korpus
Corps artillery regiment	Korpusnoy artilleriyskiy polk (kap)
Corps artillery brigade	Korpusnaya artileriysaya brigada (KABr)
Corps artillery group	Korpusnaya artileriskaya gruppa (KAG)
Corps anti-aircraft artillery group	Korpusnaya zenitnaya artilleriyskaya gruppa (KZAG)
Counter battery fire	Kontrbatareyny ogon', kontrbatereynaya bor'ba
Counter-preparation (breaking up attack)	Kontrpodgotovka
Cradle (of gun carriage, holding the barrel)	Lyul'ka
Deep operation	Glubokaya operatsiya
Defence against weapons of mass destruction	Zashchita ot oruzhiya massovogo porazheniya
Delay fuze	Distantsionnaya trubka
Deliberate fire	Metodicheskiy ogon'
Detonating mechanism	Mekhanizm vzryvaniya
Detonator	Kapsiol', detonator
Dial sight (non optical)	Uglomer
(optical)	Panorama, panoramny pritsel
Division (formation in order of 10,000 men or more strong)	Diviziya
Divisional Artillery Group	Divizionnaya artilleriyskaya gruppa (DAG)
Divisional Anti Aircraft Artillery Group	Divizionnaya zenitnaya artilleriyskaya gruppa (DZAG)
Direct fire (of gun); fire with target in view (mortar). See also semi-direct fire	Pryamoy ogon', ogon' pryamoy navodkoy
Driving band (at base of shell, to engage rifling)	Vedushchy poyasok
Drop breech (vertical wedge breech)	Vertikal'ny klinovoy zatvor
Ensign (from 1972)	Praporshchik
Experimental Design Bureau	Opytny konstruktorskiy byuro (OKB)
Fire blow	Ognevoy nalët
Fire curtain (rolling barrage)	Ognevoy val
Fire destruction	Ognevoye porazheniye
Fire for annihilation	Unichtozheniye
Fire for demolition	Razrusheniye
Fire for effect	Strel'ba na porazheniye
Fire for suppression	Podavleniye
Fire for destruction (general term, embracing the three categories above)	Porazheniye

Fire at a single (point) target	Ogon po otdel'noy tseli
Fire mission	Ognevaya zadacha
Fire (power) superiority	Ognevoye prevoskhodstvo
Fire strike	Ognevoy udar
Fissile material (in nuke)	Delyashcheyesya veshchestvo
Fixed ammunition	Unitarny patron
Formation	Soyedineniye
Flanking/observation post	Bokovoy nablyudatel'ny punkt (BNP)
Forward observation post	Peredovoy nablyudatel'ny punkt (PNP)
Forward march security element	Golovnaya pokhodnaya zastava (GPZ)
Front artillery group	Frontovaya artilleriyskaya gruppa (FAG)
Front anti-aircraft artillery group	Frontovaya zenitnaya artilleriyskaya gruppa (FZAG)
Full calibre armour piercing round	Kaliberny broneboyny snaryad
Fuze	vzryvatel'
Gas dynamic laboratory	Gazodinamicheskaya laboratoriya (GDL)
God of War	Bog voyny
Group of Soviet Forces Germany	Gruppa sovetskikh voysk v Germanii (GSVG)
Group for the study of rocket motion	Gruppa po izucheniyu reaktivnogo dvizheniya (GIRD)
Guards	Gvardeyskiy
Guards mortar (multiple rocket launcher)	Gvardyskiy minomёt
Guards mortar regiment	Gvardeyskiy minomёtny polk (Gvminp)
Guards mortar brigade	Gvardeyskaya minomёtnaya brigada (Gvminbr)
Guards mortar division	Gvardeyskaya minomёtnaya diviziya
Guards mortar unit	Gvardeyskaya minomёtnaya chast' (GMCh)
Guidance fins (mortar bomb)	stabilisator
Guided projectile	upravlyayemy snaryad
Guided missile (small)	upravlyayemy reaktivny snaryad
(large)	upravlyayemy raket
Gun	Pushka (as defined in Chapter three. As a general term for tube artillery, orudiye)
Gun artillery regiment	Pushechny artilleriyskiy polk (PAP)
Gun artillery brigade	Pushechnaya artilleriyskaya brigada (PAbr)
Gun-howitzer	Pushka gaubitsa
Gun position officer (Battery senior officer)	Starshiy ofitser batareya (SOB)
Harassing fire	Iznureniye
Head of reconnaissance (of battery, battalion, etc)	Komandir vzvoda upravleniya
Heavy artillery	Tyazhёlaya artilleriya (also used to translate artilleriya bol'shoy moshchnosti — see high powered artillery).
Heavy howitzer artillery brigade	Gaubichnaya artilleriyskaya brigada bol'shoy moshchnosti (gabr BM) or tyazhёlaya artilleriyskaya brigada (tgabr)
Held under command (of senior artillery commander)	Podruchny
High explosive (shell)	Fugasny
High explosive and fragmentation effect	Oskolochno-fugasnoye deystviye
High explosive and fragmentation shell	Oskolochno-fugasny snaryad
High powered artillery	Artilleriya bol'shoy moshchnosti

Higher Artillery Command School	Vysshee artilleriyskoye komandnoye uchilishche
Higher Military Command School	Vysshee voyennoye komandnoye uchilishche
Higher Military Engineering School	Vysshee voyennoye inzhenernoye uchilishche
Higher formation (Army, Front)	Ob'yedineniye
Horizontal wedge breech	Gorizontal'ny klinovoy zatvor
Howitzer	Gaubitsa
Howitzer artillery regiment	Gaubichny artilleriyskiy polk (gap)
Ignition delay (in rocket assisted shell)	Zamedlitel' puska
Illuminating shell	Osvetitel'ny snaryad
Incendiary shell	Zazhigatel'ny snaryad
Independent artillery battalion	Otdel'ny divizion
Independent artillery reconnaissance battalion	Otdel'ny razvedyvatel'ny artilleriyskiy divizion (ORAD)
Independent railway battery	Otdel'naya zheleznodorozhnaya batareya (otd. zh-d batr)
Independent super heavy artillery battalion	Otdel'ny artilleriyskiy divizion Osoboy Moshchnosti (oadnOM)
Independent air adjustment squadron	Otdel'naya korrektirovochnaya aviatsionnaya eskadril'ya (OKAE)
Independent air reconnaissance and adjustment regiment	Otdel'ny korrektirovochno-razvedyvatel'ny aviatsionny-polk (OKRAP)
Indirect fire	Nepryamoy ogon', ogon's zakritoy pozitsii
Integrated Fire Destruction of the Enemy	Kompleksnoye ognevoye porazheniye protivnika
Laser rangefinder	Lazerny (kvantovy) dal'nomer
Lead reconnaissance patrol or point recce patrol	Golovnoy dozor (GD)
Light artillery	Lëgkaya artilleriya, malokalibernaya artilleriya
Light artillery regiment	Lëgkiy artilleriyskiy polk (lap)
Light artillery brigade	Lëgkaya artilleriyskaya brigada (labr)
Long range artillery group	Gruppa Dal'nego Deystviya (DD)
Main Artillery Directorate (1862–1964)	Glavnoye artilleriyskoye upravleniye (GAU)
Main Rocket and Artillery Directorate (1964–)	Glavnoye raketno-artilleriyskoye upravleniye (GRAU)
Main and central Directorates	Glavnye i tsentral'nye upravleniya
Main fire unit of artillery	Glavnaya ognevaya yedinitsa artillerii
Marshal of Artillery	Marshal artillerii
Medium artillery	Srednekalibernaya artilleriya
Meeting engagement	Vstrechny boy
Metal crater (in shaped charge shell)	Metallicheskaya voronka
Military Art	Voyennoye iskusstvo
Military Doctrine	Voyennaya doktrina
Military release to service (quality control standard)	Voyennaya priyëmka
Mobile Group (Great Patriotic War)	Podvizhnaya gruppa
Mobile barrage	Podvizhny zagraditel'ny ogon' (PZO)
Mobile ground recce post (radar)	Podvizhnaya stantsiya nazemnoy razvedki (PSNR)
Mobile group (GPW)	Podvizhnaya gruppa
Mobile reconnaissance post	Podvizhny razvedyvatel'ny punkt (PRP)

Mortar	Minomët (mortir is a huge old fashioned mortar, American Civil War style)
Mortar bomb	Minomëtny vystrel
Mortar locating radar	Artilleriyskaya radiolokatsionnaya stantsiya obnaruzheniya minomëtov (ARSOM)
Mortar regiment	Minomëtny polk (minp)
Mortar brigade	Minomëtnaya brigada (minbr)
Mortarman	Minomëtchik
Muzzle brake	Dul'ny tormoz
Muzzle velocity	Nachal'naya skorost'
Neutron reflector (in nuclear warhead)	Otrazhatel' neytronov
Night action	Deystviya noch'yu
Night vision device	Pribor nochnogo videniya
Non-recoil gun	Dinamoreaktivnaya pushka (DRP), bezotkatnoye orudiye
Norm, norms	Norma, normy
Northern Group of Forces	Severnaya Gruppa Voysk (SGV)
Nuclear round	Yaderny snaryad
On one's own position (desperate measure!)	Na sebya
Operation	Operatsiya
Operational Art	Operativnoye iskusstvo
Operational Group (small roving unit for command of independent units and formations)	Operativnaya gruppa
Operational Manoeuvre Group	Operativnaya manevrennaya gruppa (from Polish Operacyjna grupa manewrowa) see also mobile group
Operational Tactical Rocket (up to 1000 km range)	Operativno-takticheskiy raket
Optical sight	Opticheskiy pritsel'
Organic (part of a given formation)	Shtatny
Paralysis	Porazheniye (usually translated destruction)
Preparation (phase of artillery support)	Podgotovka
Panorama sight, see dial sight	
Percussion cap	Kapsyul', kapsyul' vosplamenitel'
Permanent anti-aircraft fire point	Dolgovremennaya zenitnaya ognevaya tochka (DZOT)
Permanent fire point (pill box)	Dolgovremennaya ognevaya tochka (DOT)
Plunging fire	Navesny ogon'
Propellant charge	Toplilvny zaryad (solid fuel rocket), boyevoy zaryad (cartridge)
Protection (phase of fire support)	Prikritiye
Protective cone (of shaped charge shell)	Predokhranitel'ny konus
Pursuit	Presledovaniye
Radar	Radiolokatsionnaya stantsiya (RLS)
Rangefinder	Dal'nomer
Rapid firing gun	Skorostrel'naya pushka
Reactive artillery (rocket artillery)	Reaktivnaya artilleriya (RA)
Recess (in sub-calibre shell)	Poddon
Recoil system, mechanism	Protivootkatnye ustroystva

Recoilless gun	Dinamoereaktivnaya pushka (DRP), bezotkatnoye orudiye
Reconnaissance	Razvedka
Reconnaissance patrol	Dozor
Reconnaissance Destruction Complex, embracing	Razvedyvatel'no-parazhayushchiy kompleks
Reconnaissance — Fire Complex (Tactical)	Razvedyvatel'no-ognevoy Kompleks (ROK)
Reconnaissance — Strike Complex (Operational)	Razvedyvatel'no-udarny Kompleks (RUK)
Regiment	Polk
Registration point	Reper
Revolution in Military Affairs	Revolyutsiya v voyennom dele
Rocket artillery	Reaktivnaya artilleriya (RA)
Rocket assisted shell, projectile	Aktivno-reactivny snaryad
Rocket Forces and Artillery (of the Ground Forces)	Raketnye voyska i artilleriya (sukhoputnykh voysk)
Rocket launcher	Gvardeyskiy minomët (Great Patriotic War), reaktivny minomët, Boyevaya mashina (modern) (BM)
Rocket launcher brigade — see Guards Mortar brigade	
Rocket nozzle	Reaktivnaya sopla
Rocket Science Research Institute	Reaktivny nauchno-issledovatel'skiy institut (RNII)
Rocket Volley Fire System (NATO MLRS)	Reaktivny sistem zalpovogo ognya (RSZO)
Rocketeer	Raketchik
Rolling barrage (single)	Odinarny ognevoy val
(double)	Dvoynoy ognevoy val
Screw breech	Porshnevoy zatvor
Screw in head (of shell)	Privintnaya golovka
Self-propelled gun	Samokhodnaya artilleriyskaya ustanovka (SAU)
Semi-direct fire	polypryamoy ogon'
Senior artillery commander	Starshiy artilleriyskiy komandir (nachal'nik)
Services (armed)	Vooruzhënnye sily
Settings for firing	Ustanovki strel'by
Shaped charge shell	Kumulyativny snaryad
Shield	Shchitovoye prikritiye
Shock absorber	Uspokoitel' vibratsii
Smoke shell	Dymovoy snaryad
Smoke producing agent	Dymoobrazuyushchee veshchestva
Sound ranging	Zvukovaya razvedka
Special conditions	Osobye usloviya
Special Heavy Artillery (Tsarist)	Tyazhëlaya artilleriya osobogo naznacheniya (TAON)
Stationary barrage	Nepodvizhny zagraditel'ny ogon' (NZO)
Strategic Air Defence Service (to 1983)	Protivovozdushnaya oborona strany (PVO Strany)
Strategic Rocket Forces (Troops)	Raketnye voyska strategicheskogo naznacheniya (RVSN)
Sub-calibre armour piercing round	Podkaliberny broneboyny snaryad
Sub-munition (individual)	Boyevoy element
Sub-munition projectile (containing sub-munitions)	Kassetny snaryad
Sub-munition rocket warhead	Kassetnaya boyevaya chast' raketa

Sub-unit (battalion and below)	*Podrazdeleniye*
Super heavy artillery	*Artilleriya osoboy moshchnosti*
Super heavy artillery battalion	*Artilleriyskiy divizion osoboy moshchnosti (adn OM)*
Super powered artillery	*Sverkhmoshchnaya artilleriya*
Support (phase of fire support)	*Podderzhka*
Supporting (artillery assigned to a unit or sub-unit)	*Podderzhivayushchiy*
Surface-to-surface missile	*Raket klassa 'zemlya-zemlya'*
Tactical-technical instruction	*Taktiko-tekhnicheskoye zadaniye (TTZ)*
Tactics	*Taktika*
Technical criterion	*Tekhnicheskoye usloviye (TU)*
Theatre of Military Operations	*Teatr voyennykh deystvii (TVD)*
Theatre of War	*Teatr voyny (TV)*
Time of flight	*vremya poleta*
Tracer element (at back of shell)	*trassiruyushchee ustroystvo*
Trails	*staniny*
Trunnions	*Tsapfy (sing. tsapfa)*
Tube artillery	*Stvol'naya artilleriya*
Unit (regimental size)	*Chast'*
Unit of fire	*Boyevoy komplekt*
Vanguard	*Avangard (from French Avant-garde)*
Vertex height (top of a shell's trajectory)	*Vysota trayektorii*
Warhead	*Boyevaya chast'*
Weapons of mass destruction	*Oruzhiye massovogo porazheniya*

Bibliography

Russian and Polish language sources

Books

Astashenkov, P. T., *Sovetskye raketnye voyska (Soviet Rocket Forces)*, (Voyenizdat, Moscow, 1967).

Barsukov, E., *Russkaya artilleriya v mirovoy voyne (Russian Artillery in the World War)*, (Moscow, 1938).

Berkhin, I. B., *Voyennaya reforma v SSSR 1924–25 gg. (Military Reform in the USSR 1924–25)*, (Moscow, 1958).

Biryukov, Major-General G. F. and Arendarenko, I. I., *Sluzhu v raketnykh (I serve in the Rocket Forces)*, (DOSAAF Press, Moscow, 1980).

Brandenburg, General N., *500 let'ye russkoy artillerii (The 500th Anniversary of Russian Artillery)*, (St. Petersburg, 1889).

Chervonny, P. Ye, *Otprashchi do sovremennoy pushki (Introduction to Modern Artillery)*, (Moscow, 1956).

Doroshenko, S. S., *Lev Tolstoy, voyn i patriot: voyennaya sluzhba i voyennaya deyatel'nost' (Leo Tolstoy, Warrior and Patriot: Military Service and Attainments)*, (Moscow, 1966).

Fëdorov, Lieutenant-General V. G., *K voprosu o date poyavlenii artillerii na Rusi (On the Question of the Date of Artillery's Appearance in Russia)*, (Academy of Artillery Sciences, Moscow-Leningrad, 1949).

Grendal', V. D., *Ogon' artillerii (Artillery Fire)*, (Voyenizdat, Moscow, 1926).

Grendal', V. D., *Artilleriya v osnovnykh vidakh boya (korpus, diviziya, polk) (Artillery in the Principal Forms of Combat: Corps, Division, regiment)*, (Voyenizdat, Moscow, 1940).

Guk, Lieutenant-Colonel K. G., *Zakrytaya strel'ba polevoy artillerii (Field Artillery Fire from Covered Positions)*, (St. Petersburg, 1882).

Kamkov, I. A., Konoplyanik, V. M. *Voyennye akademii i uchilishcha (Military Academies and Schools)*, (Voyenizdat, Moscow, 1974).

Kartashov, N. V., *Boyevye neupravlyayemye rakety (Military Unguided Rockets)*, (Voyenizdat, Moscow, 1968).

Kazakov, K. P., *Artilleriya i Rakety (Artillery and Rockets)*, (Voyenizdat, Moscow, 1968).

Khlebnikov, N. M., *Pod grokhot soten batarey (To the Thunder of Hundreds of Batteries)*, (Voyenizdat, Moscow, 1974).

Kirey, Lieutenant-Colonel V. F., *Artilleriya ataki i oborony (Artillery in the Attack and the Defence)*, introduction by Yu. M. Sheydeman, (Voyenizdat, Moscow, 1936).

Kir'yan, M. M., ed., *Voyenno-tekhnicheskiy progress i vooruzhënnye sily SSSR (Scientific-Technical Progress and the Armed Forces of the USSR)*, (Voyenizdat, Moscow, 1982).

Kopylov, N., *Razvitiye taktiki russkoy armii s xviii do nachala xx vek (Evolution of Russian Army Tactics from the 18th to the beginning of the 20th centuries)*, (Moscow, 1957).

Korobkov, N. M., ed., *Semiletnyaya voyna: Materialy o deystvii russkoy armii i flota 1756–1763 gg. (The Seven Years' War: Documents Relating to the Operations of the Russian Army and Fleet)*, (Voyenizdat, Moscow, 1948).

Kovalenko, D. A., *Oboronnaya promyshlennost' Sovetskoy Rossii 1918–20 gg. (The Defence Industry of Soviet Russia 1918–20)*, (Nauka, Moscow, 1970).

Kutaysov, Major-General A. I., *Obshchiye pravila dlya artillerii v polevom srazhenii (General Rules for the Employment of Artillery in Field Combat)*, in Skalon (see below) Vol. 4 part 2 book 2.

Kuznetsov, P. I., *Ogon' vedet batareya (Fire Mission Battery)*, (Voyenizdat, Moscow, 1982).

Latukhin, A. N., *Sovremennnaya artilleriya (Modern Artillery)*, (Voyenizdat, Moscow, 1970).

Malakhovskiy, Ye K., *Strel'ba na porazheniye opornykh punktov (Fire for the Destruction of Defensive Positions)*, (Voyenizdat, Moscow, 1978).

Mamontov, S., *Pokhody i kony (Raids and Riding)*, (YMCA Press, Paris, 1981).

Manikovskiy A. A., *Boyevoye snabzheniye Russkoy armii v pervoy mirovoy voyne (The munitions supply of the Russian Army in World War I)*, 2 Vols. (Moscow, 1930).

Mikhaylov, O., *Ustav ratnykh pushechnykh i drugikh del, kasayushchikhsya do voinskoy nauke, sostoyashchiy v 663 ukazakh ili statyakh . . . (Regulations for Artillery and Various other Matters relating to Military Science, etc., etc . . .)*, ed. V. Ruban, published on the order of Prince Potëmkin (State Military College, 1781).

Nilus, Colonel A., *Istoriya material'noy chasti artillerii (History of Artillery Matériel)*, Vol. 2, *Field Artillery* (St. Petersburg, 1904).

Novitskiy, V. T., *Voyennaya Entsiklopediya (Military Encyclopedia)*, 18 Vols., going up to the letter 'P' (St. Petersburg, 1911–15).

Pavlenko, P. F., Bliznyuk, I. N., Smirnov, S. M., *Sovetskiye vozdushno-desantnye (Soviet Airborne Forces)*, (Voyenizdat, Moscow, 1980).

Peredel'skiy, Marshal Arty G. Ye, Tokmakov, A. I., Khoroshilov, G. T., *Artilleriya v boyu i operatsii (Artillery in the Battle and Operation)*, (Voyenizdat, Moscow, 1980).

Peredel'skiy, Marshal Arty G. Ye, *Artilleriyskiy divizion v boyu (The Artillery Battalion in Combat)*, (Voyenizdat, Moscow, 1984).

Pozdnev, A., *Tvortsy otechestvennogo oruzhiya (Founders of the Nation's Armaments)*, (Voyenizdat, Moscow, 1955).

Prochko, I. S., *Artilleriya v boyakh za rodinu (Artillery in Battle for the Motherland)*, (Voyenizdat, Moscow, 1957).

Reznichenko, Lieutenant-Colonel V. G., *Taktika (Tactics)*, (Voyenizdat, Moscow, 1984).

Robinson, A. N., ed., *Kulíkovskaya bitva v literature i iskusstve (the Battle of Kulíkovo in Literature and Art)*, (Nauka, Moscow, 1980).

Romanov, A. P., *Raketam pokoryayetsya prostranstvo (Rockets Conquer Space)*, (Politizdat, Moscow, 1976).

Shmakov, V. A., ed., *Vyshli na front katyushi (Katyushas to the Front)*, introduction by Marshal Arty Kuleshov, (Moscow Workers' Press, Moscow, 1982).

Skalon, D., ed., *Stoletiye voyennago ministerstva (A Hundred Years of the War Ministry)*, (St. Petersburg, 1902) (Many volumes).

Sotnikov, A., *Voyenno-istoricheskiy muzey artillerii, inzhenernykh voysk i voysk svyazy — kratkiy putevoditel' (The Military-Historical Museum of Artillery, Engineers and Signal Troops — a Short Guide)*, (Moscow-Leningrad, 1968).

Sovetskaya Voyennaya Entsiklopediya (Soviet Military Encyclopedia), 8 Vols. (Voyenizdat, Moscow, 1976–80).

Strokov, A. A., *Vooruzhënnye sily i voyennoye iskusstvo v pervoy mirovoy voyne (Armed Forces and Military Art in World War I)*, (Voyenizdat, Moscow, 1974).

Tikhomirov (no initial available), *Artilleriya bol'shoy moshchnosti (High Powered Artillery)*, (Moscow, 1938).

Tonkikh, A. V., *Preodoleniye protivotankovoy oborony (Overcoming Anti-tank Defence)*, (Voyenizdat, Moscow, 1978).

Triandafillov, V., *Kharakter operatsii sovremennykh armii (Character of the Operations of Modern Armies)*, (Voyenizdat, Moscow, 1936).

Tsygankov, I. S. and Sosulin, A. L., *Orudiye, minomët, boyevaya mashina (Gun, Mortar, Rocket Launcher)*, Third ed. (Voyenizdat, Moscow, 1980).

Tvardovskiy, Aleksandr, *Vasiliy Tërkin: kniga pro boytsa (Vasiliy Tërkin: a Soldier's Tale)*, (Narrative Poem, 1943–45, various editions).

Vnukov, V., *Mozhno li strelyat' na sotnyu verst? (Is it Possible to Fire at 100 Kilometres?)*, (Gosizdat, Moscow, 1927).

Voronov, N. N., *Na sluzhbe voyennoy (In the Service)*, (Voyenizdat, Moscow, 1963).

Yakovlev, N. D., *Ob artillerii i nemogo o sebe (On Artillery, and a Little about Myself)*, (Voyenizdat, Moscow, 1981).

Periodical Articles

Those most commonly consulted were:
Artilleriyskiy zhurnal (AZh) (Artillery Journal) (Tsarist).
Krasnaya zvezda (KZ) (Red Star).
Przegląd Wojsk Lotniczych i Wojsk Obrony Powietrznej Kraju (PWL i WOPK) (Polish Air and Air Defence Forces Review).
Przegląd Wojsk Ladowych (PWL) (Polish Ground Forces Review).
Tekhnika i Vooruzheniye (TiV) (Technology and Armament).
Voyenno-istoricheskiy zhurnal (VIZh) (Military Historical Journal).
Voyenny Vestnik (VV) (Military Herald).

Anashkin, I., Lieutenant-General Arty, *'Za kompleksnoye resheniye problemy'* ('For an All-embracing Solution to the Problem'), *VV* 10/1976, pp. 72–75.

Anashkin, Lieutenant-General Arty I., Kolesov, Colonel V., *'S otkritoy ognevoy pozitsii na bol'shiye dal'nosti'* ('From an Open Fire Position at Long Ranges'), *VV* 11/1982, pp. 60–63.

Anon, *'Ognevoy shchit rodiny'* ('Fire Shield of the Motherland'), *VIZh* 11/1978, pp. 11–16.

Anon, *'Polnee ispol'zovat' vosmozhnozti polkovoy i batal'onnoy artillerii'* ('To Utilise the Potential of Regimental and Battalion Artillery More Fully'), *VV* 2/1984, pp. 68–69.

Artillery Committee (Tsarist), *'O vvedenii v polevuyu artilleriyu uglomera dlya bokovoy navodki orudii'* ('On the Introduction into the Field Artillery of an *uglomer* for Horizontal Laying of a Gun'), *AZh* No. 6 (1898), Official section.

Avdeyev, Colonel M., *'Distsiplina v boyu'* ('Discipline and Reliability in Combat'), *VV* 11/1984, pp. 54–55.

Belov, Major-General M., and Shchukin, Lieutenant-Colonel V., *'Razvedyvatel'no porazhayushchiye kompleksy armii SShA'* ('Reconnaissance Destruction Complexes of the US Army'), *VV* 1/1985, pp. 86–89.

Binięda, Lieutenant-Commander Z., *'Geografia Wojenna: Ogólne pojecie Teatru Działań Wojennych'* ('Military Geography: the General Concept of a Theatre of Military Operations'), *Przeglad Morski (Naval Review)* 12/1981, pp. 3–4.

Chernukhin, Colonel V., and Tarakanov, Lieutenant-Colonel V., *'Peregruppirovka artillerii RVGK na bol'shiye rasstoyaniya po opytu nastupatel'nykh operatsii tret'ego perioda voyny'* ('Regrouping of Supreme High Command Reserve Artillery over Large Distances according to the Experience of the Third Period of the War'), *VIZh* 6/1980, pp. 10–16.

Dabolin, Colonel Ye, *'Reshaya sovmestnuyu zadachu'* ('Tackling a Joint Task'), *VV* 10/1980, pp. 74–75.

Dudarev, S., *'Artilleriya v bor'be s protivotankovymi sredstvami'* ('Artillery in Combat with anti-tank Weapons'), *VV* 5/1968, pp. 40–44.

Glushakov, Senior Lieutenant A., *'Batareya na dvukh ognevykh'* ('The Battery in Two Fire Positions'), *VV* 12/1981, pp. 62–64.

Golovin, General, *'Ustroystvo artillerii'* ('The Constitution of the Artillery'), in *Voyenny Sbornik (Military Collection)*, Vol. 7 (1925), pp. 201–18.

Ivanov, Colonel V., *'Obespechit' zhivuchest' batarey'* ('Guaranteeing the Survivability of Batteries'), *VV* 11/1972, pp. 60–63.

Ivanov, Colonel V., and Nesterov, Lieutenant-Colonel V., *'K voprosu o zhivuchesti artilleriyskikh podrazdelenii'* ('On the Question of the Survivability of Artillery Sub-units'), *VV* 10/1975, pp. 79–83.

Kaminskiy, S., *'Skorostrel'nye pushki nashey artillerii'* ('Rapid Fire Guns of our Artillery'), *Voyenny Sbornik* Vol. 59 (1870), No. 12.

Khamarchuk, A., *'Pochemu taktika?'* ('Why Tactics?'), *VV* 8/1968, pp. 44–48.

Karabanov, Colonel M., *'Uchet meteousloviy pri strel'be v gorakh'* ('The Study of Meteorological Conditions when Firing in Mountains), *VV* 2/1984, p. 62.

Kazakov, Marshal Arty K. P., *'Boyevoye primeneniye artillerii pri proryve oborony v Bobruiskskoy operatsii'* ('Military Employment of Artillery in Breakthrough of the Defence in the Bobruisk Operation'), *VIZh* 12/1980, pp. 18–24.

Kielczyński, Colonel A., Kawalec, Major W., *'Szkolenie w Ośrodku Zurbanizowany'* ('Training in Urban Centres'), three parts, *PWL*, June–August, 1983.

Kikishev, Captain N., *'Nuzhna prakticheskaya proverka'* ('Practical Checking is Needed'), *VV* 4/1976, p. 72.

Konyushko, Major-General Arty K, Bondarenko, Major A., *'Artilleriyskaya podgotovka obshchevoyskogo ofitsera'* ('The Artillery Training of the All-arms Officer'), *VV* 4/1984, pp. 54–59.

Koritchuk, Lieutenant-General Arty A. V., *'Bor'ba s protivotankovymi sredstvami v nastuplenii'* ('The Struggle with Anti-tank Weapons in the Offensive'), *VV* 6/1975, pp. 67–70.

Kravchenko, Major S., *'Artilleristy v zapolyar'e'* ('Artillerymen in the Arctic'), *VV* 12/1983, pp. 28–31.

Kuleshov, Marshal Arty P., *V. Velikoy Otechestvennoy voyne'* ('In the Great Patriotic War'), *VV* 1/1982, pp. 63–68 (part of the 600th anniversary series).

Latukhin, Colonel Engineer A., *'Vidny artilleriyskiy konstruktor'* ('Eminent Artillery Constructor'), *VIZh* 3/1982, pp. 94–96.

Litvinov, Lieutenant-Colonel B., *'Takticheskaya zrelost' komandira artillerista ('Tactical Maturity of the Artillery Commander'), *VV* 11/1984, pp. 52–53.

Makovey, Colonel O., *'Tsentral'nye artilleriyskiye'* ('Central Artillery Command Courses'), *VV* 7/1983, pp. 69–71.

Michalak, Major W., *'Lotnictwo w Dzialaniach Rajdowo-manewrowych Wojsk Ladowych'* ('Aviation in Raid-Manoeuvre Operations of the Ground Forces'), *PWL i WOPK* (Feb. 1982, pp. 5–9.

Mikhalkin, Major-General Arty V. M., Sidorenko, Colonel A., *'Kompleksnaya trenirovka'* ('Integrated Training'), *VV* 3/1977 pp. 29–33.

Mikhalkin, Colonel-General Arty V. M., *'Boyevoe primeneniye artillerii v Belorusskoy operatsii'* ('The Military Employment of Artillery in the Belorussian Operation'), *VIZh* 6/1984, pp. 25–33.

Mikhalkin, Colonel-General Arty V. M., *'Takticheskoy podgotovke artilleristov-obshchevoyskovuyu napravlennost'* ('Giving the Tactical Training of Artillery Officers an All-arms Emphasis'), *VV* 7/1984, pp. 62–65.

Mikhaylyuk, Major Engineer B., *'V interesakh vysokikh tempov nastupleniya'* ('In the Interests of the High Speed Offensive'), *VV* 4/1980, pp. 64–67.

Musial, Colonel Pilot A., *'Charakter i Znaczenie Operacji Powietrznych we Współczesnych Działaniach Wojennych'* ('The Character and Significance of Air Operations in Modern Warfare'), *PWL i WOPK* March 1982, pp. 10–13.

Musial, Colonel Pilot A., *'Rola Lotnictwa Uderzeniowego w Zabezpieczeniu Działań Desantów Morskikh'* ('The Role of Strike Aviation in Support of Sea Assault Landings'), *PWL i WOPK* May 1982, pp. 11–14.

Musial, Colonel Pilot A., *'Działanie Bojowe Lotnictwa na Korsyść Operacyjnych Grup Manewrowych'* ('Aviation Combat Operations on behalf of OMGs'), *PWL i WOPK* July–August 1982, pp. 9–14.

Nikol'skiy, Colonel-General Arty M., Ryzhenkov, Colonel G., *'Glavny Marshal Artillerii M I Nedelin'* ('Chief Marshal of Artillery M. I. Nedelin'), *VIZh* 11/1972, pp. 78–81.

Novikov, Lieutenant-Colonel A., Sebyakin, Colonel L., *'Deystviya artillerii'* ('The Action of Artillery'), *VV* 10/1982, pp. 34–38.

Odintsov, Professor Marshal Arty G., Kuznetsov, Colonel K., *'Stareyshaya kuznitsa artilleriyskikh kadrov'* ('The Oldest Forge for Artillery Specialists'), *VIZh* 12/1970, pp. 112–20.

Pavlovskiy, Army General I., *'Marshal artillerii G Ye Peredel'skiy'* ('Marshal of Artillery G. Ye Peredel'skiy'), *VIZh* 4/1983, pp. 95–96.

Peredel'skiy, Colonel-General Arty G. Ye, *'Marshal artillerii K P Kazakov'*, *VIZh* 12/1972, pp. 126–28.

Peredel'skiy, Marshal Arty G. Ye, *'O nepreryvnom ognevom porazhenii v sovremennom boyu'* ('On Uninterrupted Fire Destruction on Modern Combat'), *VV* 6/1977, pp. 82–87.

Peredel'skiy, Marshal Arty G. Ye, *'Boyevoye primeneniye artillerii v armeyskikh oboronitel'nykh operatsiyakh'* ('The Military Employment of Artillery in Army Defensive Operations'), *VIZh* 11/1979, 16–21.

Peredel'skiy, Marshal Arty G. Ye, Khoroshilov, Colonel G., *'Artilleriya v srazheniyakh ot Visly do Odera'* ('Artillery in the Operational Battles from the Vistula to the Oder'), *VIZh* 1/1985, pp. 30–34.
Struggle for Firepower Superiority in the War Years'), *VIZh* 11/1981, pp. 19–25.

Peredel'skiy, Marshal Arty G. Ye, *'Etapy na bol'shogo puti'* ('Milestones along the Highway'), *VV* 7/1982, pp. 10–13.

Peredel'skiy, Marshal Arty G. Ye, Khoroshilov, Colonel G., *'Artilleriya v srazheniyakh ot Visly do Odera'* ('Artillery in the Operational Battles from the Vistula to the Oder), *VIZh* 1/1985, pp. 30–34.

Pogonin, Colonel V., Vzaymodeystviye pri ognevom porazhenii' ('Inter-working in Fire Destruction'), *VV* 10/1984, pp. 50–55.

Pokruszynski, Colonel Dr. W, *'Operacja przeciwpowietrzna Wojsk OPK'* ('An Anti-air Operation by the Strategic Air Defence Forces'), *PWL i WOPK* May 1982, pp. 5–10.

Portugal'skiy, Colonel R., Borshchov, Major A., *'Sovershenstvovaniye metodov raboty komanduyushchikh i shtabov po organizatsii ognevogo porazheniya protivnika v nasupatel'nykh operatsiyakh'* ('Development of methods of Working by Commanders and Staff in organising Fire Destruction of the Enemy in Offensive Operations'), *VIZh* 3/1982, pp. 11–1.

Raykhtsaum, A., *'Pervy nachal'nik artillerii'* ('The First Commander of [Red Army] Artillery'), *VIZh* 11/1967, pp. 57–60.

Rokhkachev, Colonel V., *'Kassetnye boyevye chasti raket'* ('Sub-munition Rocket Warheads'), *TiV* 2/1984, pp. 8–9.

Sapkov, Colonel-General Arty L., *'Evolyutsiya taktiki i boyevogo primeneniya artillerii'* ('Evolution of Tactics and Military Employment of Artillery'), *VV* 4/1982, pp. 64–67.

Sapozhnikov, Lieutenant-General Arty A., *'Divizion-osnovnaya ognevaya yedinitsa artillerii'* ('Battalion — Main Artillery Fire Unit'), *VV* 2/1982.

Shibayev, Colonel N., *'Problemu reshat' kompleksno'* ('To Solve the Problem in an All-embracing way'), *VV* 6/1976, pp. 71–72.

Shkarubskiy, Colonel P., 'Artillery Before and Now' (Translated) *Voyennaya mysl' (Military Thought)* 2/1966.

Sidorov, Colonel-General M., *'Ognevoye porazheniye pri proryve oborony protivnika po opytu Velikoy Otechestvennoy voyny'* ('Fire Destruction During Breakthrough of the Enemy Defence According to the Experience of the Great Patriotic War'), *VIZh* 8/1984, pp. 18–23.

Strelkov, Major N., *'Podderzhka nastupleniya tankistov'* ('Supporting the Tanks' Offensive'), *VV* 3/1984, pp. 60–63.

Stroganov, Lieutenant-General Arty Ye, *'Osnovnoye ognevoye podrazdeleniye artillerii'* ('The Main Fire Sub-unit of Artillery'), *VV* 8/1979, pp. 55–60.

Stroganov, Lieutenant-General Arty Ye, *'Ognevoy udar'* ('Fire Strike'), *VV* 11/1980, pp. 67–71.

Stroganov, Lieutenant-General Arty Ye, *'Mesto komandira baterei v boyu'* ('The Place of the Battery Commander in Combat'), *VV* 5/1982, pp. 62–65.

Supreme Soviet of the USSR, *'O voinskikh zvaniyakh ofitserskogo sostava Vooruzhёnnykh Sil SSSR'* ('On the Military Ranks of Officer Personnel of the Armed Forces of the USSR'), 26 April 1984, reported in *KZ* 12 June, 1984, p. 2.

Tolubko, Army General V., *'Artilleriya 3-go Ukrainskogo Fronta v Yassko-Kishinёvskoy operatsii'* ('Artillery of 3 Ukrainian Front in the Yassy-Kishinёv Operation'), *VIZh* 8/1979, pp. 37–42.

Tsynkalov, Lieutenant-Colonel A., *'Bor'ba s protivotankovymi sredstvami protivnika v tret'em periode voyny'* ('The Struggle with Enemy Anti-tank Weapons During the Third Period of the War'), *VIZh* 7/1979, pp. 18–23.

Vorob'ёv, Major-General I., *'Oruzhiye i taktika: komandir i sovremenny boy'* ('Weapons and Tactics; the Commander and Modern Combat'), *KZ* 12 Jan. 1982, p. 2.

Voronov, Chief Marshal Arty N. N., *'Vydayushchiysya sovetskiy artillerist'* ('Outstanding Soviet Artilleryman'), *VIZh* 12/1963, pp. 58–64.

Vyshnevskiy, Colonel V., *'Batareya na marshe i vo vstrechnom boyu'* ('The Battery on the March and the Meeting Engagement'), *VV* 8/1984, pp. 56–58.

Yepifanov, Lieutenant-Colonel I., *'K voprosu o zhivuchesti artilleriyskikh podrazdelenii'* ('On the question of the Survivability of Artillery Sub-units'), *VV* 4/1976, p. 83.

Zabudkin, Colonel L., *'Kassetnye snaryady'* ('Sub-munition projectiles'), *TiV* 1/1984, pp. 36–37.

Zaytsev, General of Tank Troops M., *'Organizatsiya PVO — vazhnaya zadacha obshchevoyskogo komandira'* ('The Organization of Air Defence — a Crucial Task of the All-arms Commander'), *VV* 2/1979, pp. 23–26.

Zirka, Colonel L., *'Mesto komandira batarei v boyu — komandno nablyu-datel'ny punkt'* ('The Place of the Battery Commander in Combat — the Command-Observation Post'), *VV* 12/1982, pp. 64–65.

Other Language Sources

Books and Official Reports

British Admiralty Intelligence Papers

Adm/111/4508	Supply of Armaments and Naval Equipment to Foreign Countries.
Adm/116/1812	Situation at Vladivostok (Civil War).
Adm/116/1862	Russia — Memoranda.
Adm/116/1864	Baltic: General Situation.
Adm/116/3480	War with Russia — Naval Appreciation — 1932 (economic and naval strength).
Adm/137/1686–8	Report of the Situation at Kronstadt 1919.
Adm/223/51 Part I	Particulars of Russo-German Economic Agreement, 11/2/1940, and Naval Building Programme.
Part II	Military Strength of USSR — armaments manufacture.

Alexander, A. J., *Decision Making in Soviet Weapons Procurement*, (Adelphi Paper No. 147/8, London, Winter 1978/79).

Arndt, R. C., *Waffen und Gerät der Sowjetischen Landstreitkräfte*, (Walhalla u Praetoria Verlag, Regensburg, 1971), 4 Vols.

Bathurst, R. B., *Understanding the Soviet Navy*, (Naval War College Press, Newport, R. I., 1979).

Bazilevich, Professor K., *Russia's Art of War*, (Soviet War News Press, London, 1945).

Beaumont, Joan, *Comrades in Arms: British Aid to Russia 1941–45*, (Davis Poynter, London, 1980).

Becke, Captain A. F., *A Short Introduction to the History of Tactics*, 1740–1905, (London, 1909).

Belyayev, Lieutenant-Colonel, *Notes upon Russian Artillery Tactics in the War of 1905 with Conclusions drawn therefrom*, (trans. from the Russian *Artillery Journal*, War Office, General Staff, London, 1907).

Bethell, H. A., *Modern Guns and Gunnery*, (Royal Artillery Institution, Woolwich, London, 1905, 1907 and 1910 editions).

Biryukov G. and Melnikov G., *Anti-tank Warfare,* (translated from the Russian, Progress Publishers, 1972).

Braudel, F., *The Mediterranean and the Mediterranean World in the Age of Philip II*, 2 Vols. (Collins London, 1978).

Chief-of-Staff, India, *Reorganisation of the Headquarters Artillery Department of the Russian War Ministry*, trans. from *Novoye Vremya* of 4 Feb. 1909, (Simla, 1909).

Coates, Colonel J. B. Jr., *Wound Ballistics*, (Office of the Surgeon General, US Government Printing Office, Washington D.C., 1962).

Collins, L. J. D., 'The Military Organisation of the Crimean Tartars during the Sixteenth and Seventeenth Centuries' in Parry, V. J. and Yapp, M. E., ed., *War Technology and Society in the Middle East*, (Oxford University Press, 1975).

Cordonnier, Colonel E. L., *With the Japanese in Manchuria*, trans. from the French by Captain C. F. Atkinson, (London, 1914).

Douglas, Captain J. A., *Notes on the Russian Troops in China, 1900*, (War Office, London, 1902).

Duffy, C., *Russia's Military Way to the West: Origins and Nature of Russian Military Power 1700–1800*, (Routledge and Kegan Paul, London, 1981).

Ely, Colonel L. B., *The Red Army Today*, (Military Service Publishing Co., Harrisburg, Penn, 1953).

Erickson, J., *The Soviet High Command 1917–41*, (London, 1962).

Erickson, J., *The Road to Stalingrad*, (Harper and Row, London, 1975).

Glushko, V. P., *Development of Rocketry and Space Technology in the USSR*, trans. from the Russian (Novosti Press, 1973).

Golitsyn, Prince N. S., *Allgemeine Kriegsgeschichte aller Völker und Zeiten*, (trans. from the Russian) (Cassell, 1874), 4 Vols.

Gosztony, P., *Die Rote Armee: Geschichte und Aufbau der Sowjetischen Landstreitkräfte*, (Fritz Molden Verlag, 1980).

Grierson, Captain J. M., *The Armed Strength of Russia*, (War Office, Intelligence Staff, London, 1882 and 1886 editions).

Headlam, Major-General J., *Report on Visit to the Russian Front, 12(25) Feb to 12(25) March, 1917*. Typescript in the possession of the Royal Artillery Institution, Woolwich, London.

Headquarters United States Air Force Intelligence Reports, (AIR) 100–13/9, etc., 1948–49.

Heinl, Colonel R. B., *Dictionary of Military and Naval Quotations*, (United States Naval Institute Press, Annapolis, 1984).

Holloway, D., 'Doctrine and Technology in Soviet Armaments Policy' in Derek Leebaert, ed., *Soviet Military Thinking*, (London, 1981).

Horne, A., *The Price of Glory: Verdun, 1916*, (Penguin, London, 1978).

Hosmer, S. T., Kellen, K. and Jenkins, B. M., *The Fall of South Vietnam: Statements by Vietnamese Military and Civilian Leaders*, (Historian, Office of the Secretary of Defense, R-2208-OSD Hist, December, 1978).

House, Captain J. M., *Towards Combined Arms Warfare: A Survey of Tactics Doctrine and Organisation in the Twentieth Century*, (Combat Studies Institute, US Army Command and General Staff College, Fort Leavenworth, 1984).

Hughes, Major-General P. B., *Open Fire: Artillery Tactics from Marlborough to Wellington*, (Anthony Bird, Chichester, 1983).

International Institute of Strategic Studies, London, *The Military Balance*, various years.

Isby, D., *Weapons and Tactics of the Soviet Army*, (Jane's, London, 1981).

Jenkins, M., *Arakcheyev, Grand Vizier of the Russian Empire*, (London, 1969).

Jones, D. R., ed., *Soviet Armed Forces Review Annual*, (Academic International Press, Gulf Breeze, Florida), No. 6, 1982, and other years.

Jordan, P., *Russian Glory*, (Cresset, London, 1942).

Kenez, P., *Civil War in South Russia*, Vol. 1, 1918, (University of California Press, Berkeley, 1981).

Longstaff, Major F. V. and Atteridge, A. H., *The Book of the Machine gun*, (London, 1917).

Lederrey, Colonel E., *Germany's Defeat in the East 1941–45*, (Official History War Office, London, 1955).

Medical Statistics: Casualties and Medical Statistics of the Great War (History of the Great War), (HMSO, London, 1931).

Mellenthin, Major-General F. W. von, *Panzer Battles*, (Futura Books, London, 1977).

Miksche, F. O., *Attack!: A study of Blitzkrieg Tactics*, (Random House, New York, 1942).

Milton, John, *A Brief History of Moscovia and Other Less Known Countries Lying Eastward as far as Cathay*, (London, 1682).

Royal Artillery Institution, *Professional Visits of Artillery Officers 1861–66*, (Royal Artillery Institution, Woolwich, London, 1867).

Rutherford, W., *The Ally: the Russian Army in World War I*, (Gordon and Cremonesi, London, 1975).

Ryan, J. W., *Guns, Mortars and Rockets*, (Brassey's Battlefield Weapons Systems and Technology, Vol. 2, Brassey's, Pergamon, 1982).

Savkin, Colonel V. Ye, *The Basic Principles of Operational Art and Tactics*, (Moscow, 1972, translated from the Russian under the auspices of the United States Air Force, US Government Printing Office, Washington, D.C., 1982).

Scott, H. F. and W. F., *The Armed Forces of the Soviet Union*, (Westview Press, Boulder, Colorado, 1979), and subsequent editions.

Secretary of Defense, Washington D.C., *Soviet Military Power*, 1984 and 1985, (US Government Printing Office, Washington, D.C.).

Siegelbaum, L., *The War Industries Committees and the Politics of Industrial Mobilisation in Russia 1914–17*, (D.Phil., Oxford, 1975).

Sidorenko, Colonel A. A., *The Offensive*, (Moscow, 1970, translated from the Russian under the auspices of the United States Air Force, US Government Printing Office, Washington D.C., 1976).

United States of America — *Wartime International Agreements — Soviet Supply Protocols* — US Department of State, Washington, D.C.

Vernadsky, G., *A History of Russia*, Vol. III, *The Mongols and Russia*, (Yale University Press, Newhaven, 1953).

War Office, General Staff, *Reports of British Observers Attached to the Russian and Japanese Armies in the Field*, 3 Vols. (HMSO, London, 1907).

British War Office Intelligence Papers

WO/33/49	*Military Resources of the Russian Empire 1907.*
WO/33/712	Reports on Certain Aspects of the Military Situation in Russia &c, 1915.
WO/33/950	Archangel Front — Bolshevik Forces — Strengths.
WO/33/971	Issues made by the British Military Mission to the Armed Forces of South Russia.
WO/33/1214	*Military Forces of Soviet Turkestan 1928.*
WO/33/1461	*Order of Battle of the Military Forces of the USSR 1937.*
WO/33/1500	*Order of Battle of the Military Forces of the USSR 1938.*
WO/33/1655A	*Order of Battle 1940.*
WO/33/1684	*Order of Battle 1941.*

Whinyates, F., *From Coruña to Sevastopol: A History of 'C' Battery*, (London, 1891).

Wilson, General Sir R., *Brief Remarks on the Character and Composition of the Russian Army and a Sketch of the Campaign in Poland in the Years 1806 and 1807*, (London, 1810).

Periodical Articles

Bethell, Colonel H. A., 'The 1903 Pattern Russian Field Gun', *Journal of the Royal Artillery*, Vol. 33, (1906).

Bodansky, Y., 'New Weapons in Afghanistan', *Jane's Defence Weekly*, 9 March, 1985.

Dick, C., 'Soviet Chemical Warfare Capabilities', *International Defense Review (IDR)* 1/1981.

Dick, C., 'Soviet Operational Manoeuvre Groups — A Closer Look', *IDR* 6/1983.

Donnelly, C. N., 'The Soviet Operational Manoeuvre Group — A New Challenge for NATO', *IDR* 9/1982.

Furlong, R. D. M., 'ERFB Munitions . . .' and 'GHN 45 . . .' *IDR* 6/1982.

Hart, D. M. and Gormley, E. M., 'The Evolution of Soviet Interest in Atomic Artillery', *RUSI, Journal of The Royal United Services Institute for Defence Studies*, June, 1983.

Hoffman, Colonel K., 'An Analysis of Soviet Artillery Development', *IDR* 6 (December)/ 1977.

Keir, Major J. L., 'Direct and Indirect Fire', *Proceedings of the Royal Artillery Institution (PRAI)*, Vol. xxiv, 1897.

Kenyon, Captain L. R., 'Field Artillery Materiel on the Continent', *PRAI*, Vol. 29, 1902–03.

Ohlson, T. and Loose-Weintrab, E., 'The Trade in major Conventional Weapons', *SIPRI Yearbook 1983*, (Stockholm International Peace Research Institute, 1983).

Okunev, Lieutenant-General N. A., 'On the New Employment of Artillery and the Revolution it is Destined to Produce in the System of Modern Tactics', *Colburn's United Service Magazine*, Nos. 221 and 224, March and July, 1847, (London, 1847).

Petersen, P. A., Hines, J. G., 'Military Power in Soviet Strategy against NATO', *RUSI*, December, 1983.

'A Puzzling Weapon Captured by the Finns — the 'Non-recoil Gun', *Illustrated London News*, 6 April, 1940.

Scott, H. F., 'The Strategic Rocket Forces and their Five Elites' *Air Force Magazine*, March, 1983.

Skobelev, General, 'General Skobelev's Instructions to his Artillery before the Storm of Geok Tepe', *Translations*, etc. supplement to *PRAI*, France II, (May, 1882).

Stewart, Captain D. B., 'The Russian Field Artillery Goniometer', *Translations*, etc., *PRAI* xxxi, trans. from *Revue d'Artillerie*, September, 1904, trans. in turn from *AZh* 3/1903.

Suvorov Viktor (a pseudonym) 'Strategic Command and Control — the Soviet Approach', *IDR* 12/1984.

Tal, General Y., 'Armour — Myth and Reality', *Ha'aretz*, 20 October 1974.

Tomlinson, Major General M. J., 'Handling Artillery within the Corps', *British Army Review*, December, 1983.

Index

The letter f indicates a figure or the start of a series of figures, p a plate, a number alone a page. Where an end-note is referred to (when it contains information supplementary to the text), the page number is given, then n and then the note number, e.g. 77n21.